Ecology
for
Environmental
Professionals

ECOLOGY
FOR
ENVIRONMENTAL
PROFESSIONALS

DOROTHY J. HOWELL

QUORUM BOOKS
WESTPORT, CONNECTICUT • LONDON

Library of Congress Cataloging-in-Publication Data

Howell, Dorothy J.
Ecology for environmental professionals / Dorothy J. Howell.
p. cm.
Includes bibliographical references and index.
ISBN 0–89930–745–0 (alk. paper)
1. Environmental policy. 2. Environmental protection.
3. Conservation of natural resources. 4. Human ecology. I. Title.
GE170.H69 1994
574.5—dc20   93–5580

British Library Cataloguing in Publication Data is available.

Library of Congress Catalog Card Number: 93–5580
ISBN: 0–89930–745–0

First published in 1994

Quorum Books, 88 Post Road West, Westport, CT 06881
An imprint of Greenwood Publishing Group, Inc.

Printed in the United States of America

The paper used in this book complies with the
Permanent Paper Standard issued by the National
Information Standards Organization (Z39.48–1984).

10 9 8 7 6 5 4 3 2 1

For
Helen M. Habermann
and
in memory of
Kornelius Lems

Contents

Figures and Tables

Preface

There are few basic ecology texts intended for an audience composed of neither biologists nor ecologists. Aside from the highly appealing nature works at home on the coffee table, there are the works written to convince an audience naive in the natural sciences of a particular environmental stance. The former subsume the underlying science. The latter inevitably proceed from scant discussion of ecological principles and concepts to deceptively simplistic, direct answers to the major environmental issues facing this nation and, indeed, the whole biosphere. They usurp logic and reasoning that readers, like scientists, are entitled to conduct for themselves.

To the dismay of most outsiders, scientists can be surprisingly resistant to any suggestion that their respective fields of endeavor can be comprehended by anyone outside that field. "Anyone" includes scientists in other fields as well as the nonscientist. Ecologists have not entirely escaped conveying these impressions. The politicolegal system has promoted the attitude through its own limitations on definitions of relevant expertise. While serving a very real need in these forums, an aura of elitism remains in constraining those allowed to speak to an issue founded in the natural sciences.

The fact is that there is some justification behind this distressing aloofness. There *are* neither simple questions nor simple answers to most scientific queries of public interest. But this circumstance does not contradict two others: First, astonishing simplicity does emerge from the astounding complexity of the natural world; second, the simplicity can be communicated, with appropriate qualifications, to a naive audience in language as meaningful as it is accessible.

There is nevertheless an attendant risk of oversimplification, which in the environmental area conveys the inaccurate perception that one can intrude upon or intervene in natural processes with a predictable outcome. Paradoxically, the more specific the prediction or the broader its application, the less likely it is to be realized, especially without some alteration in affected systems no one has so much as contemplated.

For those who will be practicing in the environmental professions—indeed, *anyone* with an interest in environmental quality and the protection of natural resources—a foundation in ecology is essential. Natural resources conservation and preservation, environmental protection, and even pollution control all relate directly or indirectly to environmental amenities. Those amenities are best comprehended through the eyes of the ecologist, whether in the field or in the laboratory or ensconced in an armchair.

Without a sound basis in the relevant ecological sciences, policy will be inept. It will fail to serve contemporary missions so often stated in ecological language.

With that prelude, this is a text in the ecological sciences for environmental professionals who have managed to avoid science courses since high school—with the possible exception of the unavoidable introductory college course often represented by geology and affectionately dubbed "Rocks for Jocks." This text grows out of the lectures and class discussions developed in the Ecology and Environmental Sciences course for Vermont Law School's Environmental Law Center.

Because of the audience, there are no pictures. But there are also few figures and tables. Most significantly, the mathematical and statistical component of the ecological sciences is reduced to relative terms akin to *immense, big, little, tiny*, and *miniscule*. In short, this text is based on the belief that one need not be a scientist in order to understand and utilize scientific principles intelligently. All that is required is basic intelligence, a grasp of language, a sound sense of logic—and scientific literacy.

To teach an intelligent, well-educated, highly motivated audience naive in the natural sciences, one must avoid condescension as well as intimidation. Since the audience represents a wide variety of perspectives on the evolving environmental movement, every effort is to be expended to avoid predigesting the ecological foundation to take a stand on issues. Debate should be fostered, not predetermined. The principal goal is to place the reader in a position to graft his or her own disciplinary and ethical constructs onto that foundation and then turn to all the other relevant disciplines for their additional opportunities or constraints. From here, the reader can go on to find specifics to bring the generalities home. The advocate can find justification and the means to counter the opposition.

Much of the text is extracted from four principal sources. Some of the supplemental texts in science are sadly out-of-date for the scientist, but they have informed the author in special ways. Often, there is reference to a popularization of science or to a work frankly crossing from the scientific to the philosophical or spiritual realm. All these selections are entirely intentional. Beyond demonstrating undeniable connections, these works together reinforce the position that ecology and the environmental sciences are for everyone.

Introduction

If one accepts that the contemporary environmental movement finds its most immediate roots in the 1960s and that the national commitment to environmental amenities was most recently reinvigorated through the National Environmental Policy Act (42 U.S.C.A. 4321 *et seq.*), the 1990s are the third "Decade of the Environment." It can come as no surprise that there are numerous levels of ecology today. In addition to the science itself, ecology is claimed by everyone from politicians to poets. Ecology as one of the biological sciences can serve to inform all those interests.

Because ecology depends on all the other natural sciences and full comprehension of its adaptation into policy and law depends in turn on the nature of science, scientists, and the scientific method, the introductory background (Chapters 1 and 2) will consider the place of ecology among the natural sciences in terms of Eugene Odum's Theory of Integrative Levels. That theory observes that there are successive levels of science from pure mathematics to ecology. Each level is subject to a unique complex of natural laws by which its phenomena can be understood. Moreover, each level can only be explained in part by the phenomena of the preceding level, each level being more than the sum of its parts. Hence, the need to examine each both holistically and through reductionist techniques.

As scientists often do, we will examine ecosystems empirically, starting with the holistic approach (synecology). Specifically, we will consider the basic components of a "generic" ecosystem, that is, habitats and communities in the structural and functional unit identified as an ecosystem (Chapter 3). The specific organisms making up the community, especially the vegetation of terrestrial communities, lend themselves to prediction on the basis of global location (Chapter 4). This factor informs the environmental professional as well as the ecologist. The phenomena revealed through analysis of interactions within an ecosystem (beginning with Chapter 5) will be placed in politicolegal context.

With that empirical, holistic comprehension of an ecosystem, we will turn reductionist in order to construct an ecosystem, starting with its abiotic components, energy and materials, before adding biota (autecology) (Chapters 6 through 8). In a sense, we will be following actual patterns discerned in cosmology and in the strategy of planetary evolution and in origins of life and biological evolution (Chapters 10 and 11). We will constantly seek out connections and turn to information supplied only by natural sciences outside ecology itself.

The abiotic component of ecosystems reflects at once the simplest and the most complex levels of energy and material. Energy flows through ecological and biological systems alike, while materials cycle through them. The source of all energy on earth is most immediately the sun, but ultimately it is the Big Bang. The major material components of earth's biosphere are the atmosphere, hydrosphere, and lithosphere (Chapter 7). Each plays crucial roles in material cycling as described in biogeochemical cycles (Chapter 8). All the abiotic phenomena of ecosystems occur in three dimensions. But ecosystems are subject to a fourth dimension that must not be neglected: time (Chapters 9 and 10).

Scientists perceive strategies at all levels of planetary science. Planetary evolution begins with the Big Bang and the science of cosmology. That physical and chemical evolution continues through the geological history of the planet, ultimately yielding chemical complexes with the attributes of life. With the origin of life, a new kind of evolution commenced. What we now know as earth's biosphere is an ecosystem of planetary scale. It is the result of billions of years of abiotic evolution and millions of years of biotic evolution in interaction with each other. All the processes continue and the strategies remain in place as we humans observe and participate (Chapter 9).

Earth's biota arose from the evolving complex of energy flow and material cycling that proceeded from the initial formation of the planet. Just as organisms are a level beyond the chemistry—even organic chemistry and the still-more-complex biochemistry—the physical and chemical phenomena that affect organisms are only partially explained by physical and chemical relationships in an ecosystem. Organisms as individuals, in populations, and as communities are subject to limiting factors and interactions among those factors. Every biological system from the subcellular to an ecosystem and, almost certainly, the biosphere itself maintains a homeostasis. Each resists internal alteration imposed by external (environmental) factors by a variety of mechanisms that can be summarized in another science—cybernetics (Chapter 11).

An external factor that intrudes upon an ecosystem or any other biological system is known as a perturbation. The result of that perturbation will be mediated by subcellular processes that may go no further. Through these processes, the affected individual or individuals will counter or adapt to the perturbation. Homeostasis will either be restored or reestablished in adaptation to the perturbation. Depending on the nature and extent of the perturbation, however, its influence may be exerted beyond one or a few individuals. It may affect a whole population, the community, or the ecosystem itself.

With those considerations in mind, we will build the biotic component of an ecosystem by studying populations and then aggregations of populations culminated in a community. Populations and communities are each unique, scientifically recognized levels of organization (Chapter 12). A population is made up of all the individuals of a single species in a given geographical area. The population manifests both structure and functional features that, while dependent on those individuals, are unique to that population as a biological unit. Similarly, a community is made up of all the interacting populations in the geographical and conceptual unit we call an ecosystem. But that community, too, manifests unique structural and functional features that describe a biological unit. The community is the biological whole that is interacting with the abiotic whole to form an ecosystem.

When an ecosystem is perturbed, its biota, individually and as a community, may remain apparently unaffected. More likely, the effects are too subtle to be detected by human tools. Individually and collectively the biota may adapt. Those that cannot adapt will die (Chapter 13).

Every biological system will ultimately die. Cells arise and die constantly as the multicellular individual proceeds from conception through development to sexual maturity and into senescence. Each individual will be conceived and die as the population itself goes through the life cycle unique to it. The death of a population is known as extinction. Communities proceed through seres as each ecosystem develops and theoretically reaches its climax, whereupon a homeostasis may be maintained indefinitely. Ecosystems "die" and are replaced by others only with geological or planetary alterations occurring over lengthy time intervals—as measured by humans.

While these phenomena are perceived at the population, community, or ecosystem scale, they are actually occurring at the molecular level. Biological systems adapt, evolve, or die out through evolutionary processes currently described in terms of neo-Darwinism. These processes are mediated by the molecules ubiquitous to life: DNA (deoxyribonucleic acid) or RNA (ribonucleic acid), the molecular basis of individual and population genetics (Chapter 13). Hence, we will come full circle. From the foundations of physics and chemistry, ecosystems can be analyzed in four dimensions in terms of their component parts and holistically. But the fate of those ecosystems ultimately depends on the chemical reactions mediated by two molecules of stunning simplicity but capable of the equally stunning complexity of life.

When ecology moves into the politicolegal system, imposing a novel cultural dimension on its principles and phenomena, we can only hope that the participants will afford natural systems, nonliving and especially living, the respect they deserve (Chapters 14 and 15). Only the human organism is directly amenable to legal constraint, and then only to the extent the individual respects the law or policy to be applied. Other biological systems, including ecosystems and the biosphere itself, are subject to natural laws that must be respected by programs established in their behalf. Ecosystems will respond to intervention—natural or anthropogenic (without regard to human intent whether ignorant, benign, or malicious)—according to the constraints of natural law, which may itself be only dimly understood, if at all.

A major lesson to take from this book is that it is only with a sense of profound humility that we should purport to engage in systems ecology in order to manage natural resources. The merger of scientific with legal tools must be accompanied by mutual respect. It is only with trepidation that we can enter into yet another field of biology, applied human ecology, in achieving the missions of environmental protection and natural resources conservation or preservation upon which national law and policy are embarking.

PART I

THE BACKGROUND

1

Science, Scientists, and Scientific Method

A wonder of science is the way in which all things interconnect and merge. The inconceivably miniscule and the incomprehensibly immense are of a continuum of complexity beyond the grasp of the ordinary mind. And yet, as Albert Einstein observed, perhaps the most profound wonder of all is the very comprehensibility of the natural world.[1]

There is actually an astounding simplicity underlying the whole of the natural world. Nature is efficient, economic, and without excesses. Occam's razor actually functions: The simplest alternative explanation of a phenomenon is probably the most accurate. Undue complications (as opposed to the organization of complexes and complexity) are always more suspect in science than simplicity. The same rules work throughout the sciences. The several natural sciences reflect an organization of nature that is quite apparent upon serious observation. This organization is composed of stepwise levels, each level representing a science that incorporates the principles and concepts ("rules") from those sciences below and establishing rules constraining those above, as described by the Theory of Integrative Levels, to be described below.

Despite these interconnections and merges across the lines established by scientists, there are those who assert that the study of any of the biological sciences, including ecology, cannot be undertaken without a firm foundation in basic physics and chemistry and all the disciplines of those sciences somehow relevant to biology. Moreover, the abilities of a statistician, if not of a theoretical mathematician, are essential.

While there is some truth to these assertions, they are not entirely acceptable, as will become apparent throughout this volume. Still, just as it is useful for the environmental professional to have a sensitivity to ecological principles, if not formal training in that science, it is incumbent upon the student of ecology to foster a sensitivity to the sciences contributing to ecology.

A valuable starting point for the nonscientist gingerly approaching ecology is some comprehension of natural science itself, of the scientific method, and of scientists and their culture. The three are really inextricably associated, especially as viewed from outside the scientific community.

SCIENCE AND SCIENTIFIC METHOD

Science is a systematic approach to comprehension of the natural world. Science is a unique human endeavor quite distinguishable in its methodology from all other approaches to understanding the cosmos and its components. Science can be defined as a body of facts and truths regarding the operation of general laws. But scientific facts or truths are not so crucial as how they come into currency. The facts, hypotheses, theories, and laws of the natural sciences are continuously evolving by the cumulative application of the scientific method. Presumably, scientific explanations come ever closer to how the phenomena of the natural world are actually working and influencing one another.

Throughout its history, science has grown through the gradual acceptance that events are not arbitrary but reflect an underlying order.[2] Sequences in scientific advance begin with sets of appearances that can be organized into laws. Somewhere along the array of laws a knot will occur. The knot is a point at which several laws intersect. Symbolically, the knot itself provides unity among the array.[3]

The methodology proceeds from observations of natural systems into the collection of data by empirical and experimental means. Empirical refers to observation of a system without intrusion into its workings, whereas experimentation involves some controlled alteration of the system of interest in order to clarify how it works. In either case, hypotheses, ideally universal in application, are tested.

In principle, any number of analytical approaches may advance the hypothesis without ever fully confirming it, but it only takes one refutation to falsify or at least limit the universality of a hypothesis. Moreover, each hypothesis and its ultimate fate tend to be embedded in broad theory. They do not rest in isolation from other parts of the natural world. Science advances through a combination of deductive and inductive reasoning with the constant application of probability and other statistical manipulations. Models of phenomena follow from the statistical confirmation and refutation of hypotheses.[4] Over time, science is cumulative, despite momentary reversals and changes of direction.[5]

A striking picture of how science proceeds is derived from our changing view of the physical universe. There are three realities in this universe:

matter, space, and time. To the classical (Newtonian) physicist, they were absolutes. At the turn of the century, special relativity demanded abandonment of absolutes in relation to space and time and required an acceptance of the equivalence of matter and energy. Quantum mechanics entered the picture only a few years later to demand yet another reexamination of these few realities of the universe and their interrelationships. All are expansions of one another by which scientific comprehension is advanced in clarity, outlook, or both.[6]

Each scientist seeks the order to be extracted from appearances by looking for likenesses. Neither likenesses nor order will be immediately apparent but must be extracted. Thus, theory goes beyond any mere collection of facts. Historic discoveries result from insight into novel order. Sir Isaac Newton, for example, went beyond the pull of gravity on the apple. He realized that the force reaches beyond the tops of the trees and holds the moon in its orbit. Michael Faraday closed the link between electricity and magnetism, and today we speak of the radiation of electromagnetic energy. James Clerk Maxwell linked electricity and magnetism to light. Einstein linked time to space and mass with energy.[7]

LEVELS OF ORGANIZATION

Science is possible because we do live in an ordered universe in compliance with simple mathematical laws. The scientist studies, catalogs, and relates the orderliness in nature.[8] The order is discernible wherever we look, from the galaxies spread across the universe to the internal workings of the atom. Still, it is useful to distinguish among the sorts of order. Some of it is found in the simplicity of regularities such as those associated with the clockwork of the solar system or the oscillations of a pendulum. Another order is found in complexity (now called chaos and subject to mathematical analysis,)[9] notably in the swirl of Jupiter's atmospheric gases or of incoming waves or in the organization of living beings.

Reductionism and holism are yet another kind of order. "Reductionism seeks to uncover simple elements within complex structures, while holism directs attention to the complexity as a whole."[10] In reflecting this particular form of order, the Theory of Integrative Levels becomes a valuable guide into the sciences.

The Theory of Integrative Levels

Both scientists and students of their work who would put it to some particular use are greatly assisted by the very interconnectedness that is so important to our relationship to our environments, up to and including the biosphere. As John Muir observed, whenever we try to isolate a piece

Figure 1.1
Theory of Integrative Levels: Levels of Organization among the
Natural Sciences

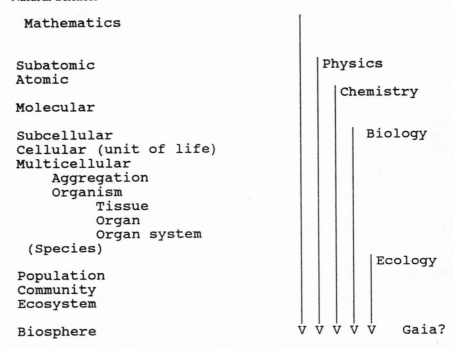

of the environment, we soon discover that it is "hitched" to everything else.[11]

There are two ways to elucidate this point and demonstrate its significance to the environmental professional. One is what Eugene Odum calls the "Theory of Integrative Levels," presented in Figure 1.1. The other is a simplified version of systems analysis that can be illustrated as a series of black boxes, as shown in Figure 1.2.

The Theory of Integrative Levels is no more or less than recognition that each level of organization within the natural sciences builds on those below in conceptual steps from pure mathematics to the planetary complex of ecosystems identified as the biosphere. In theory at least, mathematical relationships (quantification) are the foundation of all the natural sciences.

Each level consists of features at least superficially amenable to qualitative description. This narrative form can be rendered suitable to individuals outside the corresponding scientific discipline but is most often expressed within the discipline in terms of mathematics, most notably, but hardly exclusively, as statistical functions.[12]

Figure 1.2
Theory of Integrative Levels: Scientific "Black Boxes"

Scientific "Black Boxes"

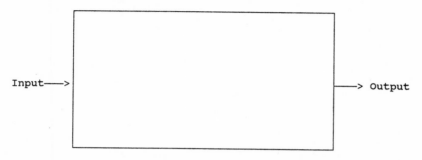

Level of Organization, e.g., Biological System

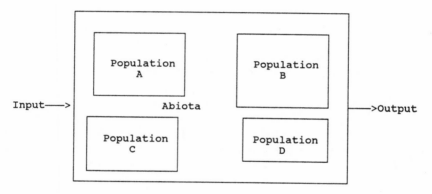

Ecosystem

Quantitative relationships build in complexity within each level to a point where a new conceptual level comes into being. The new level, while dependent on these quantitative features, can no longer be fully understood through them alone. A qualitative alteration has occurred, with a corresponding emergence of a new level of organization. Significantly, no prior level is fully abandoned as complexity builds through the steps.

Hence, theoretical subatomic physics is very close to pure mathematics, but when all the subatomic interactions are in place, new features composing a new whole are discernible. Similarly, the functioning of certain of these phenomena becomes what is identified as protons, neutrons, and electrons.

A single proton in specific interactive relationships with a single neutron becomes the next level: The combined phenomena constitute a hydrogen atom, the simplest of the chemical elements. Building on that simple foundation, the whole periodic table of atoms emerges. Two protons, two electrons, plus two neutrons are helium, and so on, up through the increasing atomic weights to the unstable (radioactive) elements.

When atoms commence to interact with each other, the results can be explained in terms of physics, but the next level of complexity, chemistry, has been reached. Molecules can be created from atoms and from other molecules through a variety of reactions mediated by the internal (physical) structure of the reactants and their products. Increasingly complex molecules can result through molecular interactions, resulting in compounds and, ultimately, polymers composed of relatively simple molecular entities repeating in specific patterns.

Chemistry has traditionally been divided into inorganic and organic. Inorganic chemistry includes the properties of the elements and reactions of elements and simple molecules or compounds such as the metals, the halogens, gases, acids and bases, and water (see Table 1.1). Organic chemistry is the study of reactions of the element carbon as it forms complex molecules in reactions with itself and especially hydrogen, oxygen, and to a lesser extent, nitrogen.

While the next level of organization, subcellular biology, requires the molecules and reactions of organic chemistry, it is ordinarily identified in terms of biochemistry and physiology. Both of these sciences, one claimed by chemistry, the other by biologists, imply a more elaborate complex than the organic chemistry upon which they are based. In essence, biochemistry describes the reactions and metabolic pathways giving rise to the physiology upon which the life of a cell or a multicellular organism depends. Physiology, then, implies a level of organization beyond, but based on, biochemistry, which in turn arises from organic chemistry. Because the complex of interconnected reactions known as life ultimately depends on the physics of atomic structure, it is unwise to neglect physics and mathematics in seeking to understand the processes of life. Nevertheless, it is both possible and essential to study and analyze biochemistry and physiology as independent levels of organization.

Similarly, it is both possible and essential to isolate for study and analysis each of the several levels of organization composing biological systems. The first of these levels is the cell itself, often identified as the unit of life. The highest level is the biosphere, although there are those who would argue that there is yet another biological system—the planet itself or Gaia (see Chapter 2). The intervening biological systems are the organism, population, community, and ecosystem. From another perspective, there are levels of organization within the organism as well. Cells are organized into tissues, which are constituents of organs, which act together in organ systems. Each level lends itself to productive and informative study, but from the perspective of the organism, it is the complex of interactions that is important.

Table 1.1
Selected Elements

Element	Symbol	Commentary
Hydrogen	H	Consisting of one proton and one electron, the simplest element; occurs as H_2 (the diatomic hydrogen gas, highly explosive), H_2O (water), a major component of organic molecules -- $(CH_2O)_n$
Helium	He	Only slightly more complex than hydrogen, consists of two protons, two electrons, and two neutrons; a gas (essentially non-reactive)
Boron	B	A trace element (essential to life) and heavy metal (toxic); a plant nutrient
Carbon	C	Occurs in three elemental forms -- diamond, coal and graphite; also occurs as gases -- CO (toxic carbon monoxide), CO_2 (essential to life), CH_4 (toxic methane); the basis of organic chemistry, in turn the basis of biochemistry, in turn the the basis of living material in the form of biochemical and physiological reactions
Nitrogen	N	Occurs as N_2 (the diatomic nitrogen gas), NO_2^- (nitrite), NO_3^- (nitrate), NH_3 (ammonia), NH_2 (amine); a major element of life
Oxygen	O	Occurs as O_2 and O_3 (the gases diatomic oxygen and ozone, respectively), H_2O, H_2NO_3 (nitric acid); an essential element in organic chemistry
Sodium	Na	Typical compounds NaOH (sodium hydroxide), NaCl (table salt)
Magnesium	Mg	A trace element and heavy metal; an essential component of chlorophyll that mediates the initial photosynthetic reaction

The Environmental Sciences

With reference to Figure 1.2, it is important to note that an arrow can be drawn from the point of input into the abiotic portion of the ecosystem or into any one of the populations representing the community of organisms. Thereafter, a veritable maze of arrows, some pointing in opposite directions, may proliferate before the one giving rise to the observable output is initiated.

It is also important to acknowledge that each population is a black box filled with individual organisms interacting with each other and with their environment. According to the Theory of Integrative Levels, the serious observer may well be required to work down through the layers of black boxes, all the way back to chemistry or physics for full comprehension of how something entered the ecosystem and was expressed as the measured output. At the same time, the serious observer will remain aware that both the input and output associated with the observed ecosystem are connected with the larger environment and, hence, potentially with the whole of the biosphere.

While it would be most difficult to isolate any of the sciences considered above as irrelevant to environmental professions, ecology is, nevertheless, the principal natural science serving environmental protection and natural resources management. Ecology commences where the individual organism ends. The ecological sciences begin with the study of populations, communities, and whole ecosystems. But these biological systems obviously do not exist in a vacuum, scientific or otherwise. Hence, the physics and chemistry of geology are important, as are disciplines associated with the phenomena of the earth's atmosphere, hydrosphere, and lithosphere (see Chapter 7).

Too often ignored is the fourth dimension, time. No environmental science is complete without some reference to applicable units of time. Ecological phenomena occur over time spans as small as milliseconds and as large as geological intervals measured in millions and billions of years.

Also to be included in sound environmental planning are the social sciences, notably including economics, sociology, political science, and even psychology, human and otherwise. While it can be reasonably argued that ecology is the prerequisite to sound environmental science, none of these other considerations can be dismissed. There are times when one of them may legitimately supersede ecological considerations.

Life and, therefore, ecology are fundamentally chemical in nature. Chemistry depends on atomic structure, with special reference to the number and placement of electrons surrounding each atom's nucleus of protons and neutrons. The electrons, whose actual paths around the nucleus are not completely determinable, do occur in levels, determined by the number of electrons. Chemical reactions occur between elements on the basis of the degree of completeness of each electron level or with the minute electric charge expressed by the atom. Covalent bonds, ubiquitous in the biological systems, represent the sharing of a pair of electrons between two atoms. Ionic bonds, also ubiquitous to biology, are related to attractions between positive and negative electrical charges. Some reactions are best understood as a combination of the two kinds of bonds.[13]

There are a few atoms and in all likelihood no molecules or compounds that are not somehow significant to the processes of biological systems, whether the effect is negative or positive (or both). Table 1.1 is a synopsis of the chemicals of particular significance to life.[14]

Among molecules, liquid water may be designated the "universal mediator" of reactions, but carbon is better described as "the elemental jack-of-all-trades." In properties, carbon lies halfway between the metals and the nonmetals. It can form compounds with almost all other elements[15]— the property that causes carbon to be the unit of organic chemistry and hence the chemical basis of life.

Carbon is uniquely able to form covalent bonds with itself and with hydrogen, oxygen, and a variety of other elements and radicals. Carbon can form straight or branched chains of linked carbon atoms, cyclic compounds of five or six carbon atoms, and the so-called aromatic compounds based on benzene. Benzene is a six-carbon cyclic molecule, where every other carbon atom is bound to the next by two instead of one electron bond.

The simplest organic molecule is methane, a single carbon atom bonded with four hydrogens. The potable alcohol, ethanol, is composed of two carbon atoms, one with three hydrogens bonded to it and the other with two plus the hydroxy radical $-OH$. It is possible to proceed stepwise from methane to essentially every known organic chemical. To do so in the laboratory is neither easy nor inexpensive, but it can be done whenever the reactions can be directed and controlled. The chemical wonder of living cells is that they have the means of synthesizing precisely the right chemical in the needed amount and at the proper rate to serve not merely their own needs but those of the whole organism.

Although it cannot actually be reduced to no more than the law of physics, life is not a matter of some novel force or other unprecedented natural laws.[16] Life is actually a particular physicochemical complex that exhibits certain characteristics unique to it, as would be predicted by the Theory of Integrative Levels (see Table 1.2). All species of organisms have the innate, genetically mediated capacities to metabolize chemical substances, to excrete the wastes of metabolism and catabolism, to replicate themselves in a characteristic pattern identified as reproduction, to respond to environmental stimuli, to move, and to adapt.

There is a kind of "missing link" between living and nonliving in viruses, just barely crossing the line into life. Viruses are particles composed of nucleic acid and protein. They are acellular and lack metabolic processes. They neither synthesize protein nor generate energy, but without either, viruses cannot grow. Yet they do reproduce themselves through altering the genetic code of the cells on which they are obligate parasites. Moreover, they can adapt and evolve. Many can actually recover from crystallization and, once reactivated, reproduce themselves.[17]

Although the individual organism within a species may lack one or more

Table 1.2
Characteristics of Life

1. Organization: specifically unique physical and chemical

2. Metabolism: Utilization of raw materials from the
   environment to produce unique pattern of structural and
   physiological elements and energy distribution

3. Excretion: Elimination of by-products of metabolism
   (wastes)

4. Reproduction: Ability to replicate (make copies of self)

5. Sensitivity: Responsiveness to environmental stimuli

6. Movement: Ability to move; motility

7. Adaptation: Ability to adjust to a variety of changes in
   the external environment

of these capacities or lack the opportunity to perform one or more of them
in a manner considered normal for the species, life is defined at the species
level and more particularly distinguished from nonlife by all of these characteristics. All contribute something to ecological processes and must be
taken into account for a full understanding of the phenomena of ecosystems
and other ecological entities.

Qualitative vs. Quantitative Analysis and the
Analysis of Unknowns

Chemists and any biologist concerned with the effects on any biological
system of chemical substances will expend substantial mental energy on
identification and quantification of unknown substances, often in mixtures.
Take, for example, a vessel containing a clear fluid. In determining the
nature of the fluid, qualitative analysis reveals the presence of gold, deuterium, hydrogen, and oxygen. The observer may next want to know something more practical: Is this mixture valuable? Is it toxic? Is it hazardous
in some other sense? To make any of these determinations, it is necessary
to quantify the various components. In this case, gold may be present at
a concentration of one part per million (1 ppm) and deuterium at 20 ppm.
The mixture is neither valuable—at least as a practicable source of the
precious metal—nor dangerously toxic—so long as it is not inhaled by
terrestrial animals. It is mostly oxygen (850,000 ppm) and hydrogen
(100,000 ppm). In fact, the fluid is seawater, the original source of life and
present-day sustainer of life.[18]

SCIENTISTS AND THE PRACTICE OF SCIENCE

From data collected through observation or experimentation or both, a hypothesis is formulated. In deductive reasoning, that hypothesis can be generally stated in terms of "If one thing is the case, then another is also" (If A, then B; A causes B.). Conclusions arising from the testing of narrowly focused hypotheses are expanded to increasingly general application through the process of inductive reasoning.

Needless to say, one scientist may not be engaged in every step of the scientific method. Moreover, since scientists are also human, insight and imagination play important roles in their individual professional lives, as do prejudices and biases. Nevertheless, science, at least over the long term, does tend to be self-correcting. One way or another, the phenomena identified with the natural sciences will make themselves known, whether or not the individual scientist understands or believes in them. Although not in some simplistic straight lines resembling the national highway system, scientific trends in comprehension and accurate descriptions of the natural world build through the systematic aggregation of those portions each discipline advances. The aggregation is composed of the scientific method and constitutes science.

Ideally, each natural phenomenon is studied from a variety of perspectives, with a constant reaffirmation of the underlying hypothesis from different means of approach depending on different sets of assumptions and premises. Constant reaffirmation elevates one or more facts to constitute a theory that may eventually become a natural law or be dropped altogether. For example, evolution in the form of neo-Darwinism is one theory of how species arise, stabilize, adapt to perturbation, and ultimately either undergo genetic change giving rise to phenotypes constituting a new species or become extinct. This theory is subject to ongoing study, modification, and reevaluation as more and more information is incorporated. Moreover, the theory is further affected by other concepts of how species may be eliminated or how new taxons may arise (see Chapter 13).

Gravity, on the other hand, is an inescapable natural law. While the mechanism of gravity is not fully understood, the fact of gravity is universally accepted among scientists. It is crucial in research ranging from the physics of fundamental particles and associated forces to the phenomena of electromagnetic radiation to cosmology.[19]

Gravity also illustrates how a science evolves. For Newton, gravity was a force, the one holding the planets in their orbits about the sun. In fact, Newton's mathematical formula for gravity can still calculate those orbits. For Einstein, gravity was curvature in spacetime. According to Einstein's mathematics, planets follow the shortest path in curved spacetime. In weak gravitational fields, the curvature in spacetime is almost perfectly flat, and Einstein's formulas give the same answers as Newton's.[20]

Gravity's lesson expands upon an early one regarding scientific advance. A theory is good to the extent that it accurately describes a large class of observations on the basis of a corresponding model with few arbitrary elements and to the extent that it makes accurate predictions regarding future observations. Theories are always provisional, never proved. With each confirmation comes greater confidence, but each disagreement calls for modification, if not abandonment.[21]

If the data generated by an individual scientist do not confirm or reaffirm the hypothesis being tested, the scientist has not failed. Instead, the hypothesis must be rejected—itself an advancement of relevant knowledge—or modified to accommodate the result. Science, like judicial rule-making, proceeds in small increments, with only the occasional profound breakthrough and new direction, each increment flowing from one or more precedents.

Often, the mission behind the practice of science goes beyond comprehension of the natural world for its own sake. The basic purpose behind these formal processes is the ability to predict events on the basis of currently acceptable hypotheses as they coalesce into theory and take on the aspect of natural law. A system about which predictions can be accurately made can be subjected to control, a crucial element of the overall process for environmental professionals, whatever their setting in the private and public sectors.

In this context, it is essential for environmental professionals to accept that science is not a democratic process. Despite the fact that "respectable" science is accepted by the majority within a scientific discipline, the majority may in fact be wrong. It requires an astute observer to distinguish the inspired individual, another Einstein, from the "crackpot." Sometimes, substantial time must pass before the distinction becomes clear, with the majority proven correct or with the formation of a new majority. The scientific phenomena remain sublimely undisturbed by the whole process.[22] They continue according to natural law in any event. They do not depend on human comprehension for their reality.[23]

There are certain characteristics of scientific fact that must be taken into account by scientists and nonscientists alike. First and foremost, it is crucial to accept that the natural processes known collectively as science are real and themselves fixed in the natural world. They cannot be altered by scientists, technologists, or participants in the politicolegal system. They can only be increasingly understood, utilized, and applied. The better we comprehend the basics of the phenomena, the more accurately we can predict the result of an alteration—perturbation or intervention—in a system of specific interest. Such predictions then become the foundation of controlling either the result or the perturbation.

With that given, it is next crucial to appreciate the reality that all scientific "fact" is tentative. Future observations and experiments based on their predecessors will almost certainly cause resultant "facts" to be clarified, modified, or even refuted. Moreover, predictability in the scientific context is limited. It, too, expands but only with continued observation and experimentation, both of which require time that scientists may have but that environmental planners do not.

In part because of the limitations of human knowledge and in part because of the tentative nature of scientific knowledge, predictability in specific circumstances is also limited, particularly at the interface of science with policy and law, a special kind of applied science. Moreover, the scientific reality itself is not subject to human control.

Finally, the phenomena science continually seeks to reveal transcend the work of the individual scientist, the discipline associated with each, and even the scientific endeavor itself. In short, no one can expect ever to have a full and complete understanding of the phenomena of a single discipline, let alone of the cosmos as a whole. Each of us works in a limited area subject to our own intellectual limitations superimposed on those of the practitioners of the field.

IMPLICATIONS FOR ENVIRONMENTAL PROFESSIONALS

Implicit to the processes of science is that every serious scientist is willing to abandon a theory when evidence contradicts it.[24] Scientists, however, are known for their professional conservatism. Resistance to novelty is no flaw but ensures that novel notions be compellingly demonstrated if not proven outright. "Maverick notions" are ordinarily unreliable, albeit momentarily tempting. The record of science chronicles only the innovations that have been shown to be right. Sooner or later, the wrong notions drop out of the collective known as science. Were it not for the conservatism, testing, and weeding-out process, science at large would be highly unreliable.[25]

These tendencies and processes together ensure that the sciences reflect the natural world with increasing accuracy. Nevertheless, they are a major source of frustration for anyone who would apply science to practical problems demanding immediate action.

Also worthy of serious reflection by environmental professionals is that even mainstream scientific results may be counter to intuition and ordinary common sense. Everyday experience can prove to be an unreliable guide into natural phenomena, which are more accurately described through resort to the abstract or to the arcane realm of mathematical manipulation.[26]

Even more difficult than working with these idiosyncracies of scientific practice is conveying these points to the nonscientist policymaker or private citizen. It can be reassuring to know that the processes of science demand the occasional "reality therapy" in maintaining a true course. The interpretations are adjusted and the accuracy of the maps into the natural world improved. For all their inadequacies, the maps science provides can be "perfectly reliable in important respects."[27] The trick, of course, is to know where reliability phases into misguided or simply wrong. Human nature is such that beliefs are relinquished only with the greatest reluctance. Sometimes, it is nearly impossible to conceive experiments that could prove it wrong.[28]

And yet, because of the process itself, science is self-correcting. Neither honest mistake nor fraud will go undetected indefinitely.[29] All scientific research is open to critical examination and testing by others within the discipline.[30]

The foregoing realities should not dissuade anyone from becoming familiar with the tenets of the science relevant to his or her professional (or personal) interest. Instead, the realities of the world projected by the natural sciences should cause one to approach an ecological system with considerable respect and a realization of the possibility that ignorant or uninformed intervention may do more damage than the harm perceived to be in need of human correction.

For these reasons, it is essential that the natural scientist who is also an environmental professional be scrupulous in the practice and the art of science. Value judgments need to be made overt, first and foremost to the scientist himself or herself. Thereupon, the environmental scientist should be prepared to honor the injunction of the Federation of American Scientists to avoid dogmatic claims, to admit and correct errors, and to reason with those in disagreement, especially in public debate.[31]

NOTES

The principal sources for this chapter are K. Arms and P. Camp, *Biology: A Journey into Life* (2d ed., 1991) (hereinafter "*Journey*"), at chapters 1–5, 18, 19, 20, and at 744; E. Odum, *Fundamentals of Ecology* (3d ed., 1971) ("Odum"), at chapter 1; R. Ricklefs, *The Economy of Nature* (2d ed., 1983) ("Ricklefs"), at chapters 1 and 2; and R. Smith, *Ecology and Field Biology* (4th ed., 1990) ("Smith"), at chapters 1 and 2.

1. *See, e.g.*, T. Dobzhansky, *Mankind Evolving: The Evolution of the Human Species* (1962), Preface, at xi.

2. S. Hawking, *A Brief History of Time: From the Big Bang to Black Holes* (1988), at 122.

3. J. Bronowski, *Science and Human Values* (1956), at 46.

4. D. Hull, *Philosophy of Biological Science* (1974), at 2.

5. S. Gould, *Wonderful Life: Burgess Shale and the Nature of History* (1989), at 207.

6. R. Augros and G. Stanciu, *The New Story of Science: How the New Cosmology Is Reshaping Our View of Mind, Art, God . . . and Ourselves* (1984), at 1, 4, and 7.

7. Bronowski, *supra* note 3, at 24–27.

8. P. Davies, *God and the New Physics* (1983), at 144.

9. *See, e.g.*, J. Glieck, *Chaos: Making a New Science* (1987); E. Porter, *Nature's Chaos* (1990); and J. Briggs, *Fractals: The Patterns of Chaos* (1992).

10. Davies, *supra* note 8, at 144–145.

11. John Muir, as quoted in M. Bean, *The Evolution of National Wildlife Law* (rev. and exp. ed., 1983), Foreword, at v.

12. It may seem odd when physicists speak of their work in terms of beauty and symmetry, and in fact they are applying these qualitative descriptions to mathematical relationships. The reknowned artist-scientist Leonardo da Vinci expressed the mathematical basis of all science in the fifteenth century. Today most of us suffer a "neurotic fear" of mathematics. This fear forms a barrier between us and full appreciation of science and of "vast areas of nature that have been revealed through painstaking research." Davies, *supra* note 8, at 221–222.

13. H. Blum, *Time's Arrow and Evolution* (3d ed., 1968), at 68 and 70–72.

14. A possible exception is helium, which is included to illustrate how the basic physical plan behind atomic structure builds on the foundation of three particles—the proton, neutron, and electron—to construct all the possible elements from hydrogen gas to carbon and its countless reactions to the most unstable heavy elements, such as uranium.

15. G. Schroeder, *Genesis and the Big Bang: The Discovery of Harmony between Modern Science and the Bible* (1990), at 121.

16. E. Schrödinger, *What Is Life?: And Other Scientific Essays* (Anchor ed., 1956), at 4. Obviously, these matters can be studied in scientific texts without the added quality provided by philosopher–scientists or those who quite deliberately enter into the metaphysical or into the spiritual realm. Moreover, some of the works cited here are woefully out-of-date from either the scientific or the legal point of views.

It is worth acknowledging, however, that science, like law, does continuously build out of precedent and that for some purposes older works are still relevant. Moreover, science and the spiritual aspect of human nature are no longer as divergent as they once were. For those with an interest in expanding human horizons through both, Paul Davies (*supra* note 8, at 66) makes a point of substantial interest:

Assuming . . . that living and non-living matter obey the same laws of physics, the mystery is how a single set of laws can produce such fundamentally different behaviour. It is as though matter can branch into two pathways, one—the living—evolving towards progressively more ordered states, and the other—the lifeless—becoming more and more disordered under the impact of the second law of thermodynamics. Yet in both cases the basic constituents—the atoms—are identical.

17. *Journey*, at 331.

18. D. Barnes, *Statistics as Proof: Fundamentals of Qualitative Evidence* (1983), at 6.

19. For popular accounts of these esoteric sciences, *see* Hawking, *supra* note 2; and D. Overbye, *Lonely Hearts of the Cosmos: The Story of the Scientific Quest*

for the Secret of the Universe (1991). In addition to opening the door to some of the most esoteric contemporary science, both works provide considerable insights into basic science, its practice, and its practitioners.

20. W. Kaufmann, *Black Holes and Warped Spacetime* (1979), at 68–69.

21. Hawking, *supra* note 2, at 9 and 10.

22. *But see* Augros and Stanciu, *supra* note 6, at 4–7, for the proposition that even the most fundamental phenomena may actually be influenced by observation. *See also* Hawking, *supra* note 2; and Overbye, *supra* note 19.

23. *See, e.g.*, Davies, *supra* note 8, at 219. Conversely, human ability to predict and control events in the natural world does depend on the degree of correspondence between the reality and human understanding of it. Sooner or later, scientific misunderstanding of a given phenomenon will make itself known.

24. *Id.*, at 6.

25. H. Bauer, *Scientific Literacy and the Myth of the Scientific Method* (1992), at 76–77.

26. Davies, *supra* note 8, at 16.

27. Bauer, *supra* note 25, at 89.

28. *Id.*, at 54.

29. C. Snow, "The Moral Un-neutrality of Science," *in Science, Technology, and Society: Emerging Relationships* (R. Chalk, ed., 1988), note 6, at 7.

30. W. Pigman and E. Carmichael, "An Ethical Code for Scientists," *in* Chalk, *supra* note 29, 34, at 35.

31. J. Edsall, "Two Aspects of Scientific Responsibility," *in* Chalk, *supra* note 29, 12, at 13.

2

The Scope of Ecology and Its Roles

THE SCIENTIFIC PLACE OF ECOLOGY

Ecologists speak of the web of life in recognition of the amazing array of relationships and interconnections through which organisms interact with their environments, a concept as narrow as the surroundings of a single cell and as grand as the biosphere.

An organism's environment even includes other organisms of its own and a wide variety of other species. The relatively new science of ecology represents the rules of the house, the name coming from the Greek phrase *oikos* ("house") *logos* ("governing rules").[1] The rules are deceptively simple, but they must be heeded by environmental professionals as well as by ecologists, even as they must be followed by biological systems.

An overview of ecology can be summed up in a few sentences.[2] An ecosystem must have resources and conditions able to support its residents through all the phases of their respective lives. Each resident is obliged to earn its keep by performing some function useful to the ecosystem. All the work of the ecosystem must be accomplished; that is, all the functional niches are to be filled. A candidate for entry into an ecosystem's biota must be accommodated to and by its fellow organisms and the abiotic environment. In the hypothetical closed ecosystem, the residents cannot leave, and new individuals or populations cannot enter to rejuvenate the community or to replace its members.[3]

In many ways, scientific efforts are like any other human endeavor—only more so. It is in the nature of both to be reductionist, if only in self-defense. The only way to take on the immensity of the natural world, building out of the paradoxical interweaving patterns from a surprisingly few straightforward foundations, is to pick apart a few of the patterns at a time.

The biota of earth and associated ecological principles and concepts are particularly complex. Simplification is an essential prerequisite on the way to comprehension.[4]

A contemporary research ecologist has bemoaned the complications experienced in attempting to work with ecological relationships. In order to begin sorting them out, the ecologist must engage in the Herculean strategy of putting some of the components under a rock while meeting with the others.[5]

Unfortunately, simplification holds hazards for the unwary "by chopping biological systems into small pieces, scientists may be destroying basic self-controlling and buffering mechanisms and actually making some aspect of them *more* difficult rather than easier to understand."[6] The wise ecologist acknowledges the role the laboratory can play in sorting out ecological realities. But there are impediments here, too. Among the most insidious is the nature of the species most suitable for study in the laboratory. In a word, they tend to be "weeds." As such, these species are more adaptable than most. "They lack the highly specific requirements that imply coevolution in organized communities."[7]

In their current state, the natural sciences are far removed from ordinary intellectual endeavor. While not as remote as the physics of subatomic particles, ecology has become distanced from the comfortable ruminations of the worlds of the naturalist, in the field or in an armchair or mesmerized before the television set. We have all lost something as a result. There was once a time (in recent centuries) when an educated person could grasp at least the outline of the whole of human knowledge and enjoy the option at least of proceeding in more personal realms upon that foundation.[8]

But since those not-so-remote times, science has outpaced us. Theories "are never properly digested or simplified so that ordinary people can understand them."[9] Even the specialist can hope only for a proper grasp of one small piece of the whole. As a result, we are bewildered by the world. But we yearn for comprehension and seriously inquire of the nature of the universe and why it is the way it is.[10]

In each of the last few decades, these yearnings have taken on new practicality as the environmental movement has become national policy codified into law. For all their remote complexity, ecology and the environmental sciences are the essential foundation for the decades of the environment—past, present, and future.

ECOLOGY AND ENVIRONMENTAL SCIENCES

Ecology and the other environmental sciences are not to be divorced from each other. In a very real sense, all the natural sciences are to some degree environmental in their application or their implications. Ecology is a legitimate contender for identification as the culmination of all the sciences. At one level, it is important to understand that physical and chemical conditions are the essence of ecology and environmental sciences. Each abiotic factor, physical or chemical, exhibits a minimum, optimum, and maximum for every biological system, from the subcellular to the ecological level. If a factor occurs below the minimum, the biological entity will be unable to function. If one occurs above the maximum, the entity will be "poisoned."

Frequently, the optimum, the quantity best serving the entity, is near the maximum tolerable. As will be discussed in greater detail in the context of transitions between the purely chemical and physical components of ecosystems and the biota, mixtures of conditions are actually affecting biological systems in rapidly altering quantitative terms, which can be difficult to follow. Thus, minima, optima, and maxima of individual components are not so readily detectable in real ecosystems as they are in isolated situations. Fortunately, the Theory of Integrative Levels serves ecology and the environmental sciences.

Within the ecosystem and its community of populations, each individual organism has the innate capacity to follow the pattern that is the life history of the species, but it will exhibit behavior patterns that, although unique, are within the constraints posed by the species and will adapt to circumstances in ways that range from momentary physiological accommodations to behavior responses. Similarly, the species itself has a life history, exhibits behavior unique to it, and can adapt to changes in the environment. So, too, do ecosystems, when studied over relatively long intervals, reveal a life history consisting more of adaptation and change than of *behavior* as that term is usually understood.

While ecosystems are structural and functional units represented by relatively stable biological communities, their boundaries are to a certain extent artificial and arbitrarily established. Aquatic ecosystems, even oceans, are inextricably linked to terrestrial systems, yet they and portions of them can legitimately be isolated for analysis without compromising the quality of the results attributed to the system as such. Similarly, although terrestrial ecosystems can be isolated and identified by several classification systems, in large part associated with a combination of latitude and altitude, there are no totally independent ecosystems. Moreover, there are "specialists" among organisms that thrive in habitats between ecosystems. There are, in short, not just overlaps but microcosms within microcosms within (and between) ecosystems. The complex of ecosystems forms the planetary biosphere. Each can influence any or all of the others. Despite the internal reality and integrity, these systems are *inextricably* connected. The environmental professional who loses sight of that reality will almost certainly live to regret the oversight.

Since everything from the physics of fundamental particles to the history of the universe is connected and is at least arguably focused in the ecosystem, it is invaluable to pause here for reflection on two extraordinarily profound aspects of the scientific endeavor: cosmology and the relationship between scientific order and the relative newcomer to science, chaos theory.

Cosmology: From the Infinitesimal to the Universal

There was a time, long before the time when legitimate ecologists could be ensconced in armchairs, when the cosmos could be expressed in five Aristotelian terms. The whole of the natural world emerged from four basic "elements"—earth, air, fire, and water—combined with two forces—gravity and levity. This was a time when matter was deemed continuous. It could be subdivided into ever-smaller bits without limit. There would never be a point at which the material of the world was no longer divisible. Later, atoms were identified and held to be indivisible. Centuries later, the precise relationships among atoms and molecules were detected. As recently as 1905, Einstein observed that Brownian motion—the constant joustling of protoplasm and other suspensions viewed with a light microscope—is actually the result of collisions between atoms and particles large enough to be visible. In another few years, the internal structure of atoms—the complexes of protons and neutrons surrounded by clouds of electrons—was discerned. Now we have discovered protons and neutrons to be precisely divisible into oddities known as quarks bearing features physicists whimsically refer to as "flavors" and "colors."[11]

All of this is quite beyond ordinary powers of comprehension. Earth, air, fire, and water are far more accessible.

At the same time, gravity, if not levity, has transformed into four forces, including some associated with subnuclear particles. In addition to the familiar, but no less mysterious, gravitational force, there is the electromagnetic force as well as the weak and strong nuclear forces. While gravity may be familiar, it is not as well understood as might be suspected. Although it is both universal and consistently a force of attraction, gravity is the weakest force and is mediated by the graviton, a virtual particle without mass.[12]

It is this infinitesimal world of vanishingly small particles and associated forces to which cosmologists turn for explanations of the origins and destiny of the universe. In a very real sense, energy and matter are wholly interchangeable, if not actually identical.[13] In a comparably real sense, ecological sciences are derivatives of both extremes in the scientific scale. The biosphere is one expression of both fundamental physics and cosmological events. But this realization does nothing to advance precision in predicting events from causes, as was once a hope, if not an expectation, among scientists.

Order and Chaos

Because of the emerging simplicity and order of the natural world, a mission was advanced for at least a moment of human history. When physical phenomena were extended into the biological and then into the psychological and social realms, a kind of giddy optimism followed. Among scientists and observers of science, there were those who sincerely believed every event explicable "in terms of antecedent events in causal chains and networks, characterizable in terms of universal laws which make no reference to the causal efficaciousness of future events or higher levels of organization."[14] In the early nineteenth century, arguments were seriously advancing the concept of a complete determinism. Scientific laws would allow predictions of "everything that would happen in the universe, if only we knew the complete state of the universe at [any] one time."[15] Since "everything" included the vagaries of human behavior, it certainly included more scientific environmental processes.

Promise or threat, such scientific predetermination has now been dismissed. Scientists and those observers of science are coming to accept that life, at the very least, is "not meant to be free from contradiction or ambiguity."[16]

It is only in this century that determinism has lost credibility in the face of advancing science. That level of order gave way to the Heisenberg Uncertainty, which has revealed that one cannot accurately know both the position and speed of subatomic particles simultaneously. The new science of quantum mechanics arises empirically from mathematical manipulation of the components of the Heisenberg Uncertainty to predict not a single, definite result but the array of possible outcomes and the likelihood of each. One of the resultant insights crucially important in ecology is that light, while composed of waves, behaves as if particulate. Light energy is emitted and absorbed only in the packets known as quanta.[17] Primarily a practical branch of physics, quantum mechanics explains phenomena as wide reaching as properties of collapsed stars, conduction of electricity, structure of atoms and their nuclei, chemical bonding, and the mechanical and thermal properties of solids.[18]

In more recent days, scientists have come to recognize that while chaos seemingly arises from the orderliness of scientific law, order is the mark of chaos. A new kind of highly mathematical science has reached the headlines and fiction,[19] not to mention volumes intended for coffee tables.[20] In the end, the important conclusion is that life consists of orderly and lawful behavior on the part of matter. Its tendency is not exclusively to proceed from order to disorder; living matter is based on keeping up existing order through metabolism. Not even large biological molecules like DNA escape or invalidate physics, chemistry, or the laws of probability.[21] But none of them can adequately explain life or predict the direction of cell, species, community, or ecosystem. The reason is embedded in chaos.

ECOLOGY, SCIENTIFIC METHOD, AND THE GAIA HYPOTHESIS

A World of Ecologies

Ecology could hardly remain untouched by novel scientific insights, on the one hand, and the political implications of an evolving environmental movement, on the other. There can be few in this country who do not subscribe to the concept of a healthy, diverse ecosystem in a state of dynamic balance. Within such an ecosystem, there are cycles and chains. Food chains connecting animal to plant direct energy outward, whereas death and decay restore energy to the earth. Whenever a change occurs anywhere within the circuit, the remaining parts must adjust to restore the balance of the whole.[22]

Such a description of ecological balance might be uttered by either a practicing ecologist or an environmental professional. It could also be a political statement, for ecology has become a matter of policy and politics.[23] This description might also be a reflection of the spiritual realm and, as such, could arise from any number of traditions, from the Judeo-Christian to the Native American to the Asian to the primal, extant as well as extinct. Ecology is no longer the sole province of the scientist working in aloof isolation.[24]

Deep Ecology

Today, three ecologies—scientific, political, and spiritual—are merged in what is called deep ecology. Yet the proponent of deep ecology need not be a scientist or even any one of the three kinds of ecologist. *Anyone* can be a deep ecologist. In fact, scientific ecology, especially as practiced by environmental professionals, is viewed by some as the antithesis of deep ecology, which is more a discipline of philosophy expressed in poetry than any other form of science.[25]

The mission of the deep ecologist is to cultivate individual but widespread ecological consciousness with an insight into the ubiquitous connections of the world around us. Deep ecology is holistic. Its message is one of appreciation, receptiveness, and trust.[26]

Whether one reacts to deep ecology with empathy or impatience, its tenets proffer much for contemplation by the environmental professional and the interested nonscientist:

1. All life has intrinsic value.
2. The richness and diversity of life have value.
3. Human life is privileged only to the extent of satisfying vital needs.
4. The relationship of humans to the natural world endangers life's richness and diversity.
5. Maintenance of life's richness and diversity mandates a decrease in human population.
6. Changes are needed to accommodate cultural diversity affecting basic economic, technological, and ideological components.
7. Ecologically sensitive ("green") societies value quality of human life over quantity of human life.[27]

How these tenets fit into the ecology of populations, especially of humans, and into the matters of the place of the biota in the strategy of ecosystems will be explored throughout this book, with special reference to the concluding chapters. Whatever the scientific realities of the ecology of the human species, deep ecologists are obligated to promote the needed sociocultural changes.[28] Surely, even these philosopher–poets will be more effective if informed by ecological realities from the scientific realm.

Gaia Hypothesis—Science or Metaphysics?

Ecologists, deep, scientific, or political, have come to recognize this planet's biosphere as a distinct level of organization arising from the interconnections among all the ecosystems. If an ecosystem is a biological system, logic is not strained through the perception of the biosphere as the highest of all biological systems. There are those who would take one more step, perhaps moving from science into metaphysics in doing so. Is the biosphere itself actually a biological entity—a living organism?

This is the position advanced by the Gaia Hypothesis.[29] There are valuable insights to be taken from Gaia, whether one is a believer or a skeptic content with stopping short of Gaia with the biosphere as nothing more (or less) than the highest level of organization. J. Lovelock propounds "that the entire range of living matter on Earth, from whales to viruses, and from oaks to algae, [can] be regarded as constituting a single living entity, capable of manipulating the Earth's atmosphere to suit its overall needs and endowed with faculties and powers far beyond those of its constituent parts."[30]

An intriguing "branch" of the Gaia Hypothesis asserts bacteria to be the primary cybernetic mechanism at Gaia's command: "The environment is so interwoven with bacteria, and their influence is so pervasive, that there is no really convincing way to . . . say this is where life ends and this is where the inorganic realm of nonlife begins."[31] According to the variant of evolutionary theory and of the Gaia Hypothesis, bacteria go beyond filling every known habitat on the earth's surface to maintain all life forms and to accelerate all biological cycles. In short, bacteria represent a complete planetary regulatory system.[32]

Biosphere or Gaia? Is the dominant taxon of earth the kingdom of Monera (bacteria) or *Homo sapiens sapiens* or some organism ecologists have overlooked? Are there practical differences among these distinctions? The individual reader must decide. Armed with the definition of life, the Theory of Integrative Levels, and an awareness of how science works and how the several ecologies fit into human endeavor, the reader will be provided in the chapters to follow with principles and concepts to inform a personal conclusion based in ecology.

Whether one believes in the Gaia Hypothesis or in a variant perspective on evolutionary theory or simply in a functioning biosphere, there is an ecological truth for acceptance by all: "[C]onsisting of life, the environment is continually regulated by life, for life."[33]

NOTES

The principal sources for this chapter are Odum, chapter 1; and Smith, chapter 1.

1. J. Allen, *Biosphere 2: The Human Experiment* (1991), at 35.

2. For a second synopsis in somewhat greater depth, *see* Odum's Great Ideas in Ecology, compiled at the beginning of the concluding chapter.

3. Allen, *supra* note 1, at 35.

4. *See id.*, at 23.

5. N. Hairston, *Ecological Experiments: Purpose, Design, and Execution* (1989), at 55.

6. Allen, *supra* note 1, at 23 (emphasis in original).

7. Hairston, *supra* note 5, at 57.

8. *See, e.g.*, E. Schrödinger, *What Is Life?: And Other Scientific Essays* (Anchor ed., 1956), at 97–98.

9. S. Hawking, *A Brief History of Time: From the Big Bang to Black Holes* (1988), at 168.

10. *Id.*, at 171.

11. *Id.*, at 63–65.

12. *Id.*, at 65, 70, 71, 72–74.

13. *See, e.g.*, P. Davies, *God and the New Physics* (1983), at 160–161.

14. D. Hull, *Philosophy of Biological Science* (1974), at 6.

15. Hawking, *supra* note 9, at 53.

16. S. Gould, *Wonderful Life: The Burgess Shale and the Nature of History* (1989), at 257.

17. Hawking, *supra* note 9, at 55 and 56.

18. Davies, *supra* note 13, at 101.

19. M. Crichton, *Jurassic Park* (1990).

20. *See, e.g.*, E. Porter, *Nature's Chaos* (1990); and J. Briggs, *Fractals: The Patterns of Chaos* (1992).

21. Schrödinger, *supra* note 8, at 68 and 70.

22. D. Lachapelle, *Earth Wisdom* (1978), at 158.

23. *See, e.g.*, C. Lollar, "AAAS Council Acts on Population Growth, RU 486, and More and 1991 Meeting," 252 *Sci.* 586 (Inside AAAS, Apr. 26, 1991). Two American Association for the Advancement of Science resolutions are relevant. One addresses environmental research and training; the other, biodiversity.

24. For more on the diverse realms of ecology, *see, e.g.*, M. Oelschlaeger, *The Idea of Wilderness: From Prehistory to the Age of Ecology* (1991), at 206, 214, 234–235, 237, 239–240, 261, and 431 note 84.

25. *See id.*, at 303–304.

26. B. Devall and G. Sessions, *Deep Ecology: Living As If Nature Mattered* (1985), at 8.

27. Compiled in Oelschlaeger, *supra* note 24, at 303.

28. *Id.*, at 303.

29. J. Lovelock, *Gaia: A New Look at Life on Earth* (1979, 1987 ed.).

30. *Id.*, at 9.

31. L. Margulis and D. Sagan, *Microcosmos: Four Billion Years of Evolution from Our Microbial Ancestors* (1986), at 92–93.

32. *Id.*, at 93–94.

33. *Id.*, at 94.

PART II

HABITATS, COMMUNITIES, AND ECOSYSTEMS: THE HOLISTIC APPROACH

3

Ecosystem as a Concept

THE GENERIC ECOSYSTEM: THE ECOSYSTEM AS A BLACK BOX

If, as was asserted in the opening chapters, an ecosystem can be seen as a black box, representing either one of the highest levels of scientific organization or a kind of biological system, what are its internal black boxes? The ecosystem's complex of inseparable interrelationships is organized in both structure and function. The two can be characterized most generally by the flow of energy through the system and the cycling of materials within it. In short, an ecosystem is made up of habitats, locations in the three spatial dimensions occupied by populations of organisms interacting in a community. If one were to construct an ecosystem, the natural point of departure is the setting composed of habitats, the physical and chemical abiota to which organisms come. The organisms—biota—are organized in relationships among individuals composing populations and the community characteristic of the setting. The resultant whole is the ecosystem.

All the relationships of this biological system are a causation network arising from interactions that are obligatory and interdependent. Close examination of an ecosystem reveals that it is actually made up of multiple smaller units, or microcosms, in which only a few organisms are directly participating, although they somehow contribute to the structure and function of the larger whole. This larger level of analysis is the holistic approach to ecology.

The distinctive biological system of the ecosystem affords each unit at this level of organization its identity. Each species present constitutes a population distributed in its particular habitat and serving the whole in a niche, a structural and functional role of which habitat is only one part.

STRUCTURE AND FUNCTION

Holistic Analysis

The contents of the black box known as an ecosystem are distributed in the abiotic and biotic realms. The former realm is characterized by low energy and inorganic compounds; the latter, by high energy and organic compounds. Energy flows through the system in patterns that follow the overall pattern describing an ecosystem as a biological unit. With the flow of energy, materials cycle between the two realms and among the components of the biota.

The major functional component of the ecosystem lies in the interaction among autotrophic and heterotrophic organisms. The principal features of this interaction are trophic structure, material cycles, and biotic diversity. Both the degree of and the participants in biotic diversity are used not only to identify but also to describe the ecosystem and its condition. Any deviations from anticipated diversity may be an indication of the health of the system or its component parts.

Working with the geological substrate, autotrophs fix light energy and utilize inorganics and some simple organics to synthesize and accumulate organics of greater complexity. The stuff of physics and chemistry is converted into living, functioning organisms. Heterotrophs utilize relatively complex organics constituting plant life for rearrangement as the large organic molecules serving their own life processes. Other heterotrophs decompose these complex materials, returning the basic materials to the substrate as increasingly simple organic and inorganic molecules.

This array of functions is intimately associated with the structural component of the ecosystem. Structure is distributed among abiotic and biotic features. Abiotic structure is physical and chemical and found among inorganic and organic substances as well as in the climate regime, characteristic interactions of light, temperature, moisture, and wind. Biotic structure is distributed among producers (autotrophic), macroconsumers (heterotrophic phagotrophs) and microconsumers (heterotrophic saprotrophs).

Neither the populations nor the community of organisms is a mere aggregation. Based on the activities and interactions of its individual members, each population is itself a unit exhibiting structure and function. The interactions among populations in an ecosystem give rise to the structure and function of its distinctive community. The whole depends on the parts—abiotic as well as biotic.

Stability, known as homeostasis, can be discerned over different time scales. Homeostasis is maintained by cybernetic mechanisms, a variety of control devices operating at every level from subcellular molecular biology to changes in the ecosystem at large. Thus, the components of an ecosystem will be shifting subtly as environmental conditions constantly alter over time measured in units smaller than seconds. Larger alterations over longer intervals may give rise to adaptations, which may either be retained or lost as new ones assert themselves.

Discernible stability notwithstanding, every ecosystem is undergoing development and, over longer intervals of time, evolution. Adaptation can be distinguished from evolution in the former's smaller time frame and temporary nature requiring no alteration in genetic structure. Adaptations are reversible and range in units of time from fractions of seconds to the lifetime of the affected biological system. By definition, evolution occurs over several generations of a given biological system and proceeds through inheritable genetic alteration.

Behind the ecosystem as a biological unit is the entire array of sciences we distribute among physics, chemistry, and biology. The biological nature of the organisms in an ecosystem determines their roles. That nature can be understood through the biochemical reactions occurring at the subcellular level and expressed ultimately at the organismal level as each individual participates in the interactions of its population and community. The energy that is driving the overall process comes from the sun and participates in the chemical reactions occurring in the cells of the biota. Put most simplistically, energy enters the black box from which emerge the products of respiration and energy in the form of heat. It is instructive to so view the generic ecosystem. In contrast, most of the material in a well-established ecosystem is available within its boundaries.

Sunlight enters along with water and carbon dioxide and a few other inorganic substances. Molecular oxygen, water, and heat exit. In a sense, this exchange can be viewed as the whole of an ecosystem, but it is hardly a satisfactory description. For increasingly satisfactory descriptions, it is necessary to explore the contents of this black box and all the black boxes of which it is composed.

Each of these analytical approaches to empirical ecology can be followed at any level, from the subatomic to the biosphere itself. Each level of biological organization from the single or individual cell to the biosphere has a life history and what can be called behavior. Each can adapt, and each can undergo evolutionary processes.

Reductionist Analysis

Analysis of structure and function becomes possible by taking a reductionist approach. Every ecosystem is made up of essentially the same components, each in patterns unique to it. There are energy circuits and their corresponding food chains and webs. There are cycles of matter in the form of biogeochemical cycles that suffuse all the components of both realms. There are patterns of diversity that can, and must, be described in terms of three-dimensional space and in terms of time as the fourth dimension. In different language, there is an economics of an ecosystem: Resources are allocated, cost-benefit ratios operate, and optimization occurs. The resources are energy and materials, the cost-benefit ratios are based on energy distribution and such considerations as competition and predation, and optimization results when organisms occupy niches.

Energy Flow. Much of what makes an ecosystem a discernible unit can actually be explained in terms of the First and Second Laws of Thermodynamics. The First Law of Thermodynamics states that neither energy nor matter can be created or destroyed. Each, however, can be transformed from one form to another. Energy, for example, is generally characterized as potential or kinetic. Energy, described as the capacity to do work, is considered potential when it is poised to do work and kinetic when it is in the process of doing work. Familiar forms of potential energy are a rock balanced at the edge of a precipice and water at the top of a gradient. Kinetic energy is represented by the actual fall of the rock or the flow of water.

Less familiar forms of potential energy are in a relaxed muscle, the internal bonds holding molecules together, and a nerve synapse. The corresponding kinetic energy of each is the contraction of a muscle to do mechanical work, the breaking of the chemical bond to release the contained energy, and the electrical charge of the activated nerve cell.[1] Each contributes to the functioning of organisms, and organisms are constantly interacting in and with their environment.

While all the energy of ecosystems comes from the sun, the forms that solar radiation takes are greatly varied. It can become biomass or wind or tide or heat. Energy in ecosystems is, then, a vivid demonstration that energy and matter are interchangeable. Energy is not created in an ecosystem but biologically fixed as it enters from outside—that is, assimilated through physical and chemical processes into a form available to life. That form is matter, the material of which biomass is composed. Similarly, matter is not created in an ecosystem but undergoes a series of alterations in chemical composition.

For every reaction of life, there is some loss of energy. This is an inescapable reality imposed by the Second Law of Thermodynamics, which can be stated in a number of different qualitative ways—accepting without further discussion the sophisticated mathematics describing the principle in precise quantitative detail. The Second Law holds that, left to itself, every system will dissipate into complete randomness—total entropy. Although chemical reactions occur, none is 100% efficient, some energy is lost in the process, usually as heat, measured as entropy. Both structure and function are constantly working against entropy. In a universe proceeding toward entropy, life is often viewed as the extreme of organization consisting of negative entropy.

The processes of energy flow through an ecosystem can then be summarized as the entry of radiant energy from the sun, some of which is reflected outward through the atmosphere, into the solar system, the galaxy, and the universe beyond, where it is lost to the planetary processes of our solar system. Some of that energy, however, becomes a part of the abiotic realm. It will warm the atmosphere and the earth to temperatures allowing life processes to occur. It will take the form of wind, which contributes to climate on a global and local scale. Some will become a part of the global hydrogeological cycle, which is an important source of both energy and material in ecosystems.

A fraction of the sun's radiant energy, specifically that occurring near the midpoint of the visible range, is captured by the biota. It is absorbed and assimilated by green plants and other autotrophic organisms. By the process of photosynthesis, the sun's light energy is converted into plant biomass. In a series of steps, that biomass may be consumed by populations of animals. When these animals excrete wastes, the waste products become nutrients to other organisms from animals to fungi and bacteria. These organisms return the materials of the biomass to the physical realm, where they can reenter the processes initiated by photosynthesis.

Material Cycling. It should have become obvious rather quickly that it is difficult to isolate one part of an ecosystem from another. While energy flow can be isolated for close analysis, the relationship to biochemistry cannot be neglected. It is chemistry, then, that describes the countless steps by which assimilated energy is distributed throughout the ecosystem by the biota. Green plants and other autotrophs initially assimilate the energy and convert it into their own biomass and use it to conduct the processes of their lives.

Homeostasis. Homeostasis is a tendency to resist change and remain in a state of equilibrium through processes of self-maintenance and self-regulation. These are the processes of cybernetics, the study of how biological systems maintain the status quo or maintain their integrity at a different level of homeostasis. Equilibria are maintained by positive and negative feedback.

Adaptation and Evolution. Despite the tendency of biological systems to restore altered order through cybernetic processes reestablishing homeostasis, no biological system, including ecosystems, is in any sense static. As a result, no description of an ecosystem or of its living components can be expected to remain accurate indefinitely. Adaptation is a constant process leading to evolution or extinction whenever perturbation exceeds the cybernetic capacities of populations. A description of an ecosystem is best acknowledged as a snapshot. It will be as accurate a representation of the real thing as the camera and film of ecological analysis allow. But tomorrow's snapshot is likely to be quite different from today's, whether the equipment is the same or an improvement.

Furthermore, although ecosystems are more than a construct to aid in scientific or other analyses, their boundaries are not so clear-cut as scientists and other observers make them. It is obvious that energy comes from outside the ecosystem in the form of light, heat, wind, and physical power of water. Energy also leaves the ecosystem. Similarly, material and even organisms may come from beyond both the convenient and the real boundaries of any given ecosystem or somehow be carried beyond them. It is helpful to consider these factors in two kinds of ecosystems—terrestrial and aquatic. The ecologist must be prepared to examine both the minutia of the ecosystem and its larger setting.

NOTES

The principal sources for this chapter are Odum, chapters 2 and 11; *Journey*, at 769–785 and 788–789; Smith, chapters 2 and 11; and Ricklefs, chapters 5 and 8 and at 98–123.

1. *Journey*, at 101.

4

Global Ecosystems

Every ecosystem depends on a mixture of abiotic and biotic components, but it is always greater than the sum of those parts. In examining global ecosystems, there are any number of points of entry. In keeping with moving from the whole to the abiota to the biota, there is some logic in moving from habitat to community and finally to the ecosystem as the resultant whole. This, after all, is the strategy of the individual ecosystem and of the biosphere.

Habitat is where an organism lives. If habitat is an organism's address, niche is its line of work and actual day-to-day employment. Communities are the living connections by which habitats are linked to an ecosystem. The ecosystem emerges as the functional biological system consisting of specific structural components. Aquatic or terrestrial, each ecosystem will follow the generic pattern provided in the last chapter but with variations unique to it and its location.

AQUATIC ECOLOGY[1]

The Habitats

From clear mountain stream to swamp, from brook to pond to sluggish river to freshwater inland sea, from shoreline to abyssal depths, from polar cold to equatorial tropics, from centimeters (or inches) to kilometers (or miles) in depth—aquatic systems represent a variety of habitats at least as diverse as their terrestrial counterparts. On the basis of salinity, three aquatic environments are recognized: freshwater, marine, estuarine.

Freshwater habitats are broadly classified as standing water (lentic) or running water (lotic). In accordance with the general rule, sharp demarcations from one habitat to another seldom occur. Moreover, a detailed nature of each will depend greatly on surrounding ecosystems, terrestrial as well as aquatic. Temperature, transparency, and current are the primary features of freshwater habitats. All three impose physical and chemical influences on the biota. Temperature ranges are relatively limited.

One of the amazing accidents or coincidences (see Chapter 10) of the biosphere is that while water freezes at 0°C (32°F), it is at its densest point at 4°C. Water is lighter above and below that temperature. The ecologically significant result is that ice floats. The significance to the biota is that large bodies of standing water often remain liquid throughout the cold seasons, allowing living processes to proceed. Another ecologically important feature associated with water's unique physicochemical properties is the turnover phenomenon. In spring and in fall, the surface and deep waters of large lakes exchange places—turn over. The result is a thorough redistribution of nutrients.

Primary producers, of course, depend on the penetration of light into the water column. Transparency of water is also a physicochemical property, but it is greatly influenced by the presence of suspended particles, chemical and living. The patterns of current, too, have physical and chemical implications to which freshwater organisms have adapted through evolutionary processes and must adapt from moment to moment and through seasonal changes.

Additional features composing freshwater habitats are concentrations of dissolved oxygen and carbon dioxide, essential to respiration and photosynthesis and important to concentrations of positive and negative ions (pH). This pH and related buffering capacity of the water are at once mediated by and crucial to the chemistry of surface waters. Chemical identity, mobility, and biological availability depend in part on whether pH is acidic, basic, or neutral. Most notable among these chemical substances are the biogenic salts, particularly nitrates and phosphates.

Strangely enough, the oceans—in which life originated and still a major source of material for terrestrial populations—are accurately described as semideserts. For lack of energy and material, the open ocean is unable to support dense communities. Still, as an array of habitats, the earth's sea is notable for its size (70% of the planetary surface), its depth, and its continuity. Barriers to movement, abiotic or biotic, do exist as a result of temperature regimes, differing salinity, and depth. Each organism will be subject to a specific tolerance range for combinations of these factors.

In addition to light and temperature, a major source of energy in marine habitats comes in the form of currents, waves, and tides. Comparable to terrestrial climatology and resultant meteorology, continuous circulation of ocean waters affects marine habitats physically, chemically, and biologically.

Literally standing between freshwater and marine habitats, and heavily influenced by both, are estuarine habitats. These are the aquatic ecotones, transitions between freshwater and marine ecosystems. As such, estuarine habitats are more than transitional; they are in some ways characteristically unique. In addition to the mingled influence of flow, currents, and tides, there are the rhythmic alterations in salinity. Although these habitats are rich in nutrients, species diversity is kept low because of the demands for wide tolerances.

Not surprisingly, there is a wide variety among estuarine habitats. Not only do they alter with the terrain and bodies of water forming them; estuaries will also be influenced heavily by their location on the globe corresponding to, and affected by, the surrounding terrestrial ecosystems.

As is always the case, care must be taken in drawing boundaries around aquatic ecosystems. It is well established that the oceans not only compose a major component of hydrogeological cycles but also bear a heavy influence on global climate and meteorological patterns. The oceans also have a substantial place in large-scale material cycling, with special reference to carbon.

The Communities

Freshwater habitats support the same kinds of food webs readily identified in terrestrial communities. There are the autotrophic producers and the heterotrophs, phagotrophic macroconsumers and saprotrophic decomposers, and microconsumers. The distribution of communities covers all three dimensions. Near the surface are communities of phytoplankton and the zooplankton, the latter only marginally more motile than the former. Throughout the body of water are the swimmers—large insects, amphibians, and fish. Some of these organisms are quite capable of moving to the surface or to the bottom substrate to feed or to proceed through the stages of their life histories.

Where currents and transparency allow, certain organisms attach to the underlying substrates along the edges of the water body and into the benthos, the substrate beneath the water column. Communities expand to include plants and animals that attach to these attached organisms. The benthos is rich in life, forming a diverse community in and on the solids. In each ecosystem, the actual taxons composing these communities are determined by the composite of abiotic features characterizing each body of water all the way from its general geological formation to the microenvironmental scale.

Marine biota also include plankton, swimmers, some attached plants, and associated plants and animals and benthic communities. Both the taxons and their representatives may be unique to the marine environments. For example, sponges and echinoderms, relatively unimportant in freshwater communities, are highly significant to marine ecology. Higher plants are rare, and insects are replaced by crustaceans. In marine habitats, large mammals travel huge distances in groups and are among both primary and secondary consumers.

Bacteria, algae, crustaceans, and fish, however, are dominant in both freshwater and marine environments. The representative communities of the two are distinct and, as always, characteristic. Moreover, communities filling the respective habitats of freshwater and marine ecosystems are quite characteristic. It is worth noting that some of the species present possess elaborate life cycles, some of which can be highly mysterious even to the most observant of researchers. This is particularly the case among marine organisms, which may fill niches in widely disparate habitats from one stage to the next.

Along the shorelines and estuaries, marine and aquatic birds are a part of the intricate food webs. Wetlands and freshwater formations support their own communities, permanent and transient. Many terrestrial mammals pass much of their time in and along such bodies of water. Aquatic fowl and the raptors are semipermanent residents. Finally, migrating flocks of fowl and songbirds depend on aquatic habitats to support them in their extraordinary intercontinental flights. But estuaries may be most significant ecologically as nurseries serving an astonishing array of populations and, of course, the sometimes-distant communities in which they participate in subsequent stages of their life cycles.

The Ecosystems

Every brook, pond, lake, stream, river, inland sea, estuary, swamp, bog, or ocean, each with its respective community, can be legitimately identified as an ecosystem. On one scale, it may be foolish to take on ecological analysis of the whole of the aquatic portion of the planet, but it is unwise to isolate any aquatic habitat from the larger environment.

Numerous ecosystems, each marked with its own community, are generally recognized by aquatic and marine ecologists. The existence of some, if not their ecological detail, is quite apparent to the most casual of observers. In freshwater systems, there are shallow (littoral) zones, open water (limnetic zones), and deep waters (profundal zones). In flowing waters, there are distinct rapids and pools, as well as more intricate or subtler formations. Each combination of distinctive habitat and corresponding community can be approached as an ecosystem, whether relatively open or relatively closed. Not to be disregarded is the complete identity of the underlying substrate, which is particularly important in the matter of potential perturbation attributable to chemical substances as either nutrients or toxins.

Lakes are large enough to exhibit temperature stratification, which will exert a major effect on the distribution of both nutrients and organisms and which will alter energy availability and demands. Ecosystems will reflect those dynamic influences in the detail of ecological structure and function.

Marine ecosystems exhibit similar zonation and stratification, ranging from shallow intertidal zones to the open ocean where there are the same kinds of geological structural formations as characterize terrestrial geology.

In terms of productivity, the estuarine ecosystems outperform both marine and freshwater counterparts. High productivity is attributed to the energy subsidies occurring only in these environments. Moreover, estuarine ecosystems are nutrient traps. Thus, they are amply endowed to serve communities rich in numbers if not diversity.

From the human perspective, estuarine ecosystems not only are a bountiful source of food but also are capable of the ecological (re)cycling of material wastes generated by human life and industry. The designers of Biosphere 2 took this function into consideration in seeking methods to cleanse human wastes from this ambitious but severely limited artificial ecosystem.[2]

It is more in keeping with ecological realities to be prepared to work from microcosm to an ever-expanding definition of the ecosystem in order to discern just what is entering and leaving the particular black box of immediate interest. Individual communities are functioning in defined ecosystems within each larger body of water. Similarly, it is essential to look beyond the body of water to larger watersheds or terrestrial ecosystems influencing and influenced by that environment and its biota.

THE TERRESTRIAL ENVIRONMENT[3]

The terrestrial ecosystem is built quite literally from the ground up. Terrestrial substrates vary widely from cooled lava or volcanic ash, bare rock, sand, and rich or poor soil. Whatever their physical and chemical nature, global substrates attract characteristic plants and microorganisms. These are the primary producers, microbial autotrophs, and the saprotrophs. Each association among these organisms is in turn associated with corresponding herbivores. Insects, rodents, birds, hoofed mammals—their identities depend on the specific plant taxons present. Communities within communities will act together, some in obligate pairings or more elaborate combinations, others in more flexible, temporal associations.

The community of carnivores will include many of the same orders and higher taxons as the herbivore community, composed of the same or different genera and species. An ecologist or a taxonomist can identify the location by describing the ecosystem and identifying the species making up its community.

It is possible to trace characteristic changes in ecosystems with distance in a line perpendicular to a shore front, lakeshore, or band of flowing water. The changing habitats support different plants, which bring different associations among the remainder of the community. Height becomes increasingly important. Low-growing plants—lichens, mosses, and grasses—give way to shrubs, bushes, and small trees, then to taller, more luxuriant, and older trees. Characteristic animal associations occur from soil to treetop. Some are permanent; others come and go in diurnal or seasonal patterns; still others are transient.

Terrestrial ecosystems depend primarily on climate and substrate. Almost all other important abiotic factors are related to that combination and to the modifications effected by the biota. For this reason, the classification of terrestrial ecosystems is important to the ecologist and to the environmental professional. Whenever one knows what should be present in a given location, it is possible to determine whether some interference with the ecosystem is occurring.

CLASSIFICATION OF TERRESTRIAL ECOSYSTEMS

Methods of Classification[4]

Because they tend to be relatively fixed in place, terrestrial ecosystems lend themselves to classification. In addition to opening the way to understanding structure, function, and strategy of an ecosystem, classification points the way to determining the condition of a specific ecosystem.

There are a variety of ways in which ecosystems have been classified, and each reflects an internal ecological logic. Zoogeography provides a classification identifying biogeochemical regions. Temperature regimes support life zones with characteristic plants and animals. Ecological associations at the species and subspecies levels give rise to biotic provinces, with an emphasis on the ranges and centers of distribution of animals. Here, plants lose no importance to the ecosystem, but boundaries are drawn from physiographic barriers rather than from types of vegetation.

Plant formations in their turn provide for biomes, which include associated animals, since animal life depends, after all, on the plant base. The biome takes into account the distinct community of plants and animals that combine in the climax community, as well as the sere proceeding to that relatively stable and long-lived ecosystem (see Chapter 10). This classification system also reflects the crucial and interacting roles of latitude and altitude. The biome is isolated through a combination of mean annual temperature and mean annual precipitation, climate tempered by local meteorology.

While each classification has its obvious advantages tempered with disadvantages, depending on the needs of researcher or observer, each should complement, if not actually confirm, the conclusions afforded by the others.

Still, there is one classification system that seems the most promising for environmental professionals: the Holdridge Life Zone System.

Based on three predominant interacting global features—latitude, altitude, and moisture regime—which are very closely related to climate, the Holdridge life zones should represent or predict climax communities throughout the globe. Each life zone, defined by climate, will support a specific kind of community, the specific taxons present further determined by local conditions.

The Holdridge system can be represented by a triangle containing six-sided figures, each representing a zone. Across the base of the triangle are humidity provinces from the arid to the humid. Along each side, temperatures decrease from base to tip, on the one side as latitude moves from equator to pole and on the other with increasing altitude. The two are comparable in effect on community type in that both distance from the equator and altitude affect temperature, expressed as biotemperature, mathematically manipulated to represent the extremes organisms tolerate. Thus, tropical latitudes are comparable to lower montane altitudes, and subpolar to alpine. The internal hexagons each represent a different kind of community. At the arid extreme, deserts occur at every latitude or altitude until the most extreme dry tundra occurs. In temperate latitudes or altitudes, moisture increases allow deserts to be replaced with desert scrub, steppe, moist forest, wet forest, and finally rain forest.[5]

A newer classification system, identifying ecoregions, is a synthesis going beyond climate type to include actual associations of vegetation and soil type. Underlying it, and an implication behind the other systems as well, is that uniformity of climate and soil should lead to similar vegetation. Disparities, then, should always reflect locally unique conditions, an early seral stage, or perturbation.

Implications for Environmental Professionals

The foregoing has been no more than the sketchiest of global ecosystems and their significance to ecologist and environmental professional. Little justice has been done the similarities, distinctions, diversity, and richness of global ecosystems.[6] Nevertheless, the connections significant to the practice of any environmental professional are extracted from the full array of those considerations. The basic structural and functional ecosystem components are to be expected, but the expected biota will be a unique and characteristic community.

The initial determinations the environmental professional must make in revealing why an expected community does not occur are the ecological history of the ecosystem, its seral stage, and the nature of the substrate supporting the community. Only when the naturally occurring features that distinguish the ecosystem have been identified is it prudent to commence a consideration of likely anthropogenic influences amenable to intervention through applied ecology, technology, or the law. When a perturbation is revealed, its ecological effects subject to the fourth dimension of time should always be carefully analyzed in preparation for introducing any intervention in the name of the environment. Ecological analysis of intervention is especially crucial in the usual circumstances where the expertise of additional disciplines will be drawn into the program.

NOTES

1. The principal source for this section is Odum, chapters 11 through 13. *See also* Ricklefs, chapter 5; and Smith, chapters 32 and 33.

2. J. Allen, *Biosphere 2: The Human Experiment* (1991), at 22, 26, 39, and 71.

3. The principal sources for this section are Smith, chapters 9 and 29 through 31; Ricklefs, chapters 5 and 6; and Odum, chapter 14.

4. The principal sources for this section are Smith, chapter 28, especially at 720–723; and Ricklefs, chapter 2.

5. Smith, figure 28.4, at 722.

6. The reader is urged to explore the rich library of natural history, of the past and by contemporary observers. In addition, there are any number of videotapes and television documentaries, as rich in image as they are in the empirical ecology they reflect. In the Ecology and Environmental Sciences course presented at the Environmental Law Center, several tapes have proven inspirational to the students. Among them are *The Creation of the Universe*, available from PBS Home Video; *Rain Forest*, available from National Geographic Video; and Hawkhill Video's *Science & Society—Future Quest* and *Ecosystems—Future Quest*. Hawkhill's *Science & Society* has proven to be particularly relevant and extremely controversial. It represents a useful exercise for any environmental professional anticipating dealing with expert witnesses in a forum of the politicolegal system.

5

Ecosystems and the Law

The preceding chapters reveal the extent to which delineation of an ecosystem through sharp, isolating boundaries is an artificial tool facilitating organized studies, empirical, experimental, or regulatory in intent. Delineation necessarily focuses on a limited array of ecological features to avoid the confounding effects arising from phenomenal complexity at this level of organization. Arising from the literally uncountable features in dynamic operation in nature, complexity is compounded by the contributions of all the levels of organization above and below the ecosystem.

But ecosystems are not entirely artificial constructs for the sake of mere convenience, scientific or political. There is a biological or scientific reality that bears some relationship, however tenuous to the construct. Reality and construct may possess entirely different boundaries and may be more ephemeral than is acceptable to scientists, not to mention politicians and bureaucrats, but the ecosystem is really there.

Specific categories of ecosystems have been recognized among scientists; counterparts can be found in, or extracted from, statutes, regulations, and associated documents regulators develop in cooperation with scientists. The question that remains for environmental professionals is whether and to what extent operating definitions of ecology and policy are coextensive. Close behind this question is the matter of the nature and extent of definitional divergence as putative ecology becomes law.

FROM ECOLOGY TO LAW: SCIENCE IN THE POLITICOLEGAL SYSTEM

Transitions from natural science to law are never easy. And among the natural sciences, ecology may prove to be the most complex. The first impediment to facile transition is the particular kind of science being incorporated into law and policy. The second impediment relates to the mechanics of incorporation.

H. Bauer would strain "science" through a "knowledge filter" by which the merely subjective and unreliable principles and concepts are eliminated to leave a filtrate of the reliable and objective.[1] Entering the filter are all the human traits marking scientists along with all the rest of us. These traits incorporate everything from conservatism to wild ideas. According to Bauer, frontier science is the result of the first filtration, which eliminates the nonsense, stupidity, and pseudoscience. From the frontier, scientific thought is filtered into the primary literature with the elimination of bias, error, and outright dishonesty. Through an additional three filters, knowledge proceeds into the secondary literature, textbook science, and ultimately into the textbooks of the future.

All too often, abstract policy and real-world regulation exist in the inadequately evaluated areas prior to filtration and at the frontier of science. Textbook science is often far behind the immediate needs of national politicolegal institutions.

As a part of this inadeqate filtration of principles and concepts or their applications to the need at hand, there is the matter of ethics as espoused, respectively, by scientists and by policymakers. Where do the environmental professionals' loyalties properly lie? To the process of ecology or other environmental sciences? To society or some segment of society? To the employer, public or private? For example, is there an obligation to encourage the sharing of data in the name of ecologically sound policy? Is there any obligation to inform the public at large of the realities of the level of organization when information available to them is skewed?[2]

On another level, how should public research dollars be distributed among ecologists? Should the distribution reflect the call for movement away from enumeration of species and preservation of habitats to elucidation of politically relevant issues such as global climate change or loss of biological diversity? Should the academically unpopular interdisciplinary approaches be fostered?[3]

Actually, these and related questions may be premature in the context of integrating ecology and environmental sciences into policy and law. The more immediate question probably lies in the level of congressional comprehension of environmental principles and concepts as reflected in relevant statutes.

Although natural resources management and related programs are more intimately connected with ecosystems, pollution is the most immediate link between ecology and law at the national level. Pollution can be physical, chemical, or biological and is subject to time considerations. Usually, pollution is described simplistically as too little or too much of one or a few factors, more often chemical than physical or biological. But heat can be a physical pollutant, and infectious or imported organisms, biological pollutants.

Ecologists will discern significant alterations long before an entire population, much less a community or entire ecosystem, is threatened. Subtle changes may occur in the abiota or in the cells of certain organisms. Over time, with continued intrusion or additional pressures, the intensity of the changes will increase and will be manifested in increasingly obvious ways. Some of those alterations will affect natural resources, portions of the abiota or biota of specific, usually economic, interest to humans.

Thus, under the law an anthropogenic agent becomes a pollutant when it affects a natural resource so as to interfere somehow with *human* interests. The significant reference is to human needs or values. At the outset, in accord with constitutional limitations on the legal system, human health comes first, followed by human welfare. Ecological amenities are a distant third in our politicolegal system. Ecosystems and their components in and of themselves come in dead last. Thus, the interests of a few populations of one species relatively high in the food chain comes first, and subtle alterations within the rest of the biosphere may be ignored until substantial damage has been done.

INTEGRATION OF ECOSYSTEM CONCEPTS
IN FEDERAL PROGRAMS

To what extent and how well are the ecosystem and related biological systems integrated into federal programs? To a great extent, the answer depends on the avowed mission of the individual program. Although conservation and preservation have been evolving since the era of Teddy Roosevelt,[4] the contemporary emphasis is as often pollution control as natural resources management. The benchmark statute of the environmental movement and the one that promised to make the requisite connections is the National Environmental Policy Act (NEPA).

NEPA

NEPA is codified at 42 U.S.C.A. 4321 *et seq.*[5] This is the statute that opens the door to connecting the national pollution control program to environmental protection. A legitimate question here is whether the Congress effectively integrated the concept of ecosystem into this crucial enactment.

The obvious starting point is in the declarations of policy. While the word *ecosystem* never appears, its presence can be felt in NEPA's declaration of purpose to

encourage productive and enjoyable harmony between man and his environment; to promote efforts which will prevent or eliminate damage to the environment and biosphere and stimulate the health and welfare of man; to enrich the understanding of ecological systems and natural resources important to the Nation[.] (NEPA sec. 2)

In establishing a national environmental policy, Congress continues to emphasize the quality of the *human* environment (see sec. 101(a) and (b)) without express reference to ecosystems. Congress left such detail to those implementing and enforcing NEPA—administrative agencies under the watchful eye of the judiciary.

Pollution Control by Environmental "Medium"

Air. Close on the heels of NEPA came the first in the array of new or substantially modified federal statutes intended to protect environmental media from pollution through control at the source. The initial statute is known as the Clean Air Act (CAA), 42 U.S.C.A. 7401 *et seq*. It is intended to protect ambient (atmospheric) air through control of industrial emissions. Early versions of the Clean Air Act speak of "mounting dangers to the public health and welfare" without express reference to any potentially affected ecosystems (CAA sec. 101, as amended through 1982). Instead, there is reference to the nation's air resources in the context of promoting public health and welfare and the productive capacity of the human population (sec. 101(b)(1)). Even in the context of health and welfare of populations of *Homo sapiens sapiens*, such contemporary issues as acid rain, global warming, and depletion of stratospheric ozone were not among environmental perturbations to be alleviated.

The focus of associated research was more on technology than on ecology or any of the other natural sciences (secs. 103–105). Nevertheless, at least the inference of an interest in healthful ecosystems is present in the name of public welfare. The matter of protection of stratospheric ozone did enter the Clean Air Act upon amendment in 1977 (secs. 150–159). Still there was no express reference to ecological considerations.

Congressional focus remained on anthropogenic changes in the stratosphere that could "cause or contribute to endangerment of the public health or welfare" (sec. 150(3)). The need to infer ecological health only in the name of human welfare—or health—lingered. Future direction is, however, at least suggested in the congressional finding to the effect that increased solar ultraviolet radiation as a result of "holes" to stratospheric ozone could increase human disease rates, threaten food crops, and most significantly to ecological concerns, "otherwise damage the natural environment" (sec. 151(a)(3)).

Improved attention to ecosystems is more promising in the charge to the National Science Foundation calling for research intended to "increase scientific knowledge of the effects of changes in the [stratospheric] ozone layer . . . upon living organisms and *ecosystems*" (sec. 154(c)).[6]

Ecosystems, Air, and the Amendments of 1990. When the Clean Air Act underwent major amendment in 1990, a substantial increase in the ecological sophistication of Congress was suggested. Definitions began to accommodate ecological features directly as well as indirectly through the public welfare route, research projects commenced to show signs of incorporating ecological realities, matters of more ecological than merely human welfare interests emerged, and regulatory programs took on an ecological component beyond any that happened to be associated with ambient air quality and designated pollutants.

The most obvious general incorporation of ecological considerations can be found in the program addressing hazardous air pollutants.[7] New subsection 112(a)(7) adds a mandate for regulating as hazardous an emission posing

any significant and widespread adverse effect, which may reasonably be anticipated, to wildlife, aquatic life, or other natural resources, including adverse impacts on populations of endangered or threatened species or significant degradation of environmental quality over broad areas.

Additionally, "welfare" throughout the statute is expanded to include effects on soils, water, vegetation, animals, wildlife, weather, and climate (sec. 302(h)).

The 1990 amendments do provide expressly and directly for ecosystem research, specifically "to improve understanding of the short-term and long-term causes, effects, and trends of ecosystem damage from air pollutants" (sec. 103(e)). Considerable sensitivity to complexity in ecosystems is discernible in congressional direction to address causes and effects associated with chronic and episodic exposures and calling for a determination of reversibility (sec. 103(e)(2)). The latter also shows some acceptance of resiliency in ecosystems—the characteristic tendency to restore homeostasis upon perturbation. Research efforts are also directed to promote improved understanding of multiple environmental stresses associated with air pollution (sec. 103(e)(3)) and, showing still greater sophistication, evaluation of effects on water quality attributable to acid deposition and other atmospheric pollutants. There is reference to wetlands, estuaries, and groundwater, all of which are or affect ecosystems that may be sensitive to airborne chemical substances (sec. 103(e)(4)). Terrestrial ecosystems are not neglected. There is reference to soils, forests, and biological diversity (sec. 103(e)(5)).

Certain ecological matters that had not been amenable to action under the Clean Air Act are expressly brought into the program. They are stratospheric ozone protection, addressed in subchapter VI; acid deposition, covered in section 112 and at subchapter IV-A; and the more general pollution deposition into surface waters. The matter of global warming is incorporated in subchapter VI (sec. 602(e)).

The ecological significance of stratospheric ozone and the corresponding basis for protective measures are assumed in section 602 in which ozone-depleting anthropogenic chemicals are listed for the purpose of monitoring and reporting (sec. 603) and actual elimination from production and consumption in the marketplace (secs. 604 and 605). There is even anticipation of a potential call for an accelerated schedule on behalf of the environment as well as of human health (sec. 606(a)(1)).

Acid deposition is the subject of continuing research, with particular reference to continuation of programs established in the Acid Precipitation Act of 1980, 42 U.S.C.A. 8901 *et seq*. Research, focusing on water quality, forests, and soil, accommodates time scales in keeping with those at which ecosystems are functioning (CAA sec. 103(j)(3)).

More general deposition of air pollutants in the Great Lakes, Chesapeake Bay, Lake Champlain, and coastal waters is addressed as part of the vastly expanded National Emission Standards for Hazardous Air Pollutants (NESHAPS) program (sec. 112(m)). Among other things, the relevant subsection calls for the sampling of pollutants in the "biota" and in fish and wildlife. *Biota* goes undefined. In the cases of Chesapeake Bay and Lake Champlain, an expansion of interest to include watersheds (sec. 112(m)(3)) suggests recognition of how one ecosystem can merge into another and of the interconnections between aquatic and terrestrial ecosystems.

At a more general level of regulation, the statutory frameworks for criteria pollutants as well as for hazardous pollutants now take into account ecological amenities above and beyond any that may be brought in through the back door of human welfare. In the case of criteria pollutants, the U.S. Environmental Protection Agency (EPA) is now authorized to assess risks to ecosystems from the listed pollutants (sec. 108(g)). In revising the congressionally established list of hazardous pollutants, the EPA may by rule address environmental effects resulting from ambient concentrations of those pollutants, from deposition and bioaccumulation and other processes (sec. 112(b)(2))—a refreshing acknowledgment that all the possibilities cannot be predicted from the splendid isolation of congressional offices.

Ecosystems and the Clean Water Act. The Clean Water Act (CWA; the Federal Water Pollution Control Act), 33 U.S.C.A. 1251 *et seq.*, as amended through 1990, followed the Clean Air Act in more than the chronological sense. The concept of ambient air finds its counterpart in water quality, while discharges to surface waters correspond to emissions into the air. In the case of water, however, ecological components were from the outset a major component of the statutory framework.

Since the contemporary origins of federal water pollution control, eco-logical systems have increasingly been integrated into emerging policy. They are found in definitions, research programs, and regulatory regimes. Taken altogether, the relevant provisions of this statute reveal attention to the flow of energy, material cycling, strategy and homeostasis, popu-lation and community interactions, and even more subtle components of the generic ecosystem as manifested in aquatic habitats. But even as this improved attention to ecology takes hold, a lingering anthropocentrism remains.

An ecological foundation is present from the opening of the Clean Water Act, with the statement of one major objective: the restoration and main-tenance of the nation's waters in terms of physical, chemical, and biological parameters (CWA sec. 101; see also sec. 104(r)). A related interim goal is water quality suitable for the protection and propagation of fish, shellfish, and wildlife (sec. 101(a)).[8]

Statutory definitions suggest more than a passing interest in ecosystem components. For effluent standards, a toxic pollutant is defined through the capacity

upon exposure, ingestion, inhalation or assimilation into any organism, either di-rectly from the environment or indirectly by ingestion through food chains, . . . [to] cause death, disease, behavioral abnormalities, cancer, genetic mutations, phys-iological malfunctions [including reproductive] or physical deformations, in such organisms or their offspring. (sec. 502(13))

This one definition reflects increased ecological awareness. Trophic levels of simple food chains or more complex food nets are recognized, as are mortality in one or more individual organisms and in whole assemblages. The more subtle reality of the importance of routes of entry breaching the integrity separating internal self from the external environment is accepted. Further, the requirement that environmental components be in contact in order to interact is also accepted. Finally, perturbation at the organismal level is acknowledged with reference to an array of biological endpoints ranging through behavioral abnormalities, physical deformation, altered biochemistry, chronic toxicity, congenital defects, and inheritable damage.

At another level altogether, the definition of biological monitoring first of all recognizes a basic intent of the Clean Water Act to address ecosystem needs and then factors implying compromise of those needs, such as ac-cumulation of chemical substances in tissues. This definition also recognizes certain ecological realities in calling for sampling at appropriate levels in the food chain with reference to the "volume and the physical, chemical and biological characteristics of the effluent" and to "appropriate fre-quencies and locations," (sec. 502(15)) in acceptance of all four significant dimensions.

Sensitivity to ecological features is found with reference to planning for reservoirs: "The need for and the value of storage for regulation of stream-flow (other than for water quality) including but not limited to . . . salt water intrusions . . . and fish and wildlife, shall be determined" by responsible agencies (sec. 102(b)(2)). Planning is encouraged to include "basins," that is, "rivers and their tributaries, streams, coastal waters, sounds, estuaries, bays, lakes, and portions thereof as well as the lands drained thereby" (sec. 102(c)(3)). Actual natural systems are addressed as whole entities. Among them are the Great Lakes System, which by definition includes the entire drainage basin of the Great Lakes themselves, a clear recognition of the necessity to expand the boundaries of an ecosystem from the microcosm of immediate regulatory interest through ever-expanding boundaries to include all the natural sources of contribution.

The statute addresses estuaries with particular attention, first in defining an "estuarine zone" as "an environmental system" including the estuary itself and "transitional areas which are consistently influenced or affected by water from an estuary." An estuary itself is defined as that portion of a river or stream "having unimpaired natural connection with open sea and within which the sea water is measurably diluted with fresh water derived from land drainage" (sec. 104(n)(4)).

The corresponding research program (sec. 320) speaks in terms of balance and of indigenous organisms. Trends are to be assessed. Both short-term and long-term conditions are taken into account. Among the research efforts are those directed to ecosystems, water quality, and designated or potential uses of estuarine systems (sec. 320(j)(1)(D)). The last factor is the most obviously directed to human interests.

Research efforts are also directed toward identification and classification of the eutrophic condition of all publicly owned lakes (sec. 314(a)(1)(A)). Although eutrophication is the natural process through which every lake proceeds, accelerated eutrophication is a nuisance situation attributed to the presence of excessive nutrients associated with human activities. Additional research authorized by Congress includes comprehensive studies of the effects of pollution on estuaries and "basic research into the structure and function of freshwater . . . ecosystems" (pure ecology) for the purpose of improving "understanding . . . [of the] ecological characteristics necessary to the maintenance" of the integrity of such ecosystems (sec. 104(n) and (r)).

Congress established River Study centers to conduct the interdisciplinary studies essential to comprehending ecological features in relationship to human needs including usage and economics. Here there is reference to the ecological phenomenon of bioaccumulation, albeit in the human contexts of "reducing the value of aquatic commercial and sport industries" and restoring and enhancing such "valuable resources" (secs. 104(s) and 104(a)).

In sum, members of Congress have demonstrated some comprehension of how chemicals move through and affect ecosystems. Organic chemicals, for example, may enter an ecosystem and serve as "exotic" nutrients or interfere with the intricate metabolism and catabolism of the biotic components of the system. Heavy metals are micronutrients, but slight excesses beyond what organisms require in their physiological processes will be toxic in terms of subchronic, chronic, or acute alterations in those processes. Congress focuses, however, on a species of immediate human interest, which may be seriously affected only after a long interval of more subtle harms with increasingly apparent biological damage, perturbation.[9]

As should be expected, actions on behalf of ecosystems are most apparent in establishing water quality standards (see sec. 303). Standards and associated implementation plans are directed to include enhanced water quality—first and foremost an ecological matter, even were the interests of a sole species, *Homo sapiens sapiens*, taken into consideration. But section 303 goes at least slightly beyond immediate human interests, with references to propagation of fish and wildlife and to thermal loads, the latter in the contexts of such factors as normal water temperatures, flow rates, and seasonal variations (sec. 303(d)(1)(D)). Here, the Congress is acknowledging the crucial fourth dimension in ecology. Recognizing that each ecosystem is somehow unique, Congress has addressed specific water quality needs of specific bodies of water.[10]

Effluent standards are not so directly connected with ecosystems, although they are in part directed to ensuring that designated water quality standards are met (sec. 302). There is an exception in the so-called guidelines on which permits to discharge into ocean waters must be based. These guidelines (sec. 403) are intended to determine degradation of waters and make specific reference to communities of organisms, notably including plankton. Additional references are to changes in marine ecosystem productivity and stability and alterations in communities' composition. In doing so, Congress implies a recognition of the varying significance of absolute amounts, concentrations, and rate of entry into a system.

Ecosystems return to the foreground in the liability provisions of section 311. Liabilities associated with spilled oil or hazardous substances include monies to be reimbursed to a natural resources trustee for replacement or restoration of such resources (sec. 311(f)(5)). Section 311 speaks in terms of harmful quantities and mitigation with reference to environmental amenities with express inclusion of organisms and their habitats within the aegis of "public health or welfare" (sec. 311(b)(4) and (9), (d), and (e)), leading the way to recognition of *Homo sapiens sapiens* as an ecological entity in need of ecosystems that are healthful to its populations. In some senses, it is only a short next step to recognizing a human requirement for ecosystems that are healthy in terms of their own immediate needs.

Additional Pollution Control Programs Addressing Ecosystems. The

Toxic Substances Control Act (TSCA), 15 U.S.C.A. 2601 *et seq.*, the Resource Conservation and Recovery Act (RCRA), 42 U.S.C.A. 6901 *et seq.*, also known as the Solid Waste Disposal Act, and the Comprehensive Environmental Response, Compensation, and Liability Act (CERCLA), 42 U.S.C.A. 9601 *et seq.*, also known as "Superfund," all followed the Clean Air and Water acts in the course of the 1970s, the first decade of the environment, with RCRA's hazardous waste regulations and CERCLA both taking effect beginning in 1980. Of the three, the TSCA pays the most direct attention to ecological amenities.

Assuming that first in reference is first in importance, Congress ranked the environment second only to human beings in its findings (TSCA sec. 2(a)(1) and (2) and (b)) of exposure to and unreasonable risks attributed to chemicals in commerce. This paired set of priorities is maintained throughout the statute. Environment is defined to include "water, air, and land and the interrelationship which exists among and between water, air, and land and all living things" (sec. 3(5)).

The kinds of toxic properties of interest pursuant to the TSCA in terms of environmental amenities expressly include "carcinogenesis, mutagenesis, teratogenesis, behavioral disorders, cumulative or synergistic effects." Additional characteristics of concern are "persistence, acute toxicity, subacute toxicity [and] chronic toxicity" (sec. 4(b)(2)(A)). These terms are not exclusively bound to human health but expressly include other biological systems.

Similarly, the RCRA calls for "environmentally safe disposal of nonrecoverable residues" (solid wastes) and associates environment closely with human health (RCRA sec. 1003(a)(9) and (b)). The hazardous component of solid waste is defined as such in part by reason of its detrimental effect on the environment (second only to human health) (sec. 1004(5)).

Ecosystems enter CERCLA by way of the natural resources route. Damages, as defined by this act, are specifically those "for injury or loss of natural resources" (CERCLA sec. 101(6)), which are defined to include land, fish, wildlife, biota, air, water, and groundwater (sec. 101(16)). Environment is that which is so defined pursuant to a variety of other national programs but essentially including all environmental media (sec. 101(8)). Hazardous substances include all those that can adversely affect environmental amenities, as defined in CERCLA's predecessor pollution control statutes (sec. 101(14)). A pollutant or contaminant is defined in terms of environmental perturbations as well as of human health concerns. The language of the definition follows that found in section 502(13) of the Clean Water Act.

CERCLA's program of strict, joint, and several liability includes liability for damages to natural resources (sec. 107(f)). This provision, however, sheds no further light on congressional understanding of ecosystems as affected by oil and hazardous materials. Section 301(c)(2) calls for two sets of procedures for determining the extent of harm. One is to establish minimal "simplified assessments requiring minimal field observation," while the other is to establish a more elaborate protocol "to determine the type and extent of short-term and long-term injury, destruction or loss." Somehow, responsible bureaucrats must consider such factors as "replacement value, use value, and the ability of the ecosystem or resource to recover."

Natural Resources Management

Because statutes addressing natural resources directly are obviously more closely linked ecological principles than are pollution control statutes, the codified foundations of natural resources law can be expected to be more accommodating of those principles. Here, that expectation will be pursued in congressional findings, missions, and definitions in selected statutes. The statutes chosen are categorized as conservation and public lands, respectively: Multiple-Use Sustained-Yield Act (Multiple-Use Act), 16 U.S.C.A. 528–531, and the Federal Land Policy and Management Act (Land Management Act), 43 U.S.C.A. 1701 et seq.

The declaration of policy of the Multiple-Use Act calls for administration of national forests for purposes of "outdoor recreation, range, timber, watershed, and wildlife and fish" (Multiple-Use Act sec. 528). Only the final three concerns bear any obvious relationship to ecological amenities as opposed to resources of value for human use, although the call for establishment and maintenance of wilderness areas is at least promising (Multiple-Use Act sec. 529). Unfortunately for ecological amenities, even reading between the lines of the definition of multiple use reveals little ecological sensitivity (Multiple-Use Act sec. 531).

Among the declarations of congressional policy in the Land Management Act is that calling for management in a

manner that will protect the quality of scientific, scenic, historical, ecological, environmental, air and atmospheric, water resources, and archeological value; that, where appropriate, will preserve and protect certain public lands in their natural condition; that will provide food and habitat for fish and wildlife and domestic animals; and that will provide for outdoor recreation and human occupancy and use[.] (Land Management Act sec. 102(a)(8))

Although this is a mixed mission well down the list of missions, it does allow for inferences of ecological amenities with resort to reading between the lines.

The import of statutory definitions is similarly mixed, with special reference to the definition here of multiple use to include the implicit, and somewhat cryptic, direction to manage public lands so that they are utilized in the combination that will best meet the present and future needs of the American people; making the most judicious use of the land for some or all of these resources or related services over areas large enough to provide sufficient latitude for periodic adjustments in use to conform to changing needs and conditions[.] (Land Management Act sec. 103(c))

Just where ecological amenities may be is far from clear.

FEDERAL PROGRAMS BASED IN
THE ECOSYSTEM CONCEPT

At least two national programs are expressly directed to resources that can be described as ecosystems. One of these programs is statutory, the Coastal Zone Management Act (CZMA), 16 U.S.C.A. 1451 *et seq.* The other must be extracted through regulatory definitions of wetlands.[11] The point of departure for the former is found in coastal ecosystems, whereas a major focus of the latter is the concept of habitat. Because the focus here is on congressional recognition of ecological concepts, only the statutory program will be addressed. The wetlands program remains extraordinarily controversial and unsettled at the point of regulatory programs and their implementation.[12]

Explorations for ecological sophistication in the CZMA will be limited to congressional missions and definitions. Congress found that the coastal zone is rich in ecological as well as other features (CZMA sec. 302(b)) and recognized that the competing demands of coastal lands and waters had led to "loss of living marine resources, wildlife, nutrient-rich areas, [and] permanent and adverse changes to ecological systems" (sec. 302(c)). Congress also recognized the fragility of associated habitats and, perhaps more important in terms of public policy, that ecological values are among those that are essential to the well-being of all citizens (sec. 302(d) and (e)). The resultant policy includes protection of ecologically meaningful natural resources such as "wetlands, floodplains, estuaries, beaches, dunes, barrier islands, coral reefs, and fish and wildlife and their habitat" (sec. 303(2)(A)).

Relevant definitions include most notably that of the coastal zone: "coastal waters (including the land therein and thereunder) and the adjacent shorelands (including the land therein and thereunder), strongly influenced by each other and in proximity to . . . shorelines . . . and includes islands, transitional and intertidal areas, salt marshes, wetlands, and beaches" (sec. 304(1)). Estuary is defined in the same terms found in the Clean Water Act (sec. 304(7)).

Just how aware of ecological principles these codified materials are will become increasingly apparent as those principles are explored throughout the remainder of the text. Upon return to matters of policy, it should become easier to read through the legal language to find and assess ecological foundations. Every return should be guided by the question: Is there such a biological entity as described by the law?

NOTES

1. H. Bauer, *Scientific Literacy and the Myth of the Scientific Method* (1992), Figure 4, at 32.

2. *See, e.g.*, L. Busch, "Science under Wraps in Prince William Sound," 252 *Sci.* 772 (May 10, 1991).

3. *See, e.g.*, A. Gibbons, "Ecologists Set Broad Priorities for 1990s," 252 *Sci.* 504 (Apr. 26, 1991). *See also* D. Howell, *Scientific Literacy and Environmental Policy: The Missing Prerequisite to Sound Decision Making* (1992), at 151–163.

4. *See, e.g.*, R. Nash, *American Environmentalism: Readings in Conservation History* (3d ed., 1990).

5. All statutory materials are taken from West's *Selected Environmental Law Statutes: 1992–93 Educational Edition*, with occasional reference to earlier editions for historical materials.

6. Section 154 was added in 1977 and amended in 1979.

7. Clean Air Act section 112—National Emission Standards for Hazardous Air Pollutants (NESHAPS).

8. This phrase is repeated at 102(a) and elsewhere throughout the statute. *See, e.g.*, secs. 303(c)(2)(A), 316(a).

9. *See* secs. 1267(4) and 118–120.

10. *See, e.g.*, CWA sec. 118(c), addressing Great Lakes water quality.

11. *See, e.g.*, 1989 "Federal Manual for Identifying and Delineating Jurisdictional Wetlands"; Proposed Revisions, 56 *Federal Register* 40440 (Aug. 4, 1991), for relevant definitions as proposed. Definitions are codified at 33 C.F.R. 328.3(b) and 40 C.F.R. 230.3(t). Incorporated into the definitions are the nature of the soil (hydric), of the hydrological formations, and of the vegetation (hydrophytic).

12. Wetlands issues, a major portion of which are associated with the rapidly changing regulatory definition of wetlands and its interpretation by which policy is intended to reflect ecology, are very much in the headlines. For an overview of where things stood in mid–1992, *see* 7 *Nat. Res. & Env.* (1) (Summer 1992).

PART III

ENERGY AND MATERIALS: THE ABIOTIC COMPONENT

6

Energy Flow

It is an inherent paradox of science that the holistic concept of ecosystem can actually be expanded through a reductionist approach supplied by physics and chemistry. Although the ecosystem is more than the sum of its constituents, details of interactions between and within the abiota and biota provide direction and insights into the structure and function of the whole.

Planet Earth was created and itself evolved out of the energy and material of the Big Bang. Life arose after ages of geological evolution leading to conditions amenable to the coalescence and persistence of certain complexes of organic molecules (see Chapter 9). In a continuing process, the biota of an ecosystem is initially determined by these abiotic features as they are uniquely combined in locations throughout the globe.

Because it is energy that drives the whole system, the energy environment will be explored first. Then material cycling between abiotic reservoirs and pools and the biota and within organisms will then be blended into the ecological mixture.

SCIENTIFIC BACKGROUND: THE ENERGY ENVIRONMENT

Energy enters the ecosystem as light and exits as heat. Energy takes numerous forms, few as obvious than the dropping of a rock off a precipice. In the biosphere, light, a portion of the electromagnetic spectrum, is kinetic energy, as are the wave particles of that entire spectrum. Mechanical energy is potential in a relaxed muscle and kinetic in the muscle contracting to move a limb or blood through the circulatory system. Chemical energy is the means whereby organisms absorb and assimilate the energy in light for work in the maintenance, growth, functioning, and reproduction of living entities.

The Laws of Thermodynamics

In order to understand the significant detail of energy flowing through an ecosystem, it is necessary to have a modest grasp of certain realities of physics. Outstanding among these are the First and Second Laws of Thermodynamics.

The First Law holds that energy and matter can neither be created nor destroyed. In essence, that reality has held true at least from the instant following the Big Bang. All the energy on earth can be traced to the thermonuclear reactions in the sun, present and past. Energy flow is mediated through conversions among types of energy with the production and rearrangements of material in cells. Similarly, preexisting material is metabolized and catabolized within organisms, with changes in chemical structure without actual material creation. In an ecosystem—or any biological entity—preexisting energy and material are fixed in a form that the biota can assimilate; energy is converted into different forms, as is matter; and the two are exchanged: Energy is converted to matter, and matter to energy.

Throughout all these processes, nothing is created out of nothing. There are specific energy and matter precursors to everything. The energy comes from the sun, and the material comes from the atmosphere, hydrosphere, and lithosphere making up the planetary biosphere. Along the way, however, energy is continually dissipated, in accord with the Second Law of Thermodynamics.

There are a number of relevant ways in which this concept can be stated for ecologists. The crucial point is that energy always tends to dissipate from a higher to a lower or more dispersed concentration. A cup of hot coffee left to its own devices never becomes hotter; it always cools to room—ambient—temperature. A sugar cube in a beaker of water dissolves, and its molecules disperse throughout the liquid. Those molecules will not reunite to re-form the sugar cube. This persistent loss of energy (organization or order) is measured as entropy (randomization). In any undisturbed system, particles (including individual chemical elements or molecules) will become as disordered as possible. Their distribution is random, the antithesis of order. Life in thermodynamic terms is a kind of negative entropy.

Additional versions of the Second Law are to the effect that no energy transfer is 100% efficient; there is always some loss, usually as heat. Thus, energy is increasingly dispersed, decreasingly available for use in the system. Finally, no process involving an energy transfer will occur spontaneously unless there is a degradation of energy content from start to finish. Chemically, the products will contain less energy than the reactants.

Electromagnetic Radiation: The Energy Spectrum

Electromagnetic radiation, particularly that portion of the energy spectrum identified with visible light, is the foundation of the energy environment in which organisms function. Radiation is defined as the emission or propagation of energy in waves through space or material. Each wave in the spectrum is defined in terms of amplitude, frequency, and wavelength. Amplitude is the height of each wave; frequency, the number of waves generated per unit time; and wavelength, the distance between peaks. Although all the parameters are interrelated, for purposes of ecological significance, the spectrum is described in terms of wavelength.

The visible portion of the electromagnetic spectrum ranges from the short wavelengths in the ultraviolet through the long wavelengths of the infrared. The longer wavelengths in the ultraviolet range remain visible to humans, but the shorter wavelengths become invisible and, indeed, are disruptive to cellular components, notably the genetic material. Ultraviolet radiation is mutagenic. From the ultraviolet, the spectrum shortens to X rays, which also are mutagenic. At the longer extreme of the spectrum, some infrared remains visible to humans but becomes invisible as wavelength approaches microwaves and radio waves.

The visible range bears a significance beyond human vision. It is within this range that biological molecules can be generated and persist for durations suitable for metabolic processes. Shorter wavelengths are too energetic and disrupt biochemical molecules. Longer ones lack sufficient energy to enter into the processes of life.

All the sun's electromagnetic energy entering the biosphere is reflected, absorbed, or converted to heat. All these fates contribute something to the planet's capacity to support life. Much light is reflected from the various surfaces it strikes. Certain wavelengths of light are absorbed by the biota and assimilated to conduct the work of the ecosystem. Others are absorbed by surrounding water or ground, contributing to temperatures in which living processes can occur. The remainder are converted to heat, which is dissipated to the surrounding environment, through the atmosphere beyond the planet, through the solar system, and ultimately, into outer space—continuing on the cosmic pathway to the entropic destiny.

In quantitative terms, sunlight reaches the biosphere with an energy content of 2 calories for each square centimeter per minute. As the light penetrates the atmosphere, much of the energy is lost. Upon reaching the surface of the earth, the energy content is reduced to 1.34 calories for each square centimeter per minute. That maximum quantity is said to exist at noon on a clear summer day. Additional attenuation is virtually certain through the presence of clouds, because of passage through water, or because of absorption by vegetation. Moreover, the sun's radiation occurs for only part of the diurnal period.

The difference between downward and upward streams of radiation is expressed as net radiation. Less radiation is released than is received because of general dissipation and also because of the evaporation of water and the generation of thermal winds. The net transfer of heat serves to maintain the temperature range in the atmosphere that is conducive to life.

Some of that light performs work or is converted to forms that themselves perform work. Prominent examples are the winds and the flow of the hydrogeological cycle. A small portion of the light is absorbed by chemical receivers in the cells of certain organisms, and this energy is converted into biomass.

Entropy and Life

None of the work accomplished by the light received from the sun, according to the Second Law of Thermodynamics, can fully utilize the contained energy. This unused energy is converted to heat, the vibration of molecules measured as temperature. The faster the vibration, the hotter the temperature.[1] The heat of the entering energy and that being released in the course of chemical reactions (a form of work) serves members of the biota as part of the environment affecting biochemical reactions.

The ecosystem is, in short, driven by the energy of the sun, but it is a highly inefficient process. Together, these two realities of physics in combination answer the biological questions of why elephants are the largest terrestrial animal and why this organism is hairless and endowed with large ears.

The elephant represents the maximum limit on terrestrial size because the heat of biochemical reactions in a larger animal could not be dissipated through the mass of elephant matter quickly enough to avoid fatal overheating at the cellular, and ultimately the organismal, level. Elephants are hairless to allow the dispersion of internal heat through the skin without the insulating effect of a fur coat. The large ears are a medium through which additional heat can be released, especially when they are flapped to enhance that release.

In the case of particularly large plants, metabolic processes are occurring only in a small portion of the whole. This limitation is obvious in the lack of leaves among the lower branches of huge trees. It would be wasteful of energy for trees to grow and maintain leaves in shaded areas where photosynthesis would be inhibited. Stated slightly more precisely, growth and maintenance would require more energy from the plant than the shaded leaves would be able to provide it.

Other adaptations for controlling energy flow in extreme climates are quite striking. In deserts, plants are relatively compact and low growing, with thickened stems, whereas animals tend to be small but lanky with prominent ears. In cold regions (alpine or subpolar), plants and animals are also small and far more compact than their desert counterparts. Animals have stubby ears, close to the body. In both regions, the relatively large ratio of surface area to mass limits the entry or loss of energy as heat. In addition, large ears radiate heat to cool the body; small ones help retain body heat.

ENERGY FLOW THROUGH THE ECOSYSTEM

The relationships among the components of an ecosystem are governed by the same natural laws that apply to nonliving systems. A major difference is in the degree of organization required for the phenomena making up living systems. From the cell to the biosphere, each succeeding level reflects greater organization than that below. Life overall is a momentary defeat of entropy. As such, life requires extraordinary amounts of energy, a condition that has been identified in terms such as negative entropy or an energy pump.

Photosynthesis and Respiration

Photosynthesis. For ecological purposes, the effective flow of energy commences with its biological fixation. If the energy of the sun simply struck members of the biota with nothing more than absorption or reflection, there would be no life. These are not effective events in terms of biological processing. Instead, a specific kind of assimilation takes place.

Green plants absorb in most of the visible spectrum (excluding the greens) and in the far-infrared, the longest wavelengths of light. Chlorophyll, the molecule of photosynthesis, absorbs more particularly in the blue and red. The energy contained in these wavelengths is biologically fixed through photosynthesis, actually a series of biochemical reactions. Those collective reactions are summarized in the formula describing the reactants and ultimate products:

$$6CO_2 + 6H_2O \overset{\text{light}}{\Rightarrow} C_6H_{12}O_6 + 6O_2$$

What the formula stands for is the combination of six molecules of the gas carbon dioxide plus six molecules of water, in the presence of light energy, for conversion into one molecule of the sugar glucose and six molecules of gaseous oxygen.

The first of the steps making up photosynthesis is the one requiring light energy, and it occurs in the presence of chlorophyll, found in cellular organelles of uniquely characteristic structure known as chloroplasts. The remaining reactions are known as dark reactions because light is no longer required.

Respiration. The apparent chemical reversal of photosynthesis is respiration:

$$(CH_2O)_n + nO_2 \rightarrow nCO_2 + nH_2O + energy$$

If the carbohydrate is a six-carbon sugar, such as the glucose formed in photosynthesis, "n" becomes "6," and the generalized formula becomes specific:

$$6CH_2O + 6O_2 \rightarrow 6CO_2 + 6H_2O + energy$$

This formula translates as one molecule of sugar reacting with six molecules of oxygen to release six molecules each of water and the gas carbon dioxide, with the release of the energy stored in the molecular bonds holding the elements of the sugar together.

Together, photosynthesis and respiration relate the processes whereby green plants capture and store energy and all organisms, including green plants, release that energy for use in their cells. It is worth noting at this stage that photosynthesis has a biochemical counterpart that requires no oxygen. That process is mediated by photosynthetic bacteria that use sulfur instead of oxygen:

$$12H_2S + 6CO_2 \rightarrow C_6H_{12}O_6 + 12S + 6H_2O$$

This formula is useful in demonstrating how the photosynthetic reaction occurs. It is the oxygen of carbon dioxide that is incorporated into the sugar. The oxygen of water, like the sulfur of hydrogen sulfide, is that which is released into the environment.

Trophic Levels: Food Chains and Food Webs

Clearly, the physics and chemistry of life are not readily isolated from each other. It is difficult to consider one without resort to aspects of the other. The same is true of life. While living organisms are much more than particularly well-organized sets of chemical reactions and physical processes, it is difficult to isolate any one of the three pieces from either of the other two.

Along the way from the entry of light into an ecosystem and the release of entropic heat, the energy is flowing through the biota while matter is cycling among all the components. There is a striking structure to this functioning whole, which will be explored further when the distribution of materials is superimposed on the flow of energy in the next chapter.

Each trophic level is made up of populations of organisms that have precisely defined places in the whole. Taken altogether, with identification of the taxons actually participating, these constituents of energy flow describe not merely some generic ecosystem but a specific one at a specific stage in its life history.

The Grazing Cycle. The first trophic level in the grazing cycle is that of the primary producers, the green plants. These organisms are the ones that fix light energy, carbon dioxide, and other inorganic substances into biologically useful forms. They are autotrophic; that is, they can convert inorganic material into organic. In fact, they cannot utilize the organics produced by other organisms.

The second trophic level is that of the primary consumers. These organisms, "grazers," are the ones that feed directly on the producers. In biological terms, primary consumers are heterotrophic. Unable to produce needed organic molecules from inorganic, they convert those generated by the producers to the biochemical molecules they need. Primary consumers are known as herbivores and are among the phagotrophs. They ingest relatively large pieces of whatever plants serve their metabolic needs. Many of these consumers are obligate herbivores; their physiology cannot be served by anything but the plants on which they feed.

The third step in this food chain of trophic levels is the secondary consumers, the first level of carnivore. These organisms feed on primary consumers, the herbivores. They, too, are heterotrophic, but their metabolic processes require organic materials as they have been rearranged by their prey organisms. The carnivores are also phagotrophs, and many are obligate carnivores.

The next and succeeding trophic levels are carnivores that feed on carnivores, but there is a limit to how many levels can be supported by an ecosystem. That limit is related to the Second Law of Thermodynamics—hence, the trophic pyramid, with biomass decreasing from the producer base to the tertiary or quaternary consumer at the top.

Organisms in the food chain, true to the First Law of Thermodynamics, are assimilating energy and using it to assimilate matter and to rearrange its organization to meet their respective physiological needs. All the processes are subject to the Second Law of Thermodynamics. Increasingly large proportions of energy are lost to entropy as it proceeds through the biomass from one trophic level to the next. Ultimately, it will require more energy than the food organism can provide, just to get it and assimilate it. The proportion of biomass bound up in each level decreases. In fact, some 80% to 90% of the potential energy is lost to entropy at each step (energy transfer). Either numbers are reduced or volume is, and the number of trophic levels is ordinarily limited to no more than five. An obvious corollary is that the shorter the chain, the greater the available energy at the top. Hence, big, fierce animals are rare in any ecosystem.[2] And trophic steps are usually limited to four or five at the most.

The doggeral below is ecologically accurate—up to a point.

> Big fleas have little fleas
> Upon their backs to bite 'em
> And little fleas have lesser fleas
> And so, ad infinitum[3]

Actually, there are two major complications here. First, some organisms are omnivores and others are facultative herbivores or carnivores. Omnivores have the biochemical apparatus to allow them to feed on both plants and animals, with a triggering of the requisite metabolic processes for assimilating the various organics being ingested. Facultative organisms can vary their diets through alternative metabolic pathways, turned on or off depending on the diet of the moment.

The second major complication is that most real ecosystems are not limited to mere food chains. Instead, there are food nets, with organisms readily feeding at more than one trophic level and numerous predator–prey interaction.

The Detritus Cycle. Because the grazing cycle is so immediately obvious, it is easy to neglect the detritus cycle mediated by detrivores. This is the cycle by which the elaborate biochemical molecules generated through the grazing cycle are restored to the abiota and become available to reenter the grazing cycle. The detritus cycle begins with consumers of carrion and of dung. Much of this cycle is mediated by series of insects and soil microorganisms. The latter, in particular, are quite invisible to the casual observer, but without them, the full material cycle would come to a halt.

While all of the organisms in the detritus cycle are heterotrophs, some are phagotrophs and others are saprotrophs. As organic materials proceed through this cycle, they are chemically converted in distinct stages to the inorganics from which the grazing cycle metabolized them.

For each link in a food chain, energy is partitioned in a manner suggesting the other links in the chain.[4] Ingestion represents the full amount of energy available to the organism. This is potential energy bound up in the material of the ingested biomass. Much of the energy is expended in the chemical processes of digestion and assimilation. In these and other cellular processes, respiration can be described as the energy used to perform the work or lost as heat and no longer available to the community. That material that has been assimilated is converted to growth and reproduction—additional biomass in the form of the ingesting organism and its offspring.

Additional energy is returned to the ecosystem throughout the life of the ingesting organism through the processes of egestion, excretion, and finally, death. Egested materials are essentially unaltered chemically and play no positive role in metabolism. Significantly, energy is required to process this material, but it contributes none to the organism.

Egestion is an energy economy in that the material unavailable to the organism is eliminated prior to entering the metabolic processes of digestion and elimination. Owls egest the inedible portions of their prey, such as fur, skin, and bones. The resultant pellets contain these materials virtually intact.

Excreted materials are the chemical wastes produced in the course of metabolic processes. Were these materials retained, they would eventually poison the organism. With death, all metabolism ceases, including defenses against detrivores. Every release of material carries energy to the detrivores.

THE MATTER OF PRODUCTIVITY

Qualitative Descriptions of Productivity

For a variety of reasons, including determinations of the condition of an ecosystem, a measurement of productivity may be in order. Generally, productivity can be defined as the amount of energy received from the sun that is retained in the biomass of the ecosystem over some specified interval of time measured in days, months, or years.

There are four ways to account for productivity. Gross primary productivity measures the total rate of photosynthesis, the full assimilation of energy by primary producers. Net primary productivity is the rate of energy storage as plant biomass in excess of respiratory utilization. This is "apparent" photosynthesis or "net" assimilation. Net community productivity is the rate of storage of organics not used by heterotrophs—plant biomass left untouched. It is calculated by subtracting heterotrophic consumption from net primary production. The fourth accounting, secondary productivities, includes rates of energy storage at the several consumer levels. Production has been replaced with conversions.

High rates of production are expected under favorable physical conditions, internal to the ecosystem and in the form of energy subsidies from outside the ecosystem. Wind and rain are energy subsidies entering rain forests. Tidal energy serves estuaries. Such subsidies are, however, not limited to naturally occurring ecosystems. They are vitally important factors in cultivated systems as well.

With agricultural ecosystems (often monoculture crops of little genetic diversity), high rates of production are related to energy subsidies from outside the system. Cultivation has always called for work beyond the immediate assimilation of solar energy. First, human labor is required, historically supplemented with that of animals. In recent times, both have been replaced to varying degrees by the fossil fuels needed to run labor-saving agricultural equipment.

The important consideration to be taken from measurements of productivity is that mere weight of biomass and counts of organisms are insufficient measures of ecosystem health. Here carefully selective quantitative measurements can provide a measure of quality. Any such effort, however, must take into account the presence of energy drains, on one hand, and subsidies, on the other. Energy drains are stresses diverting energy from the system. A familiar example is the removal of cereals, fruits, and vegetables from agricultural crops. The nature and magnitude of such important ancillary phenomena must be included in the description of energy flow and retention.

Quantifying Productivity

The ideal quantification of productivity would directly measure the flow of energy through the system. To do so, unfortunately, is difficult at best. Thus, ecologists turn to indirect methods of measurement. Significantly, no two methods measure exactly the same aspect of metabolism. Using more than one can serve as confirmation of both.

Seven methods of quantifying productivity are available. The most obvious is (1) harvesting of the crop. Also obvious are measurements of (2) oxygen or (3) carbon dioxide changes and of the (4) disappearance of raw materials. Additional methods refer to (5) pH, the use of (6) radiotracers, and (7) chlorophyll.

The harvest method measures the weight of growth from seed (set at zero) for a determination of caloric content. It is used in cultivated crops and wherever annual plants (in contrast to biennials and perennials) predominate. The method is also used in early stages of revegetation of damaged ecosystems.

The limitations of the method are not surprising. It is inappropriate where herbivores are important and actually present, where steady state has been reached, and where food is removed as it is produced. (Steady state is the condition of relatively long-lived homeostasis in a mature ecosystem.) When herbivores, including humans, are consuming or removing plant material, there will be direct and indirect effects on the rate and final extent of productivity. Once steady state is reached, productivity will diminish and cease.

Oxygen measurements compare the presence of this gas in closed vessels representing gross primary production and net community production. The amount of oxygen depletion is proportional to productivity. This system is limited to aquatic systems and cannot measure metabolism in depths beyond the photosynthetic zone. Because the community being analyzed must be contained in small vessels to allow the measurements, an unknown experimental factor is the effect of such containment. There is no guarantee that the experimental system is fully comparable to its natural counterpart.

Carbon dioxide methods measure either the uptake or the release of that gas, thus measuring net photosynthesis or respiration. The method is limited to enclosed terrestrial systems. Another limitation of the method is that the enclosure chamber can act like a greenhouse and allow the buildup of heat, which can alter the rate of photosynthesis. Moreover, the sheer size and complexity of most terrestrial ecosystems render enclosure difficult.

The pH method measures acidity as a function of dissolved carbon dioxide content and is thus limited to aquatic systems. Concentrations of this gas will decrease with photosynthesis and increase with respiration, with corresponding alterations in pH. However, this method is of limited application because water bodies have differing buffering capacities, and there is no linear relationship between pH and carbon dioxide content. A calibration curve must be established for each analysis to reflect the actual relationship between the two parameters.

If the biota of interest is not in a steady-state equilibrium, the disappearance of nutrients, for example, minerals, will provide a measure of productivity. This measurement, however, will be influenced by a whole host of additional abiotic factors, which may or may not be taken into account or even recognized.

Radiotracers, radioactive isotopes of biochemically active elements, will provide more information regarding distribution of those elements in and among cells, tissues, organisms, and the ecosystem at large than rates.

Finally, the chlorophyll method assumes with some degree of logic that the more photosynthesis is occurring, the more chlorophyll will be present.

Implications for Environmental Professionals

Productivity, naturally occurring or in agricultural or other ecosystems subject to human manipulation, if properly measured, can be informative to the environmental professional. Studies in research and applied ecology reveal certain expectations in the energy relationships in specific ecosystems. Altered relationships suggest the presence of unrecognized energy subsidies or drains. It is the environmental professional who may be called on to identify the external condition in order to determine whether the effect is amenable to correction through the marketplace or public intervention.

NOTES

Principal sources for this chapter are Smith, at 48, 124–127, and 96–100 and chapters 6 and 11; Odum, chapter 3; Ricklefs, chapter 10; *Journey*, chapters 6, 7, and 8 and at 769–785, 788–789; and P. Colinvaux, *Why Big Fierce Animals Are Rare: An Ecologist's Perspective* (1978).

1. There are three temperature scales. The most familiar is the Fahrenheit scale. The biologically crucial molecule water freezes at 32°F and boils at 212°F. Less familiar is the Centigrade or Celsius scale. Water freezes at 0°C and boils at 100°C. The scale that most directly relates to entropy is the Kelvin or absolute scale. Absolute zero or 0° Kelvin is the point at which molecules cease to vibrate. It is at −273.15°C or −459.67°F. There are two simple arithmetic formulas for converting between Centigrade and Fahrenheit:

$$C = \frac{5}{9}(F - 32)$$

$$F = \frac{9}{5}C + 32$$

2. Colinvaux, chapter 3.

3. Jonathan Swift, quoted in Odum, at 84; Colinvaux, at 22 (with "infinitem" instead of "infinitum").

4. The concept of energy partitioning as described here is adapted from Ricklefs, figure 10–4, at 149.

7

Material Cycling and Ecosystem Structure

CONNECTIONS: CYCLES AND TROPHIC LEVELS

Driven by energy, the function of an ecosystem is reflected in the structure assumed by its community of organisms in their niches that fill the trophic levels. These trophic levels also indicate the distribution of material. The resultant relationships reveal a striking degree of organization that lends itself to simplification for purposes of analysis conducted by ecologists or environmental professionals.[1]

With the flow of energy, abiotic dissolved nutrients are biologically fixed as they are assimilated into plant biomass. This biological material is eaten by herbivores that indulge in their individual versions of assimilation and biochemical conversion of the plant biomass. Herbivores are eaten by carnivores, which may be eaten by still other carnivores, each with its own unique pattern of assimilation and conversion. This grazing cycle restores certain nutrients through excretion and returns complex organics to the abiota through the formation of detritus. The detritus cycle consists of phagotrophs and saprotrophs (bacteria and fungi) that decompose the complex organics, taking these molecules stepwise back to their inorganic components, notably water and carbon dioxide from which the nitrogenous and phosphoric compounds and trace metals are released. The ultimate products of the detritus cycle are the dissolved inorganic nutrients to be assimilated by plants.

Additional connections exist between these two cycles and the abiotic environment. Detritus feeders and those that feed on bacteria and fungi are themselves consumed by certain carnivores. Symbiotic microorganisms may work in combination with plant hosts to assimilate certain nutrients directly. Autolysis, the internal enzymatic breakdown of cells, also returns dissolved nutrients to the environment, as does microbial hydrolysis. It is within this structure that the chemistry of life is taking place.

In moving from energy flow through the ecosystem to material cycling within it, the opening question might well be the fate of the glucose generated as a result of photosynthesis. In fact, the glucose is biochemically related to the Krebs citric acid cycle, the chemical center of respiration, described below. The mildly expanded and revised shorthand for the complex of reactions involved is in the two formulas:

$$CO_2 + H_2O + \text{minerals (inorganic nutrients)} \overset{\text{light}}{\Rightarrow} \text{plant production}$$
$$O_2$$
$$\text{transpired water}$$

$$\text{Sugar} \rightarrow \text{biomass (growth and reproduction)}$$
$$\text{biosynthesis}$$
$$\text{maintenance}$$
$$CO_2$$

It is highly informative now and for future reference to note that in the first formula the oxygen and water are in some senses by-products, whereas in the second, carbon dioxide is the by-product. *By-product* is legitimately translated "waste."

In ecological systems, one organism's waste is another's source of nutrients. Nevertheless, either too much waste or too much of a nutrient can be detrimental to the system and its living components. Similarly, oxygen or carbon dioxide, as representative of all essential nutrients, in the *wrong* place, that is, in the immediate environment of certain organisms, can be toxic. How a substance is going to affect an ecosystem depends entirely on its chemical nature, absolute amount, concentration, and location.

The biochemical molecules needed for all the processes of life are generated in the cells from the products of photosynthesis and respiration. The molecules of life start with simple sugars and the organic acids of the Krebs cycle, but these basic patterns are elaborated into amino acids and proteins, and an array of lipids including fats, oils, steroids, and waxes. In fact, the starting molecules give rise to the genetic molecules that effect all the other processes and to the uncannily similar chlorophyll and hemoglobin, which are the respective foundations of photosynthesis and respiration. There are, then, cycles within cycles within cycles, almost indefinitely. Moreover, the substances of all the natural sciences from physics to ecology are interconnected throughout.

In order to understand the chemistry fully, one must be aware of the physical phenomena leading to chemical reactions. The properties and reactions of both inorganic and organic chemicals lead to a fuller understanding of the biochemistry and physiology at the cellular level, which in turn renders the physiology of the organism more comprehensible. Individual organisms make up populations that are the units composing communities that describe or characterize ecosystems subject to features of space and time. Here, as always, each level of organization depends on those below, even as each new level manifests properties that could not have been predicted exclusively in terms of the predecessor science.

SCIENTIFIC BACKGROUND: BASIC CHEMISTRY

Physicochemistry

Chemical reactions depend on the physical configurations assumed by elements, molecules, and compounds. Elements are the unit of chemistry. Each element has properties unique to it, and it is the smallest unit manifesting those properties. As described in Chapter 2, the properties depend on the number and arrangement of three particles: the proton and neutron of the atomic nucleus and the electron, which occurs outside the nucleus and participates in the chemical reactions characteristic of the element.

Inorganic Chemistry

Inorganic chemistry is that of all the elements—including pure carbon and carbon dioxide but excluding carbon in certain other reactions—usually associated with life.

Inorganic chemistry is essential to ecological phenomena. One of the most important categories of inorganic chemical reactions is oxidation and reduction, or "redox," reactions. This is the chemistry of electron transfers. The generalized redox formula is:

$$Ae^- + B \rightarrow Be^-$$

In this crucial family of reactions, there is always an electron donor, the reducing agent, and an electron acceptor, the oxidizing agent. In the course of the reaction, the reducing agent is oxidized—it gives up its electrons—and the oxidizing agent is reduced—it accepts those electrons. It is important to note that this is always a two-way reaction; there is no oxidation without a corresponding reduction, or reduction without oxidation. This rule of physical chemistry holds because electrons cannot be free but are always an integral part of at least one atom.

A representative reaction is the bonding of hydrogen and oxygen to form water:

$$2H_2 + O_2 \rightarrow 2H_2O$$
$$(Ae^-) \quad (B) \rightarrow (A[+]Be^-)$$

Both molecular hydrogen and molecular oxygen have an oxidation number of zero, because in each case electrons are being shared by the paired atoms. Hydrogen, a strong reducing agent, tends to release electrons, whereas oxygen, a strong oxidizing agent, tends to accept them. Significantly, water is polar because the electrons donated by the hydrogen are held more strongly by the oxygen. Thus, this neutral molecule is more positive in the vicinity of the hydrogen and more negative in the vicinity of the oxygen. This characteristic of water is one of the many that render it essential to life.

Water is the molecule usually considered to be the single-most important to life and its processes, but other simple inorganics and the elements are also essential, as will become increasingly apparent throughout this chapter. For example, certain of the much-maligned heavy metals are actually essential to life, if only in trace quantities as micronutrients.

Organic Chemistry: Carbon, the Stuff of Life

Organic chemistry is the chemistry of carbon, especially in combination with hydrogen and oxygen. Carbon dioxide is something of a transitional compound. It, itself, is inorganic, but it is the source of the carbon backbone of all organic matter.

Carbon is unique among the elements in its capacity to seek chemical bonds for the four electrons of its outer electron shell. It can bond with one to four additional carbon atoms or with hydrogen, oxygen, or nitrogen. This ability leads to an astounding number and diversity among resultant molecules. Both factors are essential to the intricate chemistry comprising the features identified with life.

The simplest organic molecule is methane, carbon with single-bond connections with each of four hydrogens. Methane is a gas and not only the unit from which all biochemicals can ultimately be built but also one end product of catabolic processes.[2] What may seem to be subtle differences in molecular structure can result in profound differences for life. Carbon with single-bond connections with four chlorine atoms in place of the hydrogen is carbon tetrachloride, a poison. One hydrogen and three chlorines result in chloroform, a poison that humans have utilized as an anesthetic because initial toxicity takes the form of a deep induced sleep that prevents the sensation of pain.

Carbon can form single chains: the two-carbon chain is ethane when the three available electrons on each carbon are bonded with hydrogen. Replace one of those hydrogens with the hydroxyl group ($-OH$), and the result is ethanol, another toxic substance that humans utilize. Dilute ethanol is the alcohol of alcoholic beverages. Methanol, the single carbon with the hydroxyl group replacing one hydrogen, is also an alcohol, but even dilute methanol is highly toxic to humans.

Replace a hydrogen of ethane with the carboxyl group—an oxygen double bonded on the same carbon atom bonded to a hydroxyl, usually represented as COOH or

$$\underset{c}{\overset{o}{\underset{\|}{}}} -O-H)$$

—and the result is acetic acid, better known as vinegar. Acetic acid, the simplest of the organic acids, is only one of a series absolutely essential to life.

Carbon chains can include carbon atoms double or triple bonded to other carbons, and once the chain is at least five carbons long, the two ends of the chain can connect. Six-carbon chains are hexanes or hexenes depending on internal bonding between the carbons. Both chains can actually include a split instead of simply being straight. The six-carbon ring compound with each carbon atom saturated with hydrogen (that is, every carbon bound to a carbon on each side with two single-bonded hydrogens) is cyclohexane.

Each of these simple six-carbon molecules has its own set of properties, with special reference to solubility in water and in polar and nonpolar liquids, density, and melting and boiling points. Cyclohexane is comparable to its straight- (or open-) chain counterparts, but it is nonpolar with slightly higher density and boiling point. It happens to be an excellent fuel for motor vehicles. More significantly to biochemistry, hexane is readily converted into the aromatic hydrocarbon benzene, the same six-carbon chain in a ring formation with six less hydrogens and the carbons alternating single and double bonds between them. Benzene is the chemical unit of aromatics. This molecule and its aromatic five-carbon relatives contribute much to the variety requisite to cellular physiology. Each hydrogen bonded to the ring carbons can be replaced by groups such as hydroxyl or by another carbon, among other elements. A vast array of molecules can result, especially since two aromatic rings can be connected by a carbon or oxygen link or directly by sharing two carbons in common. All of these constructions of carbon play a role in living chemistry—biochemistry and physiology.

Essential to life, amino acids consist of at least two carbons in a chain. The first carbon bears a carboxyl group; the second, an amine ($-NH_2$), attached to the carbon by a single bond with the nitrogen. Most of the active amino acids contain only carbon, hydrogen, and oxygen, but two also contain sulfur.[3]

All the hundreds of proteins, of which living organisms are constructed and which, in the form of enzymes, mediate every reaction of metabolism and catabolism, are constructed of linear arrangements of twenty amino acids in polypeptide chains, synthesized through chemical condensation (described below) within cells on internal structures known as ribosomes. Biochemists identify proteins on the basis of the amino acids present; the order in which they are linked in polypeptides; and function, which depends on the elaborate three-dimensional folding that results from interactions among atomic components exposed to one another along the chains.[4]

Enzymes, the specialized protein catalysts, by definition alter the rate at which specific biochemical reactions occur, without themselves undergoing permanent change. Thus, relatively small amounts of any given enzyme are required when called upon to serve physiological needs. Some 2,000 enzymes are known to exist, and each catalyzes one specific reaction.[5] Among these reactions are condensation, hydrolysis, transfers of carbons or of active radicals or other chemical moieties, and biological oxidation-reduction reactions.

Even more elaborate combinations of carbon configurations and an array of inorganic elements are found in molecules such as chlorophyll, hemoglobin (a protein), steroids, and vitamins.

THE BIOCHEMISTRY OF ECOLOGY

The overall photosynthetic reaction should look familiar; it is a redox reaction whereby the hydrogen of water is the reducing agent and the oxygen in carbon dioxide is the oxidizing agent:

$$6H_2O + 6CO_2 \xrightarrow{\text{energy}} C_6H_{12}O_6 + 6O_2$$
$$Ae^- \quad\quad B \quad\quad\quad\quad Be^-A$$

Significantly, for biology and hence ecology, the addition of hydrogen creates energy-rich compounds such as sugars.

Respiration, in effect the chemical reversal of photosynthesis, is also a redox reaction:

$$C_6H_{12}O_6 + O_2 \rightarrow CO_2 + H_2O + \text{energy}$$
$$Ae^- \quad\quad B \quad\quad A \quad Be^-$$

It is a series of redox reactions in which carbon is being oxidized. The overall reaction is in essence a slow "burning" of sugar in which the energy of the hydrogen electrons is released; significantly, hydrogen-poor molecules are energy poor.[6] In combination, photosynthesis and respiration are a shorthand for the generation and storage of cellular energy and its release for use in cellular processes.

On one scale, these processes are reflected in the ways in which biomass is weighed for purposes of analyzing structure or function in an ecosystem or its components. Wet weight is the total biomass, including all the associated water in the cells of organisms. Dry weight measures the organic portion of the biomass, including all the inorganics incorporated in organic molecules. Ash is the inorganic component after the purely organic has been burned to CO_2 and H_2O, both of which will evaporate into the air in the heat of burning.

Carbon transfers, the buildup and breakdown of biological molecules composed of carbon chains and rings by the stepwise addition or elimination of single carbon atoms and bonded groups, are essential to the processes of life. Photosynthesis transforms the single carbon of carbon dioxide into the six-carbon compound glucose. Glucose then enters the metabolic processes of the living plant in reactions found throughout the plant and animal kingdoms. (Similar, if not identical, reactions also occur among protista, bacteria, and fungi, based on the same overall biochemical themes.)

The first step for glucose is glycolysis, whereby each six-carbon sugar molecule is broken down (hydrolyzed) into two three-carbon molecules, pyruvate. The pyruvate is further broken down to form the two-carbon group, acetyl. It is this group in association with a specific coenzyme that enters the Krebs or citric acid cycle,[7] the center of respiration in both plants and animals. In essence, this cycle constantly moves from two- to four- to six-carbon chains and back again along a precise chemical pathway. In the process, energy-rich molecules (ATP, adenosine triphosphate) are formed with the donation of electrons from hydrogen. Each time a carbon is removed from a molecule, it is as carbon dioxide. The associated hydrogen (electrons) is then carried out of the system by oxygen with the generation of water. This process provides the energy for the work of life, which is actually being carried out at the subcellular level.

When energy is required, ATP reverts chemically to ADP (adenosine diphosphate), which can return to the Krebs cycle. Indeed, most, if not all, of these individual biochemical reactions are reversible. The reverse process, however, requires the presence of an enzyme other than the one catalyzing its counterpart reaction—another deceptively simple control mechanism in the chemical complex identified as life.

Derivatives of these processes and their products are the chemical products of all the materials associated with life, including amino acids and the proteins and lipids, which include fats, oils, steroids, and waxes. Each process is mediated by the genes as they "switch" on and off. The genes are themselves specific organic chains composed deceptively simply of multiple nucleotides, each a combination of a five-carbon sugar, phosphate (PO_4^{2-}) and one of four organic bases. Each base consists of nothing more than carbon, oxygen, hydrogen, and nitrogen.[8]

Another major reaction is condensation, the joining of monomers into larger "macromolecules" with the extraction of water. The generalized formula is again deceptively simple,

$$Monomer - H + HO - Monomer \rightarrow Monomer - Monomer + H_2O$$

One of the most important condensation reactions is that which occurs between two amino acids to form a dipeptide, tripeptide, and so on, into the polypeptide proteins:

```
    NH₂  O              OH  NH₂                NH₂  O
     \  //               \  /                  \  //
   R--C--C      +        C--C--R    →    R--C--C    H + H₂O
    /    \              //    \           /    \  /
   H    OH              O     H          H   HO  N
   Amino acid         Amino acid             \   \
                                             C--C--R
                                            //
                                            O
                                        Dipeptide
```

What has happened in this representation is that the hydroxyl group in the first amino acid and one hydrogen from the amine group of the second have been split off to form water. The carbon from the first then forms a bond with the nitrogen of the second. Note that each carbon still has all four bonding sites filled and no more than those four. (All four electrons are shared for each carbon.)

If one "straightens" the dipeptide molecule, its representation better reflects its functional components:

```
                    (amine)
                    NH₂  O  H  H  OH
                     \   // /  /  /
   (specific     R--C-- C--N--C--C        (acid)
   amino acid)    /         /   \\
                 H          R    O
                        (specific
                       amino acid)
```

In the case of amino acids the condensation reactions continue, under the direction of the genetic material in the cell, to form specific polypeptide molecules, proteins. Specifically, the amine above can release an electron (one hydrogen) to combine with the hydroxyl group from a third amino acid. The acid (carboxyl) group above can release a hydroxyl group to combine with an amine hydrogen from a fourth amino acid. Thus, a polypeptide of four amino acids would be synthesized, with the release of an additional two molecules of water. This condensation process continues to form the elaborate polymers known as proteins.

The chemical reversal of condensation is known as hydrolysis, the breakdown of macromolecules into their component monomers by the restoration of water:

Monomer – Monomer + H₂O → Monomer – H + Monomer – OH

All cells hydrolyze macromolecules into their monomers and use the monomers for maintenance, growth, specific functions and reproduction. For example, a cell will break down proteins into amino acids in order to generate different proteins.

Heterotrophs cannot make their own macromolecules from "scratch," as can autotrophs, which is why herbivores must consume plants to survive. Similarly, carnivores cannot generate all their required macromolecules from scratch or directly from those generated by autotrophs. Carnivores must consume other heterotrophs that have already taken the biochemical steps carnivores cannot take. Omnivores can consume a variety of producers and consumers at more than one trophic level. Alternative biochemical pathways accommodate to the sources of the organic materials ingested.

Ecosystems, then, are composed of a community of organisms in which there are numerous cycles of closely interconnected pathways of producers, phagotrophic consumers, and saprotrophic consumers. Each cycle is connected to the abiota by green plants and by autotrophic and heterotrophic microorganisms.

The so-called scavengers—vultures, hyenas, sharks, and other (phagotrophic) consumers of carrion—can also be considered a part of the detritus circuit, but many insects and other organisms of comparable small size take some of the first steps to produce the molecules on which the communities of microorganisms feed.

Each species has a precise role in an ecosystem's trophic cycles—its niche. Some of those species can be replaced by others, depending on the specific ecosystem and its strategy over time. Other species may be uniquely capable of filling a niche in an ecosystem. If such a species is lost, that portion of the cycle is discontinued. Unless adaptations occur, the cycle will cease. If it is crucial to neighboring cycles, they will also cease. Some may adapt; others cannot. Ultimately, the whole ecosystem will adapt or be altered. If homeostasis is restored, the new community will continue to function as a recognizable unit, albeit at least subtly distinct from the original ecosystem. If the alterations exceed the system's ability to restore a homeostatic condition, the ecosystem will be lost.

How all these wondrous transformations proceed in keeping with the specific functions and changing needs of cells, tissues, organs, and the whole organism belongs in the black boxes of biochemistry, physiology, endocrinology, and a host of molecular biology disciplines well beyond the immediate scope of ecological principles. Suffice it to say that as genes are turned on and off, enzymatic reactions carry out the business at hand.

Enzymatic catalysis is the precise biological rating of biochemical reactions. Most reactions of metabolism and catabolism would never occur spontaneously or would proceed either infinitely slowly or so rapidly as to be ineffective or destructive in the biological system. The processes of life, therefore, depend on catalysis carried out by enzymes.

Both reactions whereby the products are at a lower energy state than the reactants (exergonic reactions) and those whereby the products are at a higher energy state than the reactants (endergonic reactions) are impeded by the need for a relatively large energy input—an energy "hump" that must be surmounted. Enzymes substantially reduce this hump by interacting to bring the reactants together in chemical "readiness" and then being released unchanged. In biological processes, there are numerous specific interconnections of such reactions, with the energy released by an exergonic reaction frequently driving an endergonic one. These processes occur at specific locations within the cytoplasm and subcellular structures, as required by the cell in its particular environment. For unicellular organisms, that environment is external—the abiota as it is constantly mediated by other members of the biota. For multicellular organisms, the cellular environment consists of other cells and any products they secrete in specific structural organizations building to the organism itself.

In biochemical processes, enzymatic catalysts function with cofactors or coenzymes. Cofactors are inorganic ions—often heavy metals—at the site on the protein molecule that actually serves the catalytic function. Coenzymes are nonproteinaceous organic molecules, often those characterized as vitamins or incorporating vitamins (as a "moiety") within the chemical structure. For example, the protein hemoglobin, which gives blood its red color, contains iron. It is the iron that chemically binds to and holds oxygen for distribution throughout the body and releases it as needed for the Krebs citric acid cycle. Other essential trace elements (also heavy metals important in toxicology) are magnesium in chlorophyll and copper in vitamin B_{12}.

Thus, when exploring biogeochemical cycles in the next chapter, the material cycling component of ecosystems, there are a number of specific elements and simple molecules of major interest. Primary among these elements is the carbon of carbon dioxide and of organic matter. Hydrogen and oxygen are also essential, both occurring in the biologically essential form of water, and the latter occurring not only in carbon dioxide and water but also as pure molecules: diatomic molecular oxygen (O_2), essential to respiration; and the unstable ozone (O_3), significant, on one hand, as a mutagenic agent and, on the other, as protection from another mutagenic agent, the ultraviolet wavelengths of solar radiation.

In considering these few elements and simple molecules and their seemingly countless reactions in only a few unmistakable basic patterns, the fundamental paradox emerges of the precisely structured and functional complexity of life based in deceptive simplicity. It is truly astounding.

Moreover, it can all be traced to the physical processes of the Big Bang and the formation of galaxies and solar systems. All of chemistry, inorganic and organic, is an elaboration of those physical processes.[9] We and all of life are in a very real sense the stuff of the sun, which in turn is the chemical stuff of the galaxy and ultimately of the Big Bang. "What goes around comes around" is profoundly accurate in connecting life and the cosmos.

NOTES

The principal sources for this chapter are *Journey*, chapters 3, 7, and 8; Odum, chapter 4; Smith, at 74–81, 245–282 and chapter 8; and Ricklefs, chapter 11. For additional insights into the relevant biological sciences, *see also Journey*, chapters 19–22 and 25; and Smith, chapters 8 and 9.

1. For a graphic visual synopsis of ecosystem structure and function based on combined energy flow and material cycling, *see* Odum, figure 4–11, at 104.

2. This fact is reflected in the need for sanitary landfills to include a methane collection system. The gas is constantly generated and released as the organic wastes slowly decompose.

3. For the common structure of amino acids, *see Journey*, at 45; for a list of those essential to life, consult a recent biochemistry text.

4. *See e.g.*, D. Hull, *Philosophy of Biological Science* (1974), at 26–27.

5. *See e.g.*, H. Blum, *Time's Arrow and Evolution* (3d ed., 1968), at 22.

6. Hence, the crucial difference in the human diet: Hydrocarbons "saturated" with hydrogen are energy rich, which most of us do not need, whereas those that are "unsaturated"—hydrogen poor—supply less energy.

7. For graphic representations of the Krebs cycle, *see Journey*, figures 7–2 and 7–6, at 113 and 117.

8. For visualizations of the double-helix DNA molecule, *see Journey*, at 151.

9. *See e.g.*, M. Florkin and E. Schoffeniels, *Molecular Approaches to Ecology* (1969), at 23–27.

8

Biogeochemical Cycles

PLANETARY ABIOTIC SOURCES

Holistically, in what appears to be a recurring strategy, abiotic conditions, notably including the substrate represented by geological features on the macro- and microscale, make it possible for life to arise and determine what life forms can become established. These "pioneering" organisms interact with the abiotic substrate, altering it and making way for additional or different organisms. The process may stabilize at a given stage for a measurable interval of sufficient duration to be recognized as an ecosystem, defined by its unique community.

It is instructive to examine planet Earth in terms of the three major components of the biosphere: the atmosphere, the hydrosphere, and the lithosphere. Together, they are the source of all the chemical components of life, and each has a place in every biogeochemical cycle.

Atmosphere

Essential to the maintenance of life is the earth's atmosphere. This gaseous envelope is as important to the individual organism as it is for the global biosphere. Today's atmosphere is an oxidizing one. Early in the evolution of the planet, molecular hydrogen predominated for a reducing atmosphere. Life, then, first originated in a reducing atmosphere and actually created the oxidizing atmosphere. In order to survive, organisms then had to adapt or evolve accordingly. One could argue that life itself has been a major perturbation of the global environment. One of its first influences was the poisoning of the atmosphere with its wastes. Fresh perspective on contemporary environmental crises is provided through recognition that life then proceeded to evolve in accommodation of the toxic atmosphere it generated. The biosphere we hope to preserve and protect is still being maintained by the planetary biota, including human populations.

Today, as a result of life's historical influence on the biosphere, slow oxidation in "air" is occurring constantly. Iron and other metals rust, or, more precisely, oxidize. Fire occurs with some frequency. When organic material burns, it is being rapidly oxidized. Complete burning, which occurs in the presence of ample oxygen, results in the generation of CO_2, H_2O, and energy (the heat and light of fire). If any heavy metals are present, they will be restored to the elemental form found in the ash.

There are a number of logical approaches to the earth's atmosphere. It has thermal, electrical, and compositional properties.[1] Electrically, the lower sixty or so miles from the planetary surface constitute the neutrosphere, electrically neutral and hence relatively unreactive—leaving the reactions to the chemistry and biology of the hydrosphere and lithosphere. Above the neutrosphere is the ionosphere. The ions that give this region its name would be extremely reactive were they not separated by decreasing concentrations, a reflection of the tendency toward entropy as these entities escape the atmosphere for outer space.

The temperature decreases with distance from the planetary surface. Temperatures are highest and the most dynamic below the stratosphere, especially in the lowest five to thirteen miles where weather is occurring. A thermal component can be measured as high as 100 miles from the surface, in the thermosphere. Both the concentration of ions and temperatures ordinarily measured as Centigrade or Fahrenheit continue to dissipate with distance from the planetary surface until interplanetary space of the solar system is attained.

It is illuminating to follow the chemical composition of the atmosphere from those outer reaches down toward the surface. The outermost region, from 1,500 miles in altitude and beyond, is the protonosphere, essentially molecular hydrogen. As altitude decreases, hydrogen gives way to helium, which gives way to molecular oxygen. Oxygen gives way to an oxygen-nitrogen mixture at an altitude of about 75 miles. Almost completely coextensive with the stratosphere is the ozonosphere, some 6 to 50 miles from the surface. Here the oxygen-nitrogen mix gives way to the unstable ozone molecule composed of three, rather than two, oxygen atoms.

The chemical mix from the stratosphere to the atmosphere is dynamic. The lower sixty miles are the homogeneous mix familiarly known as "air," where the winds are active. The ecosphere, the portion of the atmosphere sustaining life, is only the last two miles or so.

The ecosphere is composed mostly of molecular nitrogen, just over three quarters of the chemical content of dry air measured by volume or by weight. Nitrogen, significantly enough, is relatively stable. Molecular oxygen is just over a fifth of the content, also by volume or weight. A greater concentration of oxygen would result in an explosive atmosphere, whereas a lesser concentration would be suffocating to the predominant aerobic organisms of earth.

The noble (nonreactive) gas argon is the next-most-concentrated component, at just about 1%. Carbon dioxide is present at less than 0.5% by volume. Hydrogen, ammonia gas, and ozone are present in volumes of 0.0001% to 0.00001%. Since each of these gases is toxic to life or otherwise hazardous, albeit essential to biochemical processes, these minute percentages are significant to life and ecology for more than one reason.

Hydrosphere

The hydrosphere may be what sets Earth apart from any other planet in the solar system otherwise theoretically capable of supporting life. Neither Venus nor Mars currently possesses a hydrosphere, a factor almost certainly precluding life on either planet. Venus is also too hot and Mars too cold for most forms of life, but temperature is one of the reasons earth does have a hydrosphere. The hydrosphere at temperature regimes from the equator to the poles consists of water in three physical states: solid, liquid, and gaseous. The hydrosphere will be considered in greater detail as representative of hydrogeochemical cycles.

Lithosphere

The lithosphere is the earth itself. This sphere, the subject of geology, is the substrate for both aquatic and terrestrial life. Like the atmosphere, the lithosphere is composed of distinct layers, each having a unique role in ecological processes.

The average radius of the planet is 4,000 miles. On the top of the solid matter of the planet is the relatively fine material known as soil. This is a complex and extremely variable sediment in terms of texture, inorganic content, and organic content. Soil is usually defined by its origins or its level of fertility.

The highly heterogeneous material is divided into two categories: topsoil and subsoil. The former is a mixture of highly decomposed mineral constituents and organic material known as humus. The underlying subsoil provides nutrients and moisture for deeply rooted plants. Beneath the subsoil at varying depths is bedrock, the outermost portion of the mantle, the lithosphere itself.[2] This sixty-mile crust consists of some ten miles of bedrock. The lithosphere is 99% silicates, oxides, carbonates, and phosphates, indirectly available to the biota in that physical processes are required to raise them to the surface where they are exposed to weathering, erosion, and other mechanisms breaking them down into formations into which life can intrude.

Below this crust is the barysphere, the heavier interior of the mantle. The outer core of this region is molten rock, the source of volcanoes and of the heat of thermal waters. The inner core is also hot rock, but internal pressure is so intense that it remains solidified.

It is the bedrock that is of the most immediate significance to ecology. Nearly half of bedrock is oxygen, chemically bound in a variety of substances. More than a quarter of bedrock is silicon, relatively inactive in biological terms. Metals, such as aluminum, iron, calcium, sodium, potassium, and magnesium, are each present in concentrations approaching 10%. Other metals and hydrogen are present in amounts ranging from 0.04% to 0.1%. Among these are elements essential to life, notably carbon, sulfur, and phosphorus. Significantly, none of the three planetary sources of material contains that material in the form of relative concentrations found in the biota. To maintain its distinction from the abiota, life obviously directs substantial energy to building and maintaining its characteristic chemical organization.

WATER AND THE HYDROSPHERE

Water and the hydrosphere can be considered a biogeochemical cycle, with water representing the nutrient of interest. But water is also a major carrier and reservoir of all other nutrients.

As the liquid dihydrogen oxide, water is truly a unique substance and one particularly suited to supporting life. Physically, it is transparent to incoming sunlight but absorbs reemitted infrared to serve as an atmospheric temperature control. Through the physical process of evaporation and the biological process of transpiration, water also holds terrestrial temperatures below lethal limits for plants and animals.[3]

The atmosphere can retain more water as its temperature increases. This process stabilizes ambient temperature in the event of a sudden input of heat—as regularly occurs, for example, with sunrise.[4]

The Chemistry and Biology of Water

When water is formed by the reduction of oxygen and oxidation of hydrogen, the electrons are shared by the two elements composing the molecule, but oxygen holds them more strongly than does the hydrogen. Hence, although water has an oxidation number of zero, the two hydrogens of water tend to have a positive charge, while the oxygen tends to have a negative charge. Water is therefore polar—one of the properties making this molecule so important to life. The polarity of water makes it a good solvent for inorganics but not for organics. Hence, inorganic and simple organic nutrients dissolve in water, but organisms and their principal molecules do not. It is notable that water does, however, constitute up to 90% of the "chemical" content of organisms.[5]

Water itself readily dissociates to yield $2H^+$ and O^{2-} or, more accurately, H_3O^+ (hydronium ion) and OH^- (hydroxyl ion). These ions are highly reactive with each other and with other ions in aqueous solution. This property of water is essential to its ecological role. When the hydronium and hydroxyl ions are present in equivalent amounts, the resultant solution (environment) is neutral, designated as pH 7.0. Sometimes, however, reactions with ions in solution result in acidic conditions, where more hydroxyl than hydronium ions have entered chemical combinations that remove them from solution, leaving an excess of hydronium ions, designated as pH levels less than 7.0.

The reverse can also occur to leave an excess of hydroxyl ions in solution, a basic condition, designated as pH levels greater than 7.0. What is being measured is the concentration of hydronium ions, expressed as a negative coefficient. That is, neutrality is a concentration of 10^{-7}. A pH of 5, for example, is a 10^{-5} concentration, while pH 8 is 10^{-8}. There are more hydronium ions at the lesser pH than at the higher pH.

Each organism and many biochemical reactions depend on the pH of the immediate environment. Moreover, the availability of certain nutrients and toxic chemicals to the biota is closely related to pH. Thus, the health of an ecosystem can be affected positively and negatively by alterations in pH. Such effects can rise to the level of perturbation (too little or too much nutrient, altering toxicity of substances present), which may be natural or anthropogenic.

The Hydrogeology of Ecology

As a preliminary to biogeochemical cycles, hydrogeology serves two purposes: first, as a carrier of ecologically important chemicals; second, as a model for biogeochemical cycles. Since the processes of interest are cycles, it does not matter where the starting point of analysis is set. Water is a major constituent of the atmosphere and is found on and in the lithosphere, but water is most prevalent as oceans. The oceans contain literally billions and billions of grams of water—nearly a billion and a half billion billions of grams.

To gain perspective, a pound weighs some 454 grams, and a billion billion is more accessible when converted to exponents, sometimes known as scientific notation: 1×10^{18}. A relatively small portion of the vast reservoir of water enters the atmosphere through evaporation, some 319×10^{18} grams. Some, but not all, of this evaporated water will return to the oceans as precipitation, 283×10^{18} grams. The rest remains in the air as water vapor, with some of the water molecules forming aggregates that are sufficiently concentrated to be visible: clouds. Containing less than 40×10^{18}

grams of water, clouds are moved by net wind movement in patterns around the globe. When conditions are suitable, the water in clouds returns to land formations as precipitation, nearly 100×10^{18} grams. Some of that water runs off the land surface, to enter bodies of surface water, which ultimately make their way back to the oceans. Some of the precipitated water enters the ground and finds its way into underground waters, a system of streams, ponds, and lakes known collectively as groundwater. Together surface runoff and groundwater represent nearly 40×10^{18} grams. The remaining water percolates through the soil and enters still deeper underground systems, including cracks and pockets in bedrock. Over time, earth's sedimentary rocks have incorporated much water, physically and chemically, representing the second-largest reservoir of water on earth with a content of just over $200,000 \times 10^{18}$ grams.

What is the source of the additional water entering precipitation over land? Nearly 60×10^{18} grams come from the physical process of evaporation from land and the biological process of transpiration from the leaves of plants. Water enters vegetation through the root systems and is carried throughout the body of each organism. With it comes the inorganic nutrients needed to initiate the grazing cycle. But were that water retained in each plant, it would soon become bloated. Specialized cells in the leaves open and close to control the release of water into the atmosphere.

All those processes in equilibria with each other make up the water cycle, quite clearly composed of chemical, biological, and geological reactions or processes. Additional water movement is associated with vulcanism, is bound up in the polar ice caps, and is lost to outer space.[6]

REPRESENTATIVE BIOGEOCHEMICAL CYCLES

With the water cycle as a model, a generic biogeochemical cycle can be described. There are three major components, which, significantly enough, represent three major pieces of the generic ecosystem: available inorganic nutrients, living organisms, and organic detritus. Again, material is cycling, so analysis can commence at any point without warping logic.

This time it is instructive to begin outside the immediately active abiotic portion of the cycle, with indirectly available inorganics. This material is, in fact, the lithosphere itself, more specifically, the bedrock and even more inaccessible reaches of the earth's interior. This indirectly available matter, which is inorganic, undergoes weathering, erosion, and biological fixation in a variety of forms ranging from the physical action of deep roots to the biochemical reactions of microorganisms. This array of actions renders the inorganics available to the grazing cycle. They become biologically fixed through the process of assimilation and production through the trophic levels of each ecosystem.

Respiration, leaching, and extraction return some of the nutrients from living organisms to the available inorganic nutrient pool. Much of the material incorporated into the living mass enters the organic detritus. Some of the detritus returns to the biota through feeding by detrivores. Much of the organic material is leached, burned, or decomposed, with a release of inorganics into the pool of available inorganics and returns again to living organisms. The chemical components of some organics become indirectly available and are restored to the inorganic cycling pool through burning, leaching, or decomposition and to the organic detritus through erosion.

Some of the organics form the peat, coal, and oil that are stored indefinitely in the lithosphere. The inorganic nutrients incorporated in these organics are restored to the inorganic pool by burning. Similarly, some of the available inorganics are returned to indirectly available status through precipitation and sedimentation. They are returning to the major reservoirs: the atmosphere, portions of the hydrosphere, and the lithosphere.

Biogeochemical cycles can be represented in two lesser cycles: reservoirs and pools. As the designations imply, the difference is a quantitative one with some relationship to availability as well as to speed of movement through the environmental components. Generally, a reservoir pool is large, slow moving, and generally abiotic. A cycling or exchange pool is smaller, more active, and involves transactions between organisms and their immediate environment, sometimes considered the microenvironment. It is through all these processes—physical and chemical as well as biological—that the 30 or 40 elements known to be required by organisms are extracted from more than 100 known chemical elements, driven by the one-way traffic in energy flowing from the sun to outer space.

Carbon

The element carbon represents 0.03% of the atmosphere as the inorganic gas carbon dioxide. That gas is in constant exchange between the atmosphere and the ocean. In this and other aquatic systems, carbon's representative inorganic molecules are also in chemical equilibrium:

$$CO_2 + H_2O \rightleftarrows H_2CO_3 \rightleftarrows H^+ + HCO_3^- \rightleftarrows H^+ + CO_3^{2+}$$

This shorthand equilibrium, by which carbon dioxide can become a carbonate ion with intermediate stops at carbonic acid and a bicarbonate ion, results in a buffering capacity in bodies of water. Either an excess of acid or an excess of alkalinity will be chemically assimilated by the equilibrium to restore the system to the pH existing prior to the perturbation. Hydronium ions will react with cations in bases to remove them from the system, while the bicarbonate or carbonate ions will react with anions in acids to remove them.

In a specific ecosystem, carbon will be found as carbon dioxide, carbonates, organic detritus, and most important, living tissue. The biogeochemical cycle of carbon is already familiar. The major reservoirs are the atmosphere and the hydrosphere with cycling pools at or near the earth's surface and at the surface levels of water where light can penetrate and photosynthesis can occur. A major organic reservoir of carbon is represented by peat, coal, and oil, each of which must undergo the rapid oxidation called burning before it can reenter the atmosphere and hydrosphere and the associated exchange pools. Carbon is also in the lithosphere in the form of limestone and dissolved marine humus. All of these forms are biogenic.

In summation, most of the planetary carbon is in the abiota, primarily the hydrosphere and lithosphere. Only a small amount at any given instant can be found in either the atmosphere or the biota.

Oxygen

In contrast to carbon, oxygen represents a little more than 20% of the atmosphere. It is also present as water. Its exchange pools are the water and the atmosphere, where it is present both as carbon dioxide and as molecular oxygen. It is also a major component of a variety of inorganic compounds, designated by the chemical suffixes "-ite" or "-ate," as in nitrites and nitrates, phosphites and phosphates, carbonates, and bicarbonates. Acids and bases, organic as well as inorganic, also contain oxygen.

Biologically, oxygen can be considered a by-product or waste product of photosynthesis or as one of the three major chemical building blocks of protoplasm. The role of oxygen in respiration is one of oxidation: It accepts the electrons of hydrogen and removes them from the Krebs citric acid cycle.

The biogeochemical cycle of oxygen is as familiar as the carbon cycle, of which this element is a part. It is as nearly ubiquitous throughout the biosphere as any element can be. Less familiar forms are found chemically bound up in rock formations, including granite, marble, and quartz.

Nitrogen

Secondary only to the carbon, hydrogen, and oxygen in organic molecules is nitrogen. Molecular nitrogen, N_2, represents nearly 80% of earth's atmosphere, but it is essentially useless to the biota. Molecular nitrogen can neither be photosynthesized nor respired. It can be absorbed (principally a physical process) but not assimilated (a biological process). Yet it is prevalent in the soil as organic matter. Somehow it is drawn into the grazing and detritus cycles and converted into amino acids to generate proteins. Nitrogen is also a part of the bases encoding the directions for all life processes mediated by the genetic molecules DNA and RNA. Nitrogen is even a component of chlorophyll, used by the biota to fix carbon dioxide and light.

Nitrogen is involved in a biogeochemical cycle, but this time a logical starting point can be selected. It is the biological fixation of molecular nitrogen. In fact, the intricacies of interactions in the nitrogen cycle are a particularly lucid model for all the remaining nutrient cycles. Each movement in the cycle is actually one step, mediated by a specific organism when not subject to purely physical and chemical alterations.

Molecular nitrogen in the atmosphere is biologically fixed by genera of nitrogen-fixing bacteria. Their habitat is found within the roots of certain plants, the legumes. Here, in a symbiotic relationship, the bacteria convert nitrogen to nitrate, an anion of nitrogen combined with three oxygens. The chemical compounds known as nitrates are soluble in water. They are carried into the soil where they are absorbed and assimilated by green plants at large and thus enter the two trophic cycles as organic nitrogen, frequently in amine form. Nitrates can also be assimilated by additional genera of bacteria, the denitrifiers. They convert nitrates to nitrites (one less oxygen atom in the anion) and nitrites to molecular nitrogen, which is restored to the atmosphere.

Animals excrete urea and other organics, which are converted by soil bacteria to ammonium compounds (containing the cation NH_4^+), which nitrifying bacteria convert to nitrites (*Nitrosomonas* spp.) and to nitrates (*Nitrobacter* spp.), which can enter the soil for cycling through the grazing cycle. The nitrates can also be denitrified by additional bacterial taxons. As both plants and animals die, their nitrogenous biochemicals are acted upon by putrifying bacteria.[7]

Each biochemical step (some of which are the familiar redox reactions) in the "bio" portion of the nitrogen cycle is also an energy transfer. There is an energy barrier, surmounted by enzymatic catalysts unique to nitrogen-fixing bacteria, in the conversion of molecular nitrogen to nitrate. Each step from the nitrate through nitrite, ammonia, and amino acids to protoplasm requires external energy, because each is chemically more likely to proceed in the opposite direction. That energy comes from the sunlight or from the breaking of chemical bonds in organic matter. It is operating against entropy.

Trace (Heavy) Metals

Phosphorus is also essential to life. Organic phosphates are the immediate source of energy in the cell. ATP holds the energy ready for utilization and is converted to ADP as the energy is taken. ADP enters the Krebs cycle and is "reenergized" with a new phosphate ion. Phosphorus, chemically a metal, is found in sediments more than in the atmosphere or hydrosphere, as is the case with other metals essential to life. Iron is an active component of hemoglobin; magnesium, of chlorophyll; and copper, of vitamin B_{12}, a coenzyme. Magnesium is involved in protein synthesis in plants. It is also found in the bone of vertebrates and is essential to enzymatic reactions mediating the transfer of phosphates.

Together phosphorus with calcium actually constitute 70% of the total inorganic component of animal cells. In all organisms, phosphorus is involved in energy transfers and is a structural component of DNA and RNA. The calcium-phosphorus ratio is crucial for the utilization of certain vitamins and/or other nutrients.

In plants, calcium is involved in the association of cells and in root growth. In animals, calcium is involved in acid–base relationships and in blood clotting, the contraction and relaxation of heart muscle, and the control of fluid passage across cell membranes. The metal is a component of exoskeletons, shells, and skeletons.

The bio portion of all these biogeochemical cycles is reflected in the biomass, each in a way uniquely informative to the ecologist who would follow the fate of the chemicals involved. The relatively minute contribution of inorganics is informative in another way. Because so little is needed of each of these metals, too much in the ecosystem can be at least as harmful to the biota as too little. Thus, these trace elements that support life are also known as *heavy metals*, a term carrying a connotation of toxicity, acute and chronic. Whenever dealing with chemical substances, a number of questions are crucial not only to the ecologist but also to the environmental professional who seeks answers to questions associated with regulation and litigation.

IMPLICATIONS FOR ENVIRONMENTAL PROFESSIONALS

Chemistry is obviously as important to the environmental professional as it is to ecologists. Both will be asking the same kinds of questions about a chemical substance in an ecosystem. The first and most obvious question, the answer to which may be considerably less obvious, is, What is the chemical in chemical terms? This question can be broken down into chemical and physical components.

The identity of the unknown material is first what elements are present and in what combinations. Each combination will have unique properties, causing its actual placement in the ecosystem. A chemical substance will often occur in a mixture with the materials of the environment. By definition, the atmosphere, water, and soil are all mixtures. If in water, the substance can be in suspension or solution or somewhere in between as a colloid, each of which will have different implications for the material's physical, chemical, and hence, biological fate.

If chemical reactions are in progress, the substance may be in chemical or biological equilibrium, which will affect its availability to the biota. The next series of inquiries, which depend on accurate answers to the foregoing, address where the material is. Is it in the abiota, or has it entered the biota? Its present location determines where it is going and by what routes and through what alterations. These are qualitative and then quantitative questions. In brief, a substance will either be available or unavailable to the biota or specific organisms. Available substances are of immediate interest. Those that are unavailable are significant in terms of the mechanisms by which they may become available.

By its nature, its location in the ecosystem, its amount and concentration, and its availability, a substance may be quantitatively insufficient to have any effect on the system. As its concentration or its absolute amount increases, a progression of effects in organisms may be detected. The substance may be a nutrient in micro- or macroquantities. As such, an excess of the substance may represent nutrient enrichment that can be a perturbation of the system as a whole or in terms of a portion of the system of particular interest to the observer. Whether a nutrient or not, increasing amount or concentration may begin to cause toxic responses, which are described as subchronic, chronic, acute, and lethal as the crucial quantitative parameter increases.

These effects may be felt only in one part of an ecosystem, but they can proceed to injure additional parts or to affect the ecosystem progressively but indirectly. These phenomena are illustrated in the timely matter of acid deposition.

ECOLOGICAL EFFECTS OF ACID DEPOSITION[8]

The Chemical Pathways

The major industrial precursors of anthropogenic acid deposition are sulfur dioxide and nitrogen oxides. These ions readily react in aerosols to generate sulfuric and nitric acid, respectively. The relevant chemistry of sulfur dioxide is better known than that of nitrogen oxides.

Natural rain, water without these particular contaminants, is slightly acidic at pH 5.6 and subject to control through the dissociation of carbon dioxide. Natural waters can have a pH as low as 5, suggesting the presence of naturally occurring acidification.

Natural sources include sulfur in the lithosphere, released by volcanic action, sea salt aerosols, forest fires, and microbial decomposition. Nitrogen in the atmosphere is converted to nitrogen oxides by lightning. That compounds of both sulfur and nitrogen can be biogenic should be abundantly clear from the foregoing descriptions of the chemistry underlying ecology.

Transportation of these acids and their precursors is a physical phenomenon. They are picked up and transported from one locale to others by the prevailing winds. In Europe, studies conducted in the 1970s indicated a residence time of up to four days that carried the substances more than 600 miles from their sources. Seasonal cycles were detected. In the United States, transportation is generally out of the west, eastward and northward. Deposition then occurs in precipitation in all its forms.

History and Politics

Today, precursors to acid deposition are identified as major sources of air pollution. In the case of sulfur dioxide, 80% of that released into the atmosphere is attributed to human activity, 100% in some regions. Of that 80% to 100%, 85% is attributed to fossil fuel combustion. Nitrogen oxides also come from combustion, the most notable source being motor vehicles.

The earliest reference to anthropogenic acid deposition came from England in 1727, followed by observations of acidification associated with a Swedish smelter in operation for 500 years. The atmosphere was reportedly so corrosive that no herbs survived in the vicinity of the smelter. Widespread recognition of the effects of reduced pH did not come until the 1960s. Following an American synopsis of deposition chemistry in the mid–1950s, a continuous record of the phenomenon was initiated in 1963. Historic pH levels are necessarily inferred, not measured. Researchers disagree profoundly on the matter of trends over the last 25 years, but indirect evidence represented by acidity in Arctic ice caps suggests an increase in acidity.

Acid Deposition in Ecosystems

While there are economic and social effects of acid deposition on human artifacts, the effects of acid in ecosystems are of considerable interest as well. In forests and crops, decline and dieback of trees have been reported, possibly exacerbated by drought or dry summers. Some detrimental effects are directly the result of altered leaching of cations and other chemical entities caused by a lowered pH.

Aquatic systems are to some extent buffered. But they, too, can be adversely affected. Changes in pH can affect communities of bacteria, algae, invertebrates, and fish, altering species composition and productivity, reducing numbers, and impairing reproduction and decomposition.

Elements of the progression of effects have been reported for public consumption from field experiments.[9] The subject lake had a natural pH of 6.5. Four years into the research, pH was reduced to 5.9, and relatively obvious effects were detected in the biota. While phytoplankton remained abundant, the mix of species had altered. Freshwater shrimp had nearly disappeared, and reproduction in fathead minnows was failing. In the next two years, pH was down to 5.6. Mats of slimy algae were forming. Crayfish had become unusually vulnerable to parasites and were suffering anatomical damage. The decline in fathead minnows led to a temporary boom in another species. Ironically, the favored species was preferred by trout, which presumably benefited from the ecological alteration.

By the seventh year, pH was down to 5.0. While there was no mention of the condition of the producers, the crayfish, leeches, and mayflies had all disappeared. Reproduction among the now-emaciated lake trout ceased. Thus, in seven years, a result upon which regulators could readily base governmental controls—assuming the source of acid to be a recognizable legal entity—had occurred: the death of a population of organisms of immediate human interest. Significantly, more subtle changes earlier in the progression could have supported political action to prevent this ultimate harm. The question is the matter of political justifications and ramifications. Do we want a healthful or a healthy environment—and is there a meaningful difference? Even at such a profound level of perturbation, it was observed that at least partial recovery is rapid. Restoration of the ecosystem, however, is estimated to require hundreds of years. Clearly, the questions to be raised begin—but only begin—with ecological realities.

Unanswered Questions

Despite calls for governmental action, relevant ecological questions remain to be answered. Quantitative relationships are not clear, and relationships between sources of acid and receptors are not well known. Beyond ecology are the questions of economics and sociology.

NOTES

Principal sources for this chapter are Odum, chapter 4; Smith, chapters 8 and 9, and at 29, 74–81, 245–282; Ricklefs, chapter 11; and *Journey*, chapter 3.

1. The following descriptions of the atmosphere are taken from *Van Nostrand's Scientific Encyclopedia* (4th ed., 1968), figure 1, at 139.

2. Descriptions of the outer "crust" of the lithosphere are taken from the *Scientific Encyclopedia*, *id.*, at 1027 and 1052.

3. H. Blum, *Time's Arrow and Evolution* (3d ed., 1968), at 63–64.

4. *Id.*, at 63.

5. *Id.*, at 62.

6. *See* Odum, figure 4–8B, at 97.

7. Adapted from Ricklefs, figure 11–4, at 175, and text, at 175–180.

8. The principal source for the acid deposition section is J. Moore, *The Changing Environment* (1986), chapter 10, at 203–233.

9. J. Luoma, "Bold Experiment in Lakes Tracks the Relentless Toll of Acid Rain," *NYT*, in *Science Times*, Sep. 13, 1988.

PART IV

STRATEGY AND THE BIOSPHERE: THE FOURTH DIMENSION

9

Cosmology and the History of Planet Earth

FROM THE BIG BANG TO THE SOLAR SYSTEM

Science currently cautions us that nothing throughout the universe is static. Everything, including the universe itself, is dynamic. Not only are all natural phenomena in constant flux, but they manifest direction. In keeping with entropy, "time's arrow"[1] flows from the past through the ephemeral present into the future, never the reverse. Moreover, strategies can be discerned. Without need to call on a sentient directing agent for purposes of scientific analysis, events reveal a destination. Everything from the universe through the unicellular organism has a beginning, a series of developmental stages and, presumably, an end. The Big Bang represents the beginning of the universe and, significantly, all its contents. Stars are born, evolve, and die, as do solar systems. Planet Earth reveals a strategy that has led to the establishment of a biosphere.

The biosphere is made up of interconnected ecosystems, each representing a substrate or habitat into which living organisms invade and then proceed to succeed one another. As the arrays of organisms proceed through successional stages, they alter the abiota even as it influences them. A climax community may result and then alter with the passage of long intervals of time in something like an aging process leading inevitably to senescence. Hence, any view of a natural system, such as an ecosystem or some microcosm of or within biological entities, is truly no more than a snapshot. It is a picture of things as they were at the moment of observation—nothing more and, frequently, substantially less.

Cosmology and the Big Bang

Why, one might legitimately ask, would the greenhouse effect be in the same chapter as cosmology and the Big Bang? What possible connection can there be? One might also be tempted to ask what subatomic physics has to do with studies of the history of the universe. But, as has been noted, there is a kind of hierarchy of sciences of which ecology is an integral part. Moreover, "every atom in our bodies, every atom we touch and breathe, was created long ago deep inside a long-forgotten star. We are literally made of the dust of stars."[2]

Physicists and cosmologists currently assert that the only time that something came out of nothing occurred in the Big Bang, the theoretical creation of the universe. All forms of energy and all of matter from the hydrogen atom to the most complex biological molecule can be traced to that "singular" event. When energy became matter, it was through the fusion of hydrogen nuclei (protons) to form helium. Until recently, those two elements in combination were thought to compose more than 99% of the material in the universe.[3] Now there is reason to believe that "dark matter" is more abundant than the brightly visible stars and galaxies.[4]

It is only in recent years that projections backward in time have been amenable to scientific probing. With cosmology, physicists have joined with philosophers and theologians to ponder origins and first causes.[5]

Competing theories have constantly emerged, but it was not until the middle of this century that theories gained sufficient scientific power and experimental techniques enough sensitivity to provide meaningful data. In very recent times, the Big Bang, an extraordinary explosion some 20 billion years ago, has become the respectable *theory* of the origin of the universe and its structure and "behavior."

A variety of empirical revelations are consistent with the theory, although many mysteries remain unsolved, including that of dark matter.[6] In keeping with the practice of science, the most promising contemporary contributions have resulted from multiple contributions. Significantly enough, the theory is maintained and advanced by empirical and experimental research conducted by physicists studying relationships between the energy and material resulting from the creation of the universe and astronomers studying the resultant large-scale structures, including that of the universe as a whole.[7] These ambitious research efforts have called upon particle theorists and cosmologists to join talents.[8]

Because the importance of the fourth dimension is a particular emphasis in ecology and with constant reference to the arrow of time in flight through entropy, the relationship of time to cosmology and to the Big Bang theory is of special interest. For environmental professionals, three different arrows of time must be taken into account. From the largest to the most

intimately associated with the human environment, they are the cosmological, the thermodynamic, and the psychological.[9]

Just how far one can connect ecology to the Big Bang requires an understanding of the nature of stars, the manufacturing facilities of the universe.

Evolution of Stars

Ecology, as we have seen, depends in large part on chemistry. Chemistry,
in turn, is the study of the elements and their physical and chemical properties. But what is the source of the elements? The chemical elements are
the stuff of which stars are made. Thus, chemistry is inextricably linked
not only to the physics holding atoms together but also to the stars that
find their origins in the energy and matter released as a result of the Big
Bang.

The contemporary understanding of the life history of stars begins with
space globules.[10] Space is not a complete vacuum. Individual atoms are
scattered throughout the great vastness of the universe. At some locations,
there are more than the random average of atoms. At these locations,
there is a concomitant increase in gravity. Increased gravity draws still
more atoms with progressively intense concentration. Eventually, the globule becomes unstable, unable to support its own weight. With the pressure
of "trillions upon trillions of tons of gas pressing inward from all sides,"[11]
the mass contracts with increasingly greater pressures and densities and
correspondingly increased temperatures at the center. The gases begin to
glow and radiation filters outward in the dark red portion of the electromagnetic spectrum. This is a protostar.

Like its predecessor globule, the protostar is unstable because it cannot
support the weight of its outer layers. The inner contraction continues with
still greater increases in pressure and temperature. When the central temperature reaches 10 million degrees, hydrogen "burning" is ignited. This
is not combustion (oxidation) but the fusion of colliding protons, the nuclei
of hydrogen. With each fusion, a helium nucleus is formed, with a loss of
matter. Einstein's well-known formula $E = MC^2$ applies, and a tremendous
amount of energy is released from the lost matter, a thermonuclear reaction. Because the helium product is lighter than the hydrogen reactants,
the contraction comes to a halt, and a star has been formed.

The newly formed star will continue to burn hydrogen for billions of
years before becoming unstable again. Now rich in helium, the core shrinks
with the inevitable temperature increases. At this stage in the star's life
history, the hydrogen between the core and the surface ignites in the
thermonuclear burning. As its outer layers are pushed outward, the star
swells, with a contracting core and thin layer of burning hydrogen.

When the core reaches 100 million degrees, the helium nuclei fuse with the formation of carbon and oxygen from this thermonuclear reaction. With helium burning in the core and the shell of burning hydrogen, the star's volume increases a billionfold. As a result, the atoms of the outermost layers move farther and farther apart, with a concomitant reduction in density, pressure, and temperature. Relatively speaking, the star's surface is now big and cool. It will now evolve to a red giant with a surface temperature of 3,000 degrees.

When helium burning is depleted, the core becomes unstable yet again. Again it will contract. This time the outer helium will ignite and the inner mix of carbon and oxygen becomes inert for lack of sufficient mass to ignite any further thermonuclear reactions. This configuration, like those before it, is unstable, but this time the star pulsates in a series of expansions and contractions. Each pulse of thousands of years represents alternating cooling and contraction, the latter reigniting internal fires. In the end, the outer layers, however, will separate completely to leave a stellar corpse behind. The "nebula" is short-lived—in only a matter of 50,000 years, the expanding envelope will disperse and disappear. The star itself will shrink as its warmth radiates into space until it becomes the size of the earth, a white dwarf.

The Solar System[12]

The Milky Way galaxy was formed some 7 billion years ago, with our own solar system taking form about 4.5 billion years ago. The center of our solar system is a hydrogen-burning star. A second- or third-generation star, some 2% of the sun's matter consists of elements such as carbon and oxygen.[13] The sun is expected to continue burning hydrogen for another 5 billion years before becoming unstable. Eventually, its surface will cool to a few thousand degrees with its white-hot gases and evolve into a red giant. In the process, it will vaporize the planet Mercury, sweep away the carbon dioxide atmosphere of Venus, and devastate Earth with boiling oceans and melting rocks. Eventually, our sun will become a white dwarf, about the size of Earth.

HISTORY OF PLANET EARTH[14]

For all we know thus far in our intellectual history, Earth is unique among planets as an abode for life. While the history of this planet within its solar system can be described in terms of coincidence, random events, and statistical probabilities, a pattern can be discerned. A variety of scientists infer the history of planetary formation and geological evolution from an incomplete record left by the events, including corresponding events in the ephemeral present.

Scientists have come to conclude that the Earth has been in constant evolution, with each step depending on the lengthy past. This dependence attaches to the origin and evolution of life. As far back as the Big Bang, events in the universe as well as on Earth itself have placed important restrictions on life's nature and its evolution.[15]

The lessons of paleontology, including the remnants of paleoecology, can also be turned to prediction. The accuracy of such predictions varies wildly. Sometimes it seems as though we can only predict into some vague middle time but neither the immediate nor the distant future, a function actually of the chaos side of natural events.[16]

GEOLOGICAL EVOLUTION

Planet Earth is currently believed to be about 4.5 billion years old, measured with the completion of the lithosphere. After about 500 million years of geological evolution, life occurred in the oceans.

As is the case with every good ecosystem, life invaded while the abiota was still undergoing its own transformations. From that point on, the biosphere—lithosphere, hydroshere, and atmosphere—continued to evolve, but now it evolved in concert with the biota, each influencing changes in the other in a discernible planetary pattern.

Origins and Strategies of Life

Almost all of life is distinguished from nonlife by the production of cytoplasm, the highly organized chemical stuff of life separated from the nonliving environment by a membrane, itself an intricately functioning component of the living cell. *All* of life shares the molecule DNA or, at least, RNA. Even viruses, entities on the very border separating biology from chemistry, while lacking cytoplasm or any cellular structure of their own beyond a simple protein coat, all possess either DNA or RNA.

For those laboring under the misapprehension that life is fragile, it is illuminating to view life as a planetary membrane—the "toughest . . . imaginable in the universe, opaque to probability, impermeable to death."[17] Life is astonishing in its uniformity as well as in its diversity. There is a high probability that all of us derive from a singe parent cell. And "[i]t is from the progeny of this parent cell that we take our looks; we still share genes around, and the resemblance of the enzymes of grasses to those of whales is a family resemblance."[18]

One of the earliest innovations of Lewis Thomas's "tough membrane" was bacterial photosynthesis. From the beginning, it seems clear that geological evolution is the abiotic predecessor of life and its strategies but that ongoing geological change is in some part caused by the biota. This is a partnership that is prophetic of changes in ecosystems observed in historical times and now by ecologists.

Significantly, the pattern of succeeding ice ages alternating with warmer trends commenced nearly a billion years after bacterial photosynthesis was initiated. Early ice ages are, in fact, attributed to bacterial depletion of atmospheric carbon dioxide. Still later, certain host bacterial cells engulfed other bacteria within their membranes. At about the same time, the atmosphere was being oxygenated and converted from a reducing to an oxidating chemical mix—with devastating effects on the very life that had brought about this profound alteration.

In the course of the oxygen revolution nearly 2 billion years ago, some bacterial species died, while others survived in dark anaerobic places. Still others entered into intimate symbiotic relationships whereby one was protected by and provided nourishment for the other. It is believed that the mitrochondria in which cellular respiration occurs are the no-longer-independent descendants of the engulfed bacteria.

In another 100 million years, protoanimals were evolving, and in another similar interval, blue-green algae followed. Geologically, oxygen in the upper atmosphere was forming a layer of ozone. Protoplants evolved in yet another 100 million years, and seaweeds followed in 500 million years. Here were two more innovations: multicellular structure and sexual reproduction, the latter allowing for greater diversity of organisms within a species than is possible with asexual reproduction alone.

A series of ice ages followed. Some 670 million years ago, jellyfish and worms evolved. Their innovation is the hollow body formation that is the mark of familiar plants and animals today. The brain, a concentration of nerve cells in one end of every organism possessing it, evolved some 620 million years ago, and vertebrates followed in another 100 million years or so.

More ice ages followed around 440 million years ago, and somewhere along the line, life moved out of the water onto the land. Insects became prevalent 395 million years ago. Something more than 20 million years later, immense tsunamis struck, apparently attributable to a cosmic object hitting the ocean. In the same interval, amphibians and trees appeared, and reptiles began to move about the land masses of the time. Reptiles held sway until the next period of ice ages some 290 million years ago, followed by another global catastrophe, this time attributed by some to the assembly of a supercontinent or to a collision with a comet. Nearly all species of marine animals were annihilated, and all the large terrestrial mammal-like reptiles were wiped out.

A scant 50 million years later, dinosaurs were taking their turn at dominance among animals, and the first flowering plants appeared. At 170 million years ago, the earth went through a greenhouse phase. This period represents a global boom in petroleum formation, the result of deaths among the immense biomass.

Birds appeared 150 million years ago. Shortly thereafter—by the geological scale—there was a major fall in sea level associated with another round of mass extinctions. But during this interval, the flowering plants commenced to support new animals, the mammals.

Less than 100 million years ago, more than half the known global oil reserves were created as the continents flooded and submerged the vast growth of plant life.

Nearly 70 million years ago, primates were present, according to fossil findings. Yet another catastrophe occurred, during which the dinosaurs became extinct. It is not known whether a comet or giant asteroid struck Earth or whether the agent "killed quickly or slowly, by shock wave, poison, heat, cold, the obscuration of the sun, or prolonged ecological disturbance." Whatever the agent, it "dusted the entire planet with exotic chemicals. For about ten thousand years afterward the oceans were dead."[19]

Another cosmic impact followed as the plant entered another cold spell, and the distinct pattern of summer and winter emerged. Twenty-nine million years ago sea levels fell, and on the emerging land, grass became prevalent—"the edible carpet."[20] Ape and monkeys split into two distinct evolutionary lines, and antelopes appeared, the ancestors of domestic cattle and sheep.

Fifteen million years ago yet another cosmic object hit what is now Europe. At this time, Antarctica entered into a deep freeze that has persisted into the contemporary time. Intensive volcanic activity marked this interval. From 10 million years ago to nearly 7 million years ago, glaciers spread into Alaska and the southern portions of the North American continent. Following thousands of years of drying and flooding from spills from the Atlantic Ocean, the Mediterranean Sea normalized.

Five million years ago the common ancestor of contemporary gorillas, chimpanzees, and humans arose and

life came up with another, quite different response to . . . geographic and climatic changes. In one primate line, an evolutionary adaptation to changing circumstances became an adaptation to every circumstance. The eventual outcome was an animal so unspecialized in its habits that it could live in any setting whatsoever[.]²¹

The genus *Homo*, capable of "consuming plants, meat, rocks, trees, iron, coal, uranium,"[22] was on its way.

Origins and History of *Homo sapiens sapiens*

Some 3.25 million years ago the current pattern of ice ages commenced in cycles of 90,000 years. In the course of this geological cycle, *Homo habilis*, the maker of stone tools, arrived. This species took up scavenging some 2 million years ago, and another species, *Homo erectus*, took up hunting in another 100,000 years. Fire making followed in 500,000 years, and *Homo sapiens* arrived in Europe 600,000 years ago. In another 50,000 years, the thirtieth of the current ice ages descended with warm interludes commencing 500,000 years ago.

In another 300,000 years, *Homo sapiens* domesticated an animal recognizable as modern cattle. A false ice age occurred in the relatively brief span of no more than a century, and shortly thereafter, the predecessors to the modern human race arose. After another false ice age, *Homo sapiens sapiens* was evolving in Africa. Geological upheaval—a major volcanic explosion, climatic oscillations, and the thirty-fifth modern ice age—intervened.

Then, some 60,000 years ago, humans were practicing herbal medicine, and 40,000 years ago, modern humans, the users of language, appeared. Soon thereafter humans began devising calendars, and the Neanderthal became extinct.

These new members of the genus *Homo* formed communities, tamed dogs, and survived the end of the ice age. Along the way, they began to practice decidedly modern techniques including irrigation, copper smelting, and the construction of stone buildings. Thus, humanity discovered and made use of what we call chemistry today. They also tamed horses and instituted taxes, the latter at least associated with the beginnings of class distinctions. By 5,500 years ago, two diverse inventions furthered the cause of human populations: the wheel and writing.

In historical times, humans have suffered the bubonic plague and the Black Death, but they invented printing. The astronomical telescope was created, and science was formalized during the seventeenth century. Oxygen was discovered as recently as 1771, and the germ theory of disease was presented in 1863.

The beginning of the fossil-energy revolution is marked at 1825. In 1885, the automobile became available to a few intrepid motoring pioneers. Antibiotics were discovered in 1940; gene structure, in 1953; and space craft were being built by 1957. The green revolution in agriculture is placed in 1961, and gene splicing at the molecular level began in 1973. In 1977, *Homo sapiens sapiens* deliberately eliminated another species from the biosphere: The smallpox virus was eradicated.

Milestones in the History of the Biosphere

Every person, whether environmental professional or simply having a personal interest in one or more levels of ecology, will isolate a few events that can be distinguished as milestones in planetary history. From the ecological perspective, every step in the global strategy is crucial to life, if not actually mediated by some portion of the biomass, and each step can represent a crisis in homeostasis. Particularly critical events must start with the Big Bang, the ultimate source of all energy and material in the universe. From that ultimate source, the next critical step is the formation of the lithosphere of earth in combination with the cooling of the planetary surface to the range in which H_2O exists as a liquid.

The next critical steps were the origin of life and the incorporation of certain bacterial cells into others with the formation of membranes, separating life from nonlife. The oxygen revolution was perhaps the single most important ecological crisis. The next critical step was the evolution of an organism that was to be the ancestor of primates, represented today by gorillas, chimpanzees, and humans.

In terms of geological time and past events, rapid manifestation of crises has attended the development of the human species. Language, communities, and culture are a combination unique to this particular primate. It is human culture that evolves, and rapidly, rather than the organism itself. Most recently, humanity has undergone or perpetrated a particularly critical step—the formalization of science out of a mixed background of magic, religion, and industry. The great crises for humans, then, are the advent of hunting and gathering, settling in communities as tillers of the soil, entering in rapid succession the industrial and scientific revolutions, and many would add, the information revolution associated with computer technologies.

Many would argue that the absolutely essential response to ecological crises, today at least allegedly anthropogenic in origin, is a restoration of humanity's connection to the biosphere. Nowhere is that restoration more significant than it is in terms of climate change.

CLIMATE, GLOBAL WARMING, AND THE GREENHOUSE EFFECT[23]

The Issues and Questions

In order to examine contemporary issues associated with the so-called greenhouse effect in terms of anthropogenic causes, it is essential to place the effect in geological and climatological perspective. To do so requires a return to the matter of energy flow through ecosystems to explore the balance between entering and departing radiation, including heat.

The temperature range of the atmosphere is critical to, and maintained in large part by, the living component of the biosphere. Yet, as has been discussed at some length, the biosphere is itself evolving. Moreover, it is proceeding through cycles discernible in units measured by seasons, years, centuries, and the vast geological intervals. The latter include the "recent" planetary pattern of ice ages and intervals of warming.

The greenhouse effect of contemporary usage is asserted to be an anthropogenic perturbation that acts by interrupting the dissipation of energy from ongoing ecological processes and by the rapid utilization and resultant dissipation of the energy stored over geological time in the form of "fossil fuels."

That contemporary greenhouse effect is subject to substantial scientific, technological, economic, political, and legal scrutiny. But the issues and questions are not always sorted into those distinct categories.

The questions before us can be stated in a kind of hierarchy from the large and impersonal to the highly personal: Is the perceived greenhouse effect a phenomenon of biosphere evolution and strategy, of lesser climatic cycles, or of very recent anthropogenic origin? Or is it some complex amalgam of all those phenomena? Can direct and indirect effects of some potentially devastating, albeit transitory, trend of global warming be accurately predicted in terms of human activities, let alone in terms of ecosystems and the biosphere at large? If such a trend is at least partially attributable to human activities, can those sources of the perturbation be isolated and identified generally and specifically? Then, the question, which goes beyond science, is whether we can prevent anthropogenic global warming or even reverse the perceived trend. Even further removed from science, although inextricably connected, is whether we *should* take action to halt or reverse the contemporary trend of global warming. What if, for one example with some precedent, we are entering another mini–ice age?

Have we the knowledge and the wisdom to determine whether prevention or reversal is either necessary or desirable, assuming either is possible? Can we make intelligent, informed choices among alternative responses? Assuming affirmative responses to the foregoing series of queries, have we the means to make the requisite choices through existing institutions of science, technology, politics, economics, and law?

Just as the questions range, so do the putative answers. Political, economic, and social responses make sense only when tailored in the first instance to the realities of the phenomenon. An imminent climatic change at a geological scale calls for very different adaptations in human populations than does a disproportionate meteorological alteration attributable to certain specific human activities. Only when the choices have been so tailored does it make sense to apply them in the identified institutions of human endeavor.

The Answers . . . Thus Far

On the Geological and Global Scales. Weather prediction has never been an easy endeavor. To attempt prediction, it is necessary to understand the atmosphere, itself an incredibly complex system of air and moisture in motion. Prediction can be categorized as a problem in fluid dynamics, probably composed of no less than hundreds of equations. The new science of chaos theory goes so far as to suggest that no matter how facile one becomes at solving the array of equations, we will find weather inherently unpredictable more than two to three weeks in advance.[24]

If we cannot predict weather, how can we hope to predict global warming *and* determine its source? Have *any* of the pertinent questions been answered? According to James Hansen of the Goddard Institute for Space Research, two or three essential questions have been answered. It is his position that no one can dispute that global increases in temperature have been statistically significant since 1965. That the warming is consistent with models predicting greenhouse warming is similarly undisputed. What is in dispute is the matter of cause and effect. In sum, any number of mechanisms could be behind the changes individually or in combination.

It makes sense to commence any responsible inquiry with the solar system and relevant earth sciences. These sciences reveal that incoming energy is radiation of short wavelengths, mostly in the range visible to the human eye. Atmospheric gases absorb this radiation only weakly. Outgoing radiation is mostly in the infrared, which is readily absorbed—and hence retained—by the atmosphere. Theoretically, without the atmosphere, global temperature would drop some 35°C.

While we still do not comprehend how solar variability influences either weather or climate, we do attribute geological patterns in terms of planetary orientations to the sun. At least in part, these patterns are related to variations in the tilt of the planet, the direction of its axis of rotation, and the shape of its orbit around the sun.

We also know that global temperature was 3° to 4°C warmer 5 to 15 million years ago and that over the millennia atmospheric carbon dioxide has been determined by the equilibrium of this gas between the atmosphere and the oceans. Significantly, atmospheric concentrations have been inferred to be 200 ppm during glacial intervals and 270 ppm during interglacial. This difference can explain about half the difference of 10°C. Also significant is the understanding that the planetary norm is glaciations of some 100,000 years with interglacial separations, such as that in which we now live, of only a few thousand years. It appears that climate changes on this scale can be abrupt and that mini-warming or -cooling periods have occurred. "Little ice ages" are a phenomenon of recent history.

During past interglacial intervals, temperatures in North America were 2° to 3°C higher than they are now, and tropical species inhabited what are now temperate areas. At least some of these warm intervals are attributed to phenomena other than carbon dioxide concentration. It is worth noting in passing that seasonability has also been both stronger and weaker than is experienced at present. Research and debate are associated with these phenomena, but no explanatory mechanism has been devised. Not only are cause and effect subject to controversy, but timing and duration of global climatic phenomena are also revised from time to time as new information or new interpretations come forward. There is even serious attention to the fact that every 180 years eight of the planets in the solar system are on the side of the sun opposite the Earth. Arguably, the result of that particular alignment could be earthquakes and extreme weather on Earth.

In Historical Context. At the outset, it is worth noting that the study of anthropogenic climate change is only about fifty years old. Nevertheless, it is held probable that atmospheric concentrations of carbon dioxide were at 270 ppm in 1850 and began to rise with industrial burning of fossil fuels. Prior to that time, the concentration is believed to have been constant. From 1950 to the mid–1980s, the concentration increased from 310 ppm to 340 ppm.

In a comparable interval of 100 to 200 years, natural variation in temperature has been 0.5° to 1.0°C, but it is worth noting here that trends have been measured on a global scale only since 1880. Since then, decreases in temperature occurred between 1880 and 1930; the interval from 1930 to 1960 was marked by relatively stable temperatures; from 1960 into the 1970s, temperatures showed a small increase; and increases occurred from the 1970s into the 1980s.

Adaptations of the biota to the climate of historical times have been possible because of relative stability. Thus far at least, little alteration in life spans from trees to humans have been noted. At least until now, plant and animal migrations have not been blocked by development, and human migrations involved relatively few individuals subjected to fewer political barriers.

Prognostication. Against this background, carbon dioxide concentration is now at 350 ppm and increasing by some 0.4% each year.[25] On an annual basis, some 5 to 6 billion tons of carbon are released from the burning of fossil fuel into an atmosphere containing some 700 billion tons of carbon dioxide. Some carbon, of course, is stored in the biota and lithosphere, but simultaneously with the burning of fossil fuels, an unknown quantity of deforestation is occurring. This loss is also a loss of biotic carbon dioxide assimilation, allowing further increases in atmospheric concentration.

On a smaller scale, respiration is increasing as temperatures increase. Calculations indicate that the rate of respiration is increasing faster than that of photosynthesis. The latter is affected primarily by the availability of light, water, and nutrients as well as by the presence of chlorophyll, whereas the former, while dependent on available water, is particularly sensitive to temperature.

Those who engage in prognosis assert that for each doubling of carbon dioxide concentration, a temperature increase of 3.5° to 4.5°C follows. For every global increase of 1°C, temperature zones shift by 100 miles. By the year 2030, a 2°C increase is then predicted to move these zones 200 miles. Migrations to suitable habitats could occur except where blocked by natural phenomena such as oceans and mountains[26] and by social or political features such as agriculture and urbanization. Among human populations, about one half of all individuals inhabit coastal areas, which are expected to be inundated.

The Uncertainties. The considerable uncertainties associated with the contemporary greenhouse effect are attributable to incomplete scientific understanding of the array of relevant phenomena. Over the last several hundred thousand years, there has been nothing analogous to today's greenhouse gases. In order to make predictions, inferences are required. One approach takes the form of climate models, by which present events are calculated for comparison with actual experience. Where reconstructions of the past are available, those events are computed for comparison to present experience. Another approach is to use the planets Mars and Venus for comparison, the one with less and the other with more capacity for trapping heat than Earth.

Whatever the quality of such predictions, it is essential to integrate them with other geophysical phenomena. In one case, the influence of sunspot activity, the effect on climate is simply unknown in terms of presence, absence, or extent. The phenomena dubbed El Niño and La Niña are relatively new to climatology and thus something of mysteries in themselves. Then there is the matter of volcanic activity and its effects on global climate, including temperature. In the end, how can decisions be made on behalf of human populations, let alone the biosphere, when short-term global temperature changes may in fact be headed up or down naturally, and may as well be tempered as exacerbated by anthropogenic events? This is the uncertainty facing those responsible for policy, especially policy affecting ecosystems, and for the environmental professionals who serve the policymakers.

Where Do We Go From Here? The first step is a familiar one—the unpopular but essential need for expanded research efforts. Popular or not, it is essential to know more of large-scale oceanic circulation, of phenomena as disparate as processes regulating soil moisture and those responsible for cloud formation, of the influences of biogeochemical cycles on atmospheric composition, and of processes regulating sea ice.

When we have a better grasp of the underlying scientific realities, we can turn that knowledge to such crucial matters as the choice between adaptation and prevention—or even the much-maligned "do nothing" or "wait and see" responses. It is often said that greater harm will follow if we mistakenly take one of the latter approaches in the face of perceived environmental threats than if we are mistaken in an active response such as the former approaches. But here is a situation where doing something at tremendous expense to institutions and individuals itself could go beyond any such harm to exacerbate the effects of natural trends that were never imagined, let alone predicted. That prospect should cause us to be less inclined to dismiss scientific uncertainty in the rush to do what is momentarily deemed the right thing. That is a telling incentive for societal scientific literacy, especially in ecology and the environmental sciences—at least to the point of appreciating the implications of uncertainty.

WHERE ARE WE GOING? THE BIG BANG AND BLACK HOLES IN SPACE

At the beginning of this chapter, our ability to predict our ecological future from the foundation of relevant sciences was called into question. Among any number of practical problems of inadequate or inaccurate prognostication is that associated with global warming. Proponents of the Gaia Hypothesis might assert that it does not matter what we do: Whatever it is will be the mechanism intended by Gaia for survival of the planet.

We recognized the evolution of the biosphere to be directional, part of a global strategy over which human institutions may actually have no control for better or for worse. In terms of the strategy of our species, each of us must decide how we will respond to that knowledge.

Global marketplaces and governments are, after all, populations within populations. Each is made up of individuals. We are only just beginning to learn how to adjust our behavior to maintain our microcosms on behalf of our ecosystems. We are only just beginning to glimpse possible biospheric perturbations brought on by our numbers, distribution, and consumptive habits. Further insights into the ecological aspects of human populations will be suggested in Chapters 12 and 14.

We would do well to take immense care in predicting where we and our fellow members of the biosphere are going, especially when we would take upon ourselves redirection of the perceived strategy. We should act with the humility demanded by the immensity of what time's arrow has wrought and holds for the future. The relevant times are infinite, at least from the limited perspective of a human lifetime. Even the duration of human presence on earth is humbling in the face of cosmology.

Whatever we do, however long our species endures, the ultimate fate of the *planet* is not in our hands. Earth's fate is linked to that of the sun.[27]

To contemplate the cosmos is to reinforce the lesson of humility. It is possible, according to cosmologists, that every black hole—a star so immense it collapsed into infinite density from which neither gravity nor light (and hence spacetime) can emerge—is another big bang. Thus, there may be parallel universes with parallel solar systems with their respective planets Earth. One can speculate, along the lines of decades of science fiction, that some of the species corresponding to humans have done better than we in discovering and applying ecology to their own biospheres. On the other hand, they may have done far worse—or had no lasting impact at all.

Should a black hole someday swallow up our galactic neighborhood, what we have done to or for this planet is hardly going to be particularly significant.[28]

It is time we developed a better sense of our place in the natural world. We leave the realm of the natural world for those of philosophy and theology when we would usurp the omniscience and omnipotence prerequisite to running biospheric strategy.

NOTES

1. This phrase comes most directly from the title of Harold F. Blum's 1968 popularization of the concepts of evolution and entropy, *Time's Arrow and Evolution* (3d ed.)

2. W. Kaufmann, *Black Holes and Warped Spacetime* (1979), at 20.

3. P. Davies, *God and the New Physics* (1983), at 21.

4. J. Gribbin, *Blinded by the Light: New Theories about the Sun and the Search for Dark Matter* (1991), at 181–182.

5. *See* S. Brush, "How Cosmology Became a Science," *Sci. Am.* (Aug. 1992), 62.

6. Among the mysteries is the meaning of dark matter in the universe. This contemporary cosmological mystery is so deep that there is uncertainty over the order of magnitude by which its quantity exceeds that of the bright stars and galaxies. In fact, dark matter may actually make up the bulk of the universe. It is believed to "consist of exotic particles never yet detected here on Earth." Gribbin, *supra* note 4, at 182.

7. Brush, *supra* note 5, at 62–64.

8. Gribbin, *supra* note 4, at 181.

9. S. Hawking, *A Brief History of Time: From the Big Bang to Black Holes* (1988), at 115 and 145.

10. The principal source for the evolution of stars is Kaufmann, *supra* note 2, at 5–18.

11. *Id.*, at 8.

12. *Id.*, *supra* note 2, at 10, 15, and 18; and N. Calder, *Timescale: An Atlas of the Fourth Dimension* (1983), at 104–107.

13. Hawking, *supra* note 9, at 120.

14. This history is taken from Calder, *supra* note 12.

15. Blum, *supra* note 1, at 76.

16. For more on paleontology and paleoecology and their implications for our own future, *see, e.g., Journey*, at 308–313; S. Gould, *Wonderful Life: The Burgess Shale and the Nature of History* (1989), at 25, 35, 47–48, and 208; L. Margulis and D. Sagan, *Microcosmos: Four Billion Years of Evolution from Our Microbial Ancestors* (1986), at 34 and 49–53.

17. L. Thomas, *The Lives of a Cell: Notes of a Biology Watcher* (1974), at 3.

18. *Id.*, at 5.

19. Calder, *supra* note 12, at 125.

20. *Id.*, at 130.

21. *Id.*, at 137.

22. *Id.*

23. The literature of the greenhouse effect can be distributed among a number of categories particularly relevant to the environmental professional as suggested below. As is suggested in the citations below, the sources of information range accordingly.

The Relevant Phenomena
R. Kerr, "Volcanoes Can Muddle the Greenhouse," 245 *Sci.* 127 (1989).
R. Pool, "Is Something Strange about the Weather?" 243 *Sci.* 1290 (1989).
R. Kerr, "How to Fix the Clouds in Greenhouse Models," 243 *Sci.* 28 (1989).
R. Kerr, "The Global Warming Is Real," 243 *Sci.* 603 (1989).
R. Kerr, "The Weather in the Wake of El Niño," 240 *Sci.* 883 (1988).
R. Pool, "La Niña's Big Chill Replaces El Niño," 241 *Sci.* 1037 (1988).
M. McCarthy, "Is the Crazy Weather Still Another Sign of a Climatic Shift?" *Wall St. J.*, Oct. 24, 1988, at B3.
R. Kerr, "Sun, Weather, and Climate: A Connection?" 217 *Sci.* 917 (1982).
J. Kwitny, "A Controversial Theory of the Weather," *Wall St. J.*, Mar. 9, 1982.
R. Kerr, "El Chichon Forebodes Climate Change," 217 *Sci.* 1023 (1982).

Its Effects
P. Thomas, "Warming Trend Found to Have Global Impact," *Wall St. J.*, Oct. 21, 1988.
L. Roberts, "Is There Life after Climate Change?" 242 *Sci.* 1010 (1988).

Its Sources
L. Roberts, "Global Warming: Blaming the Sun," 246 *Sci.* 992 (1989).
K. Trenberth, *et al.*, "Origins of the 1988 North American Drought," 242 *Sci.* 1640 (1988).
J. Bishop, "New Culprit Is Indicted in Greenhouse Effect: Rising Methane Level," *Wall St. J.*, Oct. 24, 1988, at A1.
R. Kerr, "Carbon Dioxide and the Control of Ice Ages," 223 *Sci.* 1053 (1984).

Institutional Response
P. Ingrassia and J. White, "Debate over Pollution and Global Warming Has Detroit Sweating," *Wall St. J.*, May 4, 1989, at A1.
D. Abrahamson, *The Challenge of Global Warming* (1989).
W. Booth, "Johnny Appleseed and the Greenhouse," 242 *Sci.* 19 (1988).

(Editorial) Opinion
P. Abelson, "Climate and Water," 243 *Sci.* 461 (1989).

24. R. Kerr, "Hansen vs. the World on the Greenhouse Threat," 444 *Sci.*, 1091 (1989).

25. Carbon dioxide is not the sole greenhouse gas. At least a quarter of the warming attributed to atmospheric gases is attributed to methane, nitrous oxide, ozone, and chlorofluorocarbons (the notorious "CFCs" believed to be placing the ozone layer at risk).

26. It is unclear whether deserts and unsuitable soils will be amenable to timely modification by migrating biota.

27. Blum, *supra* note 1, at 200.

28. *See, e.g.*, Hawking, *supra* note 9, at 83–93; and Kaufmann, *supra* note 2, at 88 and 99–101.

10

Development and Evolution
of Ecosystems

When turning from biospheric strategy to the counterparts at the ecosystem level, additional perspective on the ecology of human populations is provided. We have encountered the argument that any fragility in life as a planetary force is illusory. There is no need for resort to Gaia in arguing for the toughness and longevity of life. What may be far more delicate is our own species.[1]

PLANETARY ECOLOGICAL DEVELOPMENT

Returning for the moment to particle physics, the ecologist is advised that slightly stronger nuclear forces would render hydrogen rare. With a reduction in the amounts of the simplest element, long-lived stars like our sun could not exist, and there would be no water, if they did. Slightly weaker nuclear forces would preclude nuclear ignition of hydrogen. Without ignition, no heavy metals would emerge, and carbon-based life could not exist. Without the exclusion of one electron by another, there would be no chemistry.

Similar accidents or coincidences abound throughout the sciences, and they all hold implications for ecology. Among these coincidences are those that allow water to exist as a liquid, carbon atoms to form complex organics, and hydrogen atoms to form readily breakable bonds between molecules. In almost every case, no more than a slight increase or decrease in a single parameter would render life not different from that which we acknowledge as such but *impossible*.[2]

Once life emerged, the strategy of the biosphere could not fade out of being. Instead, life itself imposes the strategies requisite to its own continuation "against the mischief of the world."[3]

In the consolidation of apparent accidents and coincidence as a discernible strategy of the biosphere, the ecologist might well return to the boundary between life and nonlife, the cell. Not only is the cell the structural and functional unit of all life; it stands representative of those levels of organization that are biological systems. Metabolism, occurring within the cell, requires the same kind of delicately balanced environment that consistently distinguishes the biotic from the abiotic. "Cells are the life-support chambers that contain this special environment. A living cell keeps its chemical composition steady within narrow limits, a condition known as homeostasis."[4] It is the cellular membrane that separates the living cell from its environment.[5] The evolution of the membrane may then be the final step in the emergence of a biota from a planet of geological processes described exclusively through physics and chemistry.

This ultimate transition in the planetary continuum stretching all the way back to the Big Bang and indefinitely into the future is obviously a crucial step in planetary strategy. Earth may truly be unique in the universe. The unique agent of planetary strategy is now life, and all of life is itself a continuum linked by the molecules of inheritance. Astonishingly,

[o]ur DNA is linked in an unbroken sequence from the same molecules in the earliest cells that formed at the edges of the first warm, shallow oceans. Our bodies, like those of all life, preserve the environment of an earlier earth. We coexist with present-day microbes and harbor remnants of others, symbiotically subsumed within our cells.[6]

While life is maintaining its identity and its separation from the nonliving, it is also maintaining the biosphere. If this is indeed a strategy, it is particularly obvious in the atmosphere. First, in the distant past, life brought on a global pollution crisis, "the oxygen holocaust."[7] Through photosynthesis, atmospheric carbon dioxide was depleted at a juncture when molecular hydrogen was escaping and hydrogen sulfide becoming insufficient. Life accommodated to the changes it had brought on even as it was stabilizing them.

Water, the abundant dihydrogen oxide, has replaced hydrogen sulfide in photosynthesis, with a release of oxygen instead of sulfur. But oxygen is toxic because of its high reactivity with organic matter![8] Nevertheless, life adjusted so successfully that atmospheric molecular oxygen went from a concentration of well under 1% to 21%. The cyanobacteria initiated the controlled combustion—oxidation–which is aerobic respiration.[9]

Strategy or mere coincidence, molecular oxygen in the atmosphere holds today at 21%. Were it lower, aerobic organisms would suffocate. A few percent higher and living organisms would undergo spontaneous combustion.[10] Strategy or coincidence, it is oxygen that "filters out the very bands of ultraviolet . . . most devastating for nucleic acids and proteins, while allowing the penetration of the visible light needed for photosynthesis."[11] Strategy or coincidence, the ozone layer now protects living entities from mutation, which is perceived today as a hazard to life. Before that protective layer was generated, living entities were undergoing frequent mutations leading to evolution through speciation, perceived today as beneficial because the processes have resulted in the familiar biota of our own time.

There is no reason to believe planetary strategy has ceased. The process is, however, too slow for contemporaneous measurement by individual human populations. A comparable strategy can be perceived among ecosystems. Such strategies are not merely significant in terms of immediate environmental conditions. They are a continuation of and a mediator of biospheric strategy.

ECOSYSTEM STRATEGY

Just as the planet and its biosphere have manifested a direction in their lengthy and partially mutual histories, each ecosystem manifests a strategy. If there were no such direction with discernible steps theoretically leading to the so-called climatic climax community, there would be no biomes by which terrestrial ecosystems can be classified. Furthermore, such a strategy informs of diversions, with special reference to those caused by anthropogenic intrusions into ecosystems.

A major long-term strategy behind ecosystem development is coevolution involving two or more organisms. Distinct communities arise because certain plants and their herbivores have evolved in mutual relationships, as have parasites and hosts and the microbial symbionts of a wide variety of animals—including humans as well as their domestic species. In fact, today's symbionts can be viewed as particularly successful parasites. Whenever two or more organisms act to their mutual benefit, each is more likely to have a multigeneration future than is possible when one is lethal to another.

Aquatic

Life is believed to have originated in the oceans. Recent evidence suggests that the geological processes from which life arose there still exist. Oceanographers have observed the mingling of magma, steam, and gases at underwater seams between continental plates. Where the cold, dark ocean floor is mostly barren, at these seams communities based on sulfur bacteria thrive.[12]

In fact, succession continually occurs in aquatic environments but is far less obvious to the casual observer than in terrestrial ecosystems. Marine ecosystems are apparently well established, yet fluid, with notable succession occurring primarily where land meets sea or fresh water meets saline. Because of geological alterations, such areas tend to be in flux with predictable ecological accommodations adapting to altering habitats and niches. Examples of such alterations are the slow, ponderous movement of continents, the "traveling" of barrier beaches, volcanic upwellings, and alterations brought about when severe weather makes landfall.

In freshwater ecosystems, succession is mediated by two forces in tension with each other. Geological features provide direction, while the biotic tend to slow the resultant processes or to stabilize the ecosystem. Geological forces cause erosion and the filling of lakes, altering streambeds and contiguous terrestrial habitats and carrying a lake through the process of eutrophication, resulting ultimately in a terrestrial habitat in which invasion and succession will proceed.[13]

In a sense, succession in the waters of the planet is heavily influenced by geology and hydrogeology and forms a part of terrestrial strategy as well. This is especially the case over lengthy intervals. Aquatic communities, then, seem to relate far more to place and a human time frame than to geological time.

Terrestrial[14]

A succession of organisms and of influences between organisms and the abiotic environment occurs in both aquatic and terrestrial systems, but the terrestrial systems are those that tend to define a planetary region in ecological terms.

Each terrestrial ecosystem starts with an array of abiotic conditions. First and foremost are those of the climate, dependent on latitude and altitude. Organisms invade and succeed one another, as temperature and moisture regimes allow, but success and succession depend on the substrate—the chemical composition and physical state of the land—although it is itself modified by the resident biota over time.

Because terrestrial succession takes the form of an orderly process of community development, it is reasonably directional and, therefore, predictable. Succession results as invading organisms establish themselves while modifying the physical environment, and those organisms and their modifications make way for other organisms. In a series of steps known collectively as the sere, community composition alters along predictable lines. The abiotic environment determines the pattern, establishes the rate of change, and may set limits on how far the sere can go. It is a changing community, however, that controls the actual process. The sere is expected to culminate in a stabilized ecosystem, which will remain in place as long as the climate does not alter and no perturbation seriously alters the homeostasis.

The relatively transitory communities are recognized as seral stages, also known as developmental or pioneer stages. The terminal stabilized community is known as the climax community. The relatively short-term strategy of an ecosystem is comparable to that of the biosphere over the long term. Obviously, the two strategies are inextricably interconnected.

Criteria of succession have been identified. They are community energetics and structure, organismal life histories, nutrient cycling, selective pressure, and overall homeostasis. As succession progresses, the effects of production and respiration become balanced with the generation of greater biomass over time. A relatively large biomass comes to be supported for each unit of energy. Net production, however, is relatively low, and there are food webs rather than simple food chains. The detritus cycle becomes a primary component of the whole.

With the alterations in energy relationships, community structure is altered toward a large total component of organic rather than inorganic matter. Inorganic nutrients are found in the biomass. Both taxonomic and biochemical diversity increase in well-organized patterns of distribution and behavior—niches become intricately distributed. An increased variety of species accompanies a reduced dominance by one or a few species.

As the community so alters, individuals are subject to characteristic modifications. Narrow niche specialization is accompanied by the appearance of large organisms with lengthy and complex life histories. Nutrient cycling undergoes related alterations. Mineral (inorganic) cycles are more closed than open, and nutrient exchange within the biota slows. As these alterations occur, the detritus becomes increasingly important in the biogeochemical cycles.

Selective pressures are affected by feedback controls on growth and enhanced quality in production, often expressed as diversity or stability. Overall, homeostasis does become relatively stable, that is, a steady state exists. Internal symbiosis has developed, nutrients are conserved, and the system becomes resistant to perturbations. In short, the system is subject to low entropy and maintains a high level of information. The overall strategy is believed to be one of movement toward as large and diverse an organic structure as possible within the limits set by available energy input and prevailing physical conditions.

The climax community is the theoretical—and sometimes actual—final, stable community for each sere. This community is self-perpetuating and in equilibrium with the physical habitat of the ecosystem. The theoretical single climax community of a given global setting will be realized wherever local physical conditions are not so extreme as to modify the controlling effect of the regional climate.

In many locations, that theoretical community will not become established. Instead, there will be a pattern of edaphic climaxes, the perpetuation of one or more communities intermediate along the sere. Another pattern is that of the catastrophic or cyclic climax, often maintained under the influence of humans or their domestic animals.

Two kinds of succession are recognized: primary and secondary. Primary succession is the natural process manifested in an area not previously occupied by life. Secondary succession is that which proceeds upon the removal of an existing community, natural or anthropogenic.

EDAPHIC CLIMAX: IMPLICATIONS FOR
ENVIRONMENTAL PROFESSIONALS

In some ecosystems, the sere pauses or halts indefinitely in one or more edaphic climaxes. A variety of conditions will preclude progress to the climatic climax while allowing the maintenance of a relatively stable one. Climate itself may represent seemingly minor differences from one location to another. On one scale, north- and south-facing slopes on the same elevation will support noticeably different plant communities.

On another scale, microclimates in soil temperature and moisture regimes will support correspondingly distinct communities of microorganisms. Between the two extremes there will be unique plant communities. Similarly, soil and communities of larger organisms are affected by the intricate physicochemical relationships among soil chemicals and particles, including the chemistry of products; pH; and mobility of elements, ions, and more complex substances.

Edaphic climaxes are naturally occurring. A disclimax is the community resulting from a human intervention that prevents the sere from reaching the theoretical climatic climax. (A less accusatory description is anthropomorphic subclimax.) Excessive harvesting or overgrazing by domestic herds are well-recognized disclimaxes.

In addition to the foregoing, cyclic or catastrophic climax communities are recognized. The agent here may be a biological one, but the best known is fire. Fire, often caused by lightning, routinely clears forests of thick underbrush. Not only does this clearing maintain the community and promote the reproduction of certain populations, but it also acts as a preventative. Frequent brushfires prevent the devastation of crown fires.

Thus, the ecological aftermath of brushfires is not mere renewal or restoration, as is the case with a crown fire, but a component of ecosystem strategy. Although recognized by ecologists as such, forest fire has been a point of major contention among environmental professionals. The Yellowstone fires of the late 1980s brought the controversies to the political process and to the headlines.[15]

NOTES

The principal sources for this chapter are Odum, chapter 9; Ricklefs, chapter 22; and Smith, chapter 25.

1. L. Thomas, *The Lives of a Cell: Notes of a Biology Watcher* (1974), at 3.

2. R. Augros and G. Stanciu, *The New Story of Science: How The New Cosmology Is Reshaping Our View of Mind, Art, God . . . and Ourselves* (1984), at 69.

3. L. Margulis and D. Sagan, *Microcosmos: Four Billion Years of Evolution from Our Microbial Ancestors* (1986), at 57.

4. *Journey*, at 57.

5. *Id.*

6. Margulis and Sagan, *supra* note 3, at 20. Among those remnants are the chloroplasts of plants and the mitochondria of all cells.

7. *Id.*, at 99–114.

8. *Id.*, at 100–102.

9. *Id.*, at 108–109. Notably, some organisms remain capable of switching between hydrogen sulfide and water for photosynthesis. *Id.*, at 102.

10. *Id.*, at 111.

11. Thomas, *supra* note 1, at 147.

12. Margulis and Sagan, *supra* note 3, at 47–48.

13. Odum, at 295.

14. The principal source for the discussion of terrestrial ecosystem strategy is *id.*, chapter 9.

15. *See, e.g.*, R. Rudner, "Even as It Burns, Yellowstone Is Reborn," *Wall St. J.*, Aug. 25, 1988, at 14; S. McMurray, "Back to Life: Yellowstone Park Begins Its Renewal," *Wall St. J.*, Sep. 23, 1988, at 1; P. Reynolds, "Yellowstone Fires Seen as a Renewal: Plants, Even Animals Will Benefit," *Boston Globe*, Jul. 31, 1988, at 1; and L. Wiseman, "Yellowstone Inferno Could Have Been Averted," *Wall St. J.*, Letters to the Editor, Sep. 22, 1988, at 39.

PART V

LIFE ON PLANET EARTH: THE BIOTA

11

Transition: Homeostasis and Limiting Factors

ABIOTIC INFLUENCES ON THE BIOTA

With regard to environmental constituents, the organisms in an ecosystem either are in a transient state, during which the constituents of the surrounding environment are rapidly changing in some particular way, or are in a steady state. While relatively constant, a steady state should not suggest stasis among or within organisms. The only static biological system is a dead one! The condition is better described as a kind of dynamic equilibrium whereby the inflows of energy and materials balance the outflows in terms of biological effects and their quantification.

As has been suggested throughout this text, every equilibrium is the net sum of many distinct but connected chemical reactions. First and foremost among them are photochemical reactions. All the rest are thermochemical reactions. Not surprisingly, photochemistry is driven and limited by light intensity. Thermochemistry, as the name implies, is driven and limited by temperature regimes.[1]

Since each observation of the ecosystem is in effect a snapshot, the steady state as well as one recognized as transient may be ephemeral. Living organisms are notoriously resistant to being pinned down. Thus, the discussions to follow may be more a reflection of limitations on observation than of the richness of detail in ongoing natural processes. Nevertheless, the phenomena associated with limiting factors, ranges of tolerances, and interactions among them provide essential detail in connecting organisms to the abiota. Moreover, the added detail informs comprehension of associations among organisms.

As a point of departure, terrestrial, marine, and freshwater ecosystems are primarily subject to characteristic regimes of interacting factors. For terrestrial ecosystems, the regime is light, temperature, and water, the latter in terms of both precipitation patterns and availability. The marine regime is light, temperature, and salinity, whereas that for freshwater ecosystems is light, temperature, and concentration of molecular oxygen. All ecosystems are regulated by the availability and distribution of mineral (inorganic) nutrients and their rates of movement through the biogeochemical cycles.

Limiting Factors

Limiting—or regulating[2]—factors are best discerned when an ecosystem is more accurately described as being in steady state than in a transient one. Odum has proferred two "laws" to describe the effects on organisms of limiting factors. The first is Liebig's "Law" of the Minimum; the second, Shelford's "Law" of Tolerance. Both principles are stated as *quasi*-laws, because they do not rise to the level of the relatively fixed concept of a law in the usual scientific sense. Rather, each constitutes no more than a vastly simplified expectation of a specific ecological relationship, which may be manifested at least briefly despite the daunting complexity of real interrelationships and despite the ephemeral nature of any such relationship. Regardless of the imposing caveats, the two laws remain worthy of attention because they do assist in understanding events in an ecosystem.

According to Liebig's Law of the Minimum, when an ecosystem is subject to steady-state conditions, the essential material, or other factor, available in the amount most closely approaching the critical minimum for the subject biological system will tend to be the factor limiting that biological system. Limiting factors are usually analyzed at the level of a species or population or of the individual organism, although the immediate and most direct effect may be occurring at some other level of organization. As might be expected, that limiting factor is not often among macronutrients. More subtle factors tend to be limiting.

This law is said to be less applicable, not inapplicable, under transient-state conditions. It is likely, however, that it is the observer's inability to detect and measure such fleeting limitations when conditions are rapidly altering. In all likelihood, one and then another and still others will be briefly limiting as environmental conditions change and organisms respond to the changes.

Indeed, comprehension of limiting factors generally is frustrated by the very dynamic interactions that constitute ecosystems and their components. For example, if the observer is monitoring modifications in the rate of utilization of a factor believed to be limiting, the effort can be frustrated by such matters as the high concentration or availability of another substance or factor. Such naturally occurring phenomena alter biological responses from the molecular level to the level manifested as behavior. Moreover, the observer may not even be aware of the presence, let alone the influence, of another factor. From the perspective of the biological system, there is the matter of the tremendous ability to substitute, often at the level of molecular biology, where alternative metabolic pathways may be available, depending on chemical and physical circumstances.

Tolerances and Ranges

Shelford's Law of Tolerance is probably the more accurate reflection of natural complexity. It holds that first the presence and then the success of an organism depend on the completeness of a complex of conditions. The absence or failure of an organism, then, is a function of qualitative or quantitative deficiency or excess with respect to any one of several factors approaching that organism's limit of tolerance for it.

More precisely, each organism—whether the individual or the species population—is subject to an ecological minimum, maximum, and optimum for any specific environmental factor or complex of factors. The range from minimum to maximum represents the limits of tolerance for the factor or complex. Significantly, if all known factors are apparently within their respective ranges for the subject organism and yet it fails, it is necessary to consider additional factors or a more complete array of interrelationships, including interactions with other organisms.

When faced with any such situation, it is essential to remember yet another caveat, a biological reality to be taken seriously: "[S]tudies in the intact ecosystem must accompany experimental laboratory studies, which, of necessity, isolate individuals from their populations and communities."[3] Put another way, it is essential for field biologists to consider the wisdom to be discovered in the laboratory and for biologists ordinarily bound to the laboratory to be aware of the ecological reality associated with the processes they are investigating.

There are significant corollaries to the Law of Tolerance. An organism may have a wide range of tolerance for one factor but a narrow range for another. Logic suggests that organisms with wide ranges of tolerance for many, if not all, factors will be the most widely distributed. Within an organism or species, when conditions are nonoptimum for one factor, limits of tolerance for others may be narrowed. Tolerance is most likely to be limited during periods of reproduction.

Evolution of narrow limits constitutes one form of specialization and reflects greater efficiency, but it does so at the expense of adaptability. These are the kinds of factors that contribute to increased diversity in the community as a whole.

It is crucial to bear in mind that organisms are not slaves to their environment. As will be explored in greater detail in Chapter 12, they can adapt. Adaptation as such is ordinarily physiological, temporary, and read-ily reversible. A genetic alteration is more likely to be permanent and nonreversible. Such a genetic alteration is a step toward speciation and Darwinian evolution. A particularly interesting phenomenon is the so-called genetic fixation of local types within any taxon, but especially prev-alent at the species level. Isolation of such a type from the parent stock can also result in speciation.

On the practical level, limits of tolerance provide an opening to the ecologist or to the environmental professional for studying and compre-hending complex ecological systems. These conditions allow a determi-nation of factors that are operationally significant to a biological system and of how factors can affect the individual, the population, or the com-munity. The methods include observation, analysis, and experimentation. Wisdom further dictates not only that the observer move back and forth between lab and field but also that each professional interact with specialists from other disciplines in the relevant sciences and technologies.

Unfortunately, these are ideals that were not being met two decades ago:

In the training of biologists during the past 40 years, there has been an unfortunate cleavage between the laboratory and the field, with the result that one group tended to be trained entirely in laboratory philosophy...while another group tended to be trained quite as narrowly in field techniques. Modern ecology, of course, has become especially relevant to our times because it breaks through this artificial barrier and provides a meeting ground for the biochemist and physicist on the one hand and the range, forest, or crop manager on the other![4]

It is up to practicing environmental professionals to minimize any such cleavages, with special reference to the natural sciences in relationship to social and political sciences and practitioners of law. The days of balkan-ization among the environmental disciplines should have been left far be-hind. Never has modern ecology been so relevant to the times as it is now and in the foreseeable future. That the disciplinary barriers are artificial in terms of ecological entities is becoming increasingly apparent.

One impetus for better integration of other sciences and a variety of analytical approaches to ecology into the environmental sciences is the matter of interactions. No limiting factor exerts its effects in isolation. Tolerances and ranges influence each other, often altering the extent of limitation if not the identity of "the" factor limiting a biological process.

Interactions

Interactions of predominant and therefore obvious significance are those among temperature, moisture, concentrations of oxygen and carbon dioxide, and the availability of nutrients. Obvious or subtle, these influences may well be significant at any level from the subcellular to the biospheric. Nevertheless, it is always wise to retain the notion that, ultimately, these dynamic events are actually biochemical in nature, determined and controlled by the genetic complement of the individual and that of the species—the gene pool.

Limiting or regulating factors in ecosystems can be placed in classes. In doing so, however, the interconnectedness of their respective influences must always be kept in mind.

For example, light and temperature are important limiting factors affecting photosynthesis. When light is operating as a limiting factor, the process is relatively insensitive to temperature. In light near a species' optimum, the rate of photosynthesis will increase as much as fivefold for every temperature increase of 10°C. In light near the maximum for the species, its range of tolerance for temperature extremes will be narrowed. In fact, each species will possess a characteristic optimum combination of light and temperature.[5]

With regard to light intensity, there are two steps of significance to the relationship between photosynthesis and its metabolic partner, respiration. First, there is the compensation point, the intensity at which the two processes are in balance. The oxygen released in the course of photosynthesis is equivalent to the oxygen assimilated through respiration. Second, there is the saturation point, the intensity at which the photosynthetic rate no longer responds to increasing intensity. The biological system is "saturated" with light and cannot effectively utilize any more of that form of energy.

Perhaps the most important factor is water or moisture. Water is the physical, chemical, and biological entity that is a physiological necessity for all protoplasm. Next to water, the most important factor for life is temperature. The range of tolerance for life is astounding——200°C to +100°C, well below the freezing point to slightly above the boiling point of water.

Most species, however, are individually far more restricted in their tolerance for temperature extremes. Generally, the upper limit is more critical than the lower, as might be inferred from the sensitivity to temperature of biological molecules such as proteins, especially enzymes. Paradoxically, organisms tend to function more efficiently as the upper limit is approached. Thus, a stimulation of biological processes can occur, rapidly followed by morbidity and mortality as the upper limit of tolerance closely follows.

Populations of any given species are likely to be found in areas where there is a relatively narrow range of temperature at some characteristic point along the extensive range encompassing all species. That range is smaller in water than on land. A variety of adaptations accommodate the temperature range. Some species, especially among microorganisms, are able to go into a kind of suspended animation, or dormancy, allowing their survival for lengthy intervals at a temperature that would otherwise be lethal.

In summary, temperature is universally important to life and often a limiting factor. As a result, temperature regimes can be responsible for zonation and stratification, respectively, the horizontal and vertical distribution of organisms in the ecosystem. Nevertheless, it is easy to overemphasize the importance of temperature simply because it is among the easiest environmental factors to measure.

As might be expected, the most obvious complex of interactions among environmental factors is found in regimes of combined temperature and moisture. On the global scale, these regimes are represented by climate. But regimes of temperature and moisture also occur on decreasing scales, down to microclimates affecting microcosms measured in inches or millimeters. It is worth noting that temperature becomes more severely limiting—that is, the range of tolerance will be reduced—at extreme moisture conditions.

Other interactions occur among atmospheric gases in terms of their occurrence and availability in soil as well as in water. While atmospheric water vapor undergoes large variations over space and time, the portion of the atmosphere that is identified with the biosphere or ecosphere tends to be stable or remarkably homeostatic. The relationship between carbon dioxide and oxygen tends to be limiting to many of the higher plants. Within known limits, moderate increases in carbon dioxide tend to increase photosynthesis, as do decreases in oxygen. In fact, oxygen inhibition of photosynthesis can occur, a negative feedback mechanism believed to be effected by the reversal of a chemical reaction between oxygen and a metabolic intermediate in the overall photosynthetic process.

Oxygen concentrations can be severely limiting in both soil and water ecosystems, although the chemistry of oxygen in combination with that of carbon dioxide is quite distinctive in water. Here, pH is a crucial factor. Biological systems are subject to specific ranges of tolerance for pH, which not only exerts a direct effect on the processes of life but also alters the chemistry of important nutrients and the toxic properties of chemical substances, including those that are macro- or micronutrients.

Immediately, yet another pattern of interaction comes into play in aquatic ecosystems. Temperature is a determinant of concentrations of a gas in water. Chemistry, specifically the nature and quantities of dissolved and suspended substances, is another. Currents and water pressure determine the distribution and local concentrations of gases and of nutrients as well. Populations adapted to local conditions, especially at boundaries separating ecosystems, can take on traits unique to them. Such populations are known as ecotypes. As Odum has noted, "The possibility of genetic fixation in local strains has often been overlooked in applied ecology;

Table 11.1
Elements Essential to Life

Essential	Photosynthesis	Other Metabolic Functions
Iron	Manganese	Manganese
Manganese	Iron	Boron
Copper	Chlorine	Cobalt
Zinc	Zinc	Copper
Boron	Vanadium	Silicon
Molybdenum		
Chlorine	**Nitrogen Metabolism**	
Vanadium		
Cobalt	Molybdenum	
	Boron	
	Cobalt	
	Iron	

restocking or transplanting of plants and animals may fail because individuals from remote regions were used instead of locally adapted stock[.]"[6]

Such patterns will have noticeable effects on communities, which will respond with distinct morphological and physiological adaptations. In terrestrial ecosystems, wind plays a role comparable to water currents. Moreover, wind can cause a loss of water through increased transpiration, perhaps causing water or a nutrient carried in water to become limiting to a plant. Morphological, physiological, and behavioral adaptations to both extremes in the availability of water have evolved in terrestrial plants and animals.

Similarly, the biogenic salts, most notably those of nitrogen and phosphorus, represent chemical regimes in which organisms must function. Salts are the chemical products of the neutralization of acids and bases. Both dissolve readily in water and dissociate into positive and negative ions, which recombine to form salts, products that are substantially less soluble than the reactants. The negative ion of the acid combines with the positive ion of the base. For example, hydrochloric acid (HCl) and sodium hydroxide (NaOH), a base, both dissociate in water to release the ions H_3O^+, Cl^-, Na^+, and OH^-. From these ions, sodium chloride (table salt, NaCl) is produced. (The hydronium and hydroxide ions also combine to produce water.)

The nitrogen salts are crucial to life, and salts of phosphorus are among the most frequently encountered limiting factors. The macronutrients also include salts of potassium, calcium, sulfur, and magnesium. Of course, it is the micronutrients, components of enzymes and coenzymes—notably the trace elements—that may be limiting and for which ranges of tolerance may be small. This is an explanation of why a heavy metal is both essential to life and extremely toxic (see Table 11.1).

The metal molybdenum,[7] for example, can be limiting to the whole ecosystem. An added concentration of 100 parts per billion (ppb) in a mountain lake can increase photosynthesis. But at the same time, the resultant concentration is high enough to be inhibitory to the growth of phytoplankton. The *net* effect here would be crucial: Would increased photosynthesis or decreased growth prevail, or would the two in effect cancel each other out with no *net* change?

In this context, it is essential to be aware of the influences of such unpredictable[8] factors as storms and hurricanes. Not only will these meteorological factors affect the distribution of material; they can affect organisms directly. Protective behavior patterns have evolved.

In addition to all the foregoing, there are factors such as currents and pressures exerting their influences on organisms. Finally, soil itself and fire represent additional interacting factors affecting organisms.

For terrestrial organisms and the benthic communities of aquatic ecosystems, soil (or sediment or other substrate) represents a crucial combination of interacting abiotic factors. In addition to inorganic and organic content, such factors include the size of particles composing the soil and the resultant texture and porosity. Fire is an important limiting factor.

Implications for Environmental Professionals

The Practical Side of Limiting Factors. The matters of limiting factors and, especially, tolerance ranges have major implications for ecologists and for environmental professionals alike. Well-established limiting factors can be put to practical use.

Not surprisingly, regimes of combined temperature and moisture are of particular practical import. Climographs, polygons, take form when monthly average moisture is plotted against monthly average temperature and the twelve points connected. When plotted for specific regions and then combined with a corresponding climograph representing tolerances for a population, certain questions can be answered (at least prima facie). Among them, What climax community is expected? Where can a species be successfully introduced? In what years will a pest be particularly active?[9]

Climographs for the coastal and northern regions of some states are strikingly different. They never overlap. One region is subtropical with a pronounced wet and dry season, while the other's seasonal temperature differences are more pronounced than seasonal patterns of rainfall. The climax community for the former region is broad-leaved evergreen forest of live oak and Spanish moss[10]; that in the latter is temperate deciduous forest. Obviously, if one or the other community is not found, some factor, natural or anthropogenic, could represent a perturbation, once other natural factors have been taken into account.

In the case of the deliberate introduction of an alien species, the climographs for the two other states largely overlap that of the species' natural habitat. One state, however, is hotter, with greater rainfall from spring to summer. The other is cooler, with comparable rainfall in the winter. The species was successfully introduced only in the second state, suggesting two possible explanations: Either the species is more tolerant for cool temperatures than for a hot, wet season, or the latter conditions were more extreme than the former.

In the case of a pest organism, both optimal and favorable climographs were available for comparison to climographers drawn for two different years in a region where oranges are an important crop. In one year, regional conditions were always drier than the optimum, sometimes with cooler temperatures. In one month, it was drier than favorable for the population. In the other year, both conditions were usually within the optimum range. For part of the year, temperatures were cooler but remained within favorable limits. In this second year, as would be predicted by comparing climographs for the pest and for the region, damage to the orange crop was much more severe than in the first.

The Interdisciplinary Nature of Ecology. One of the strengths of today's science of ecology is its demolition of artificial barriers among scientific disciplines. As ecological interactions are explored, the ecologist is hopelessly isolated if he or she is not engaged in an occasional meeting with a physicist or a biochemist. The environmental professional goes even further and may actually be responsible for the management of a crop, forest, or rangeland. That professional must not only be steeped in ecology and related natural sciences; management implies the addition of at least economics, politics, and law, if not sociology and even psychology. And superimposed over the whole are the ethics of each profession as well as personal and even national environmental ethics. It is essential that each piece in this management puzzle be afforded due respect. No one piece is the sole source of answers.

Nowhere is the full array of ecological sciences more apparent than in interactions among the abiotic factors *limiting* or *regulating* the biota. Moreover, a truly profound inference from the interactions just among atmospheric gases is that the resultant complex is no random accident or mere coincidence, as was noted at the opening of Chapter 10. Whatever the array of mechanisms bringing about this precise balance, living as well as nonliving, its manifestation is treatment to biospheric homeostasis and cybernetics.

HOMEOSTASIS AND CYBERNETICS

By now it should be abundantly clear that organisms are no "slaves" to the environment in which they find themselves. Organisms are constantly adapting themselves *and* modifying their environments so that limiting effects are at least accommodated if not alleviated or eliminated altogether.

Organisms and other biological systems are constantly seeking the stability known as homeostasis. They do so by internal cybernetic processes.

From this situation, it is easy to fall into one of two logical traps: teleology and anthropomorphism. Teleology is the fallacy of attributing sentient intent where it does not exist. Anthropomorphism, equally fallacious, goes further to impose human intent or sensibilities on nonhuman entities either abiotic or biotic. To the conservative scientist, Gaia crosses at least the teleological line. But even in doing so, the concept still provides valuable insight.

At the cellular level, decisions as to the edibility or otherwise of things encountered, and as to whether the environment is favourable or hazardous, are vital to survival. They are, however, automatic processes and do not involve conscious thought. Much of the routine operation of homeostasis, whether it be for the cell, the animal, or for the entire biosphere, takes place automatically, and yet it must be recognized that some form of intelligence is required even within an automatic process, to interpret correctly information received about the environment. . . . Indeed, all cybernetic systems are intelligent to the extent that they must give the correct answer to at least one question. . . .

There is a spectrum of intelligence ranging from the most rudimentary, . . . to our own conscious and unconscious thoughts during the solving of a difficult problem.[11]

Each level of biological organization engages in processes whereby that stability known as homeostasis is maintained. Even a minute change in the environment will trigger mechanisms that act to restore that stability or to establish a new homeostasis as conditions require. These mechanisms are the subject of the science of cybernetics.

Every biological system is capable of alteration through cybernetic mechanisms to meet environmental modification. But here, too, there are limits and ranges of tolerance. When those are exceeded, the system has been perturbed. Here, there are also ranges: Some perturbations can be accommodated; others will disrupt a biological system to the point of death.

With particular reference to energy in the ecosystem, there is a distinct pattern of considerable relevance here. The tendency in such a natural, enclosed system, through which energy is flowing, is for the community members to undergo shifting alterations and mutual adjustments leading to a degree of stability. These directional shifts, alterations, and adjustments actually are occurring in each affected individual organism through internal, self-regulating mechanisms. Each mechanism—physical, biochemical, physiological, or behavioral—tends to return the biological system to the constancy of homeostasis. Energy transfers in the unperturbed ecosystem in homeostasis tend to flow in one direction at a steady rate that is characteristic of the specific ecosystem.

In combination, these relatively minute mechanisms interact throughout the community in a kind of ripple effect[12] upon stimulation by any outside influence. In a sense, homeostasis, if not the ecosystem at large, is in a constant state of perturbation in one constituent or another. Perturbation, however, is only recognized by the casual observer when a population, community, or whole ecosystem manifests symptoms of stress. By then, the cybernetic processes are, or have been, stressed beyond their ranges of tolerance.

PERTURBATION

Perturbation can be natural, or it can be anthropogenic. It is any disruptive intrusion into a biological system sufficient to overwhelm homeostasis or to impose a new homeostatic condition deemed detrimental, usually from some human perspective. For the environmental professional, the system most obviously of interest is the ecosystem.

Today, we are beginning to comprehend that it is not enough to respond to perturbation in the name of healthful ecosystems. Instead, the goal of the environmental professions is a healthy ecosystem. If the mission is not in the name of the ecosystem for its own sake, we have gained the wisdom to acknowledge that only healthy ecosystems can be healthful.

NOTES

The principal sources for this chapter are Odum, chapter 5 and at 33–36; and Ricklefs, chapter 10.

1. *Journey*, at 139.

2. "Limiting" bears a connotation of detriment, while "regulating" suggests beneficial. The latter may be more accurate in that biological systems work with the factors to be considered in the text.

3. Odum, at 107.

4. *Id.*, at 113. Note that the early 1970s represent the beginning of the modern era of the environmental movement, when ecology commences to be integrated into economic and social regulation at the federal level. Contemporary environmental professionals must themselves be prepared to integrate a number of disparate disciplines with the principles and concepts of their primary profession. Indeed, we have not made much discernible progress since the early 1970s when this edition of Odum was published.

5. *See, e.g., Journey*, at 143. In this context, it is particularly instructive to recall that only the initial photosynthetic reaction is mediated by light. All the subsequent reactions—the "dark" reactions—are independent of light.

6. Odum, at 109.

7. Molybdenum is essential to enzymatic nitrate reduction and nitrogen fixation by plants and is a component of animal enzymes. *Journey*, at 682 and 453.

8. Extreme weather is unpredictable in two different, but highly relevant, senses—when and where it will actually strike and with what severity. The frequency and distribution of storms (wind, rain, or snow) are subject to a degree of prediction

based on seasonal and diurnal patterns, historical and recent. Hurricanes are less predictable but more frequent at specific seasonal intervals.

9. These studies are adapted from Odum, figure 5–10, at 125.

10. *Id.*, figure 14–19, at 399.

11. J. Lovelock, *Gaia: A New Look at Life on Earth* (1979, 1987 ed.), at 146.

12. The ripple analogy is less than perfect: Ripples in water or sand tend to dissipate with distance from the point of origin. In an ecosystem, ripples stimulated at some point may not dissipate at all. In some cases, the effect will be enhanced or exacerbated from the point of origin. Bioaccumulation, or bioconcentration, is a case in point.

12

Ecology of Aggregations

Among the features unique to life is the manner in which organisms are distributed. That distribution is essentially *never* random. "Never" is a word as infrequent in the vocabulary of scientists as it is in that of the lawyer. For that reason alone, aggregations are of particular interest to environmental professionals.

Working against the randomization otherwise imposed by entropy and the laws of thermodynamics, organisms occur in associations exhibiting interrelated structure and function, the influences of which are manifested at the ecosystem level. Thus, just as the cell and the entire individual organism represent levels of organization, so do populations of individuals of the same species and communities of populations characterizing ecosystems, culminating in the ultimate biological level of organization, the biosphere.

Throughout its life, the individual organism will occur in a habitat, serving in a niche in characteristic ways. The aggregation of organisms forming a population also occurs in characteristic patterns associated with habitat and niche, as does the aggregation of populations composing the community. The resultant patterns can be studied and analyzed at any level of organization. They are better understood, of course, when the observer is aware of the contributing levels of organization. Moreover, all four dimensions must be taken into account. The patterns will change over the three dimensions of space and over time, the latter measured in fractions of seconds all the way to units of geological time.

It can be productive, then, to commence with either extreme, the individual or the whole community, as long as the holistic and reductionist approaches are both taken into account. Here we will begin with popu-

Table 12.1
Statistical Functions of Populations and Corresponding Attributes of Individuals

Statistical Function	Attribute of Individual
Density	Existence
Natality	Birth
Mortality	Death
Age distribution	Age
Biotic potential	Reproductive activity
Dispersion	Physical location
Growth form	Life history

lations and build to the community. But then we will return (in the next chapter) to the individual in order to reexamine the ecology of adaptation and evolution.

POPULATION ECOLOGY[1]

A population is defined as an aggregation of organisms of the same species occupying a particular space over a given interval of time. For purposes of this definition, a species is a natural aggregation of organisms in which the individuals can exchange genetic information.[2] In addition, a population is a biological system uniquely characterized by statistical functions and certain genetic characteristics. The statistical functions are density, natality, mortality, age distribution, biotic potential, dispersion, and growth form. The genetic characteristics are adaptiveness, reproductive (or Darwinian) fitness, and persistence (the probability of leaving descendants over long periods of time).

Statistical Functions

Since populations are composed of individual organisms and thus depend on those organisms for their features, it is informative to consider a population's statistical functions in comparison with the corresponding attributes of an individual (see Table 12.1).

The density of a population, based on the existence of the individuals composing that population, is the number of organisms per unit of space. Density depends on the interaction of the other statistical functions even as it itself contributes to them. There will be a characteristic density for each population in an ecosystem against which actual density can be compared as a measure of the "health" of that population, with implications for the health of the larger community and the ecosystem itself.

Most immediately, density interacts with natality and mortality, the population's birth rates and death rates, respectively. Natality is a phenomenon determined by a variety of factors inherent to the population and its component individuals and imposed by the environment in which they are interacting. Inherent features are the age of sexual maturity and the theoretical number of young per birth and over the interval of reproductive activity characteristic of the species. These inherent features are modified by the actual age of sexual maturity among the individuals in combination with actual opportunities to breed and actual births.

Mortality is determined by comparable inherent and environmental features. Each population is characterized by an expected longevity among its individuals—the predicted maximum age at death. Individual life expectancy, however, actually alters in a characteristic pattern with the age of the individual organism. The actual mortality rate in the population thus depends on the actual age at death among individuals and is closely related to the cause of death. Few animals die of old age, although plants and microorganisms may actually fulfill their life expectancies in the absence of perturbation.

Similarly interconnected with natality and mortality and closely associated with density is the age distribution of a population, expressed as the age classes of the individuals. Age classes are made up of all the individuals in a specified age range. Again, there are characteristic patterns to this statistical function that reveal the health of the population and reflect on the health of the community and ecosystem.

An excess of aged individuals no longer capable of reproduction suggests the imminent demise of a population. Large numbers of young suggest a healthy population, but an excess would suggest the possibility of premature death among them, also an unhealthy sign. The age classes of the sexes may also be an indication of the prospects of the population.

Biotic potential is the maximum reproductive power of a population, unlikely to be realized in a healthy community. This function is closely related to the carrying capacity of the ecosystem but will be tempered by the population's interactions with other members of the community.

Dispersion of the population depends on the location of the individual organisms and the activities in which they are engaging. There are two levels of ecological factors determining activity and location. Habitat and niche as manifested as actual home ranges or territories of individuals are initially determinative. These determinative factors, however, will be modified through the population's age distribution and depend on such time factors as the time of day and the season of the year.[3] On the individual level, such additional factors as feeding habits, success in finding a mate, and success in producing offspring will all exert their effects on dispersion. Also significant are individual behavioral patterns that will be expressed within limits characteristic of the species.

Random distribution is at most rare. The other extreme—uniform distribution—suggests severe competition or antagonism. The most common pattern can be described as clumping. When not acting in isolation from their own kind, organisms of the same species tend to be distributed in pairs, clones, families, pods, schools, prides, or herds. Significantly, any attempt at statistical analysis of populations must accommodate, or "fit," the patterns assumed by the organisms themselves. Any lack of such fit will compromise analysis, with concomitant disruption of interpretations and conclusions.

Finally, each population manifests a growth form. The corresponding attribute of the individual is life history, which is predicted by species identity. The actual life history of the individual will depend on such factors as its prenatal environment; its actual development thereafter; and its progress through immaturity, sexual maturity, and senescence or old age. In a manner analogous to, and dependent on, the actual life histories of its members, a population grows, differentiates, maintains itself, and exhibits definite (and definitive) organization and structure.

While a population has no prenatal period, it is subject to development, and there are characteristic intervals of immaturity, maturity, and at least theoretically, senescence. Two major growth forms are recognized. Some populations exhibit a rapid exponential increase in numbers, coming to an abrupt halt as some limiting factor intervenes—the J-shaped growth form. Other populations exhibit an S-shaped form. Their numbers increase slowly before entering an exponential phase, which is followed by a gradual slowing.

Whether the expected form will occur will depend on all the features and factors, biotic as well as abiotic, influencing the population and its individual members. Growth forms can be disrupted by any number of factors, some of which can rise to the level of perturbation. As always, time is a crucial parameter. Groupings and patterns may undergo changes over specific intervals characteristic of the population.

From the foregoing points, it should be apparent that while absolute numbers of individuals in a population may indeed be important, changes in those numbers may be far more informative. In the first instance, there are both theoretical and actual upper and lower limits on population size itself. Too few organisms suggests the possible imminence of extinction.

The upper limit on population density depends on environmental conditions. Most significant among the external conditions are energy flow and the trophic levels. Internal conditions, such as the size of the organism and its rate of metabolism, are also significant to the upper limit on population numbers.

Too many members subjects the individuals and the population itself to a variety of stresses, which in the extreme can be lethal. At sublethal levels, stresses can stimulate responses ranging from those promoting survival of the species to those promoting detrimental abnormalities. Some organisms (including the Chincoteague ponies made famous by author Marguerite Henry) become stunted. Smaller organisms require less energy and less food than their normal counterparts. In others (including at least one species of deer), the female's body resorbs the developing fetus. Resorption can be deemed a positive response because the female avoids the stress imposed by the demands of a growing fetus. One potential member of the population is lost, but perpetuation of the species is advanced by the female's survival and the increased likelihood of additional offspring under more tolerable conditions in the future. In some populations (including laboratory populations of rats), crowding results in abnormal behavior that can include cannibalism among the adults and of newborn litters by their mothers.

Genetic Characteristics

The gene pool of a population will support a characteristic range of phenotypes initially manifested at the molecular level and then throughout the ranges of features defining the species. These features range from the biochemical and physiological to behavioral. Each feature, as well as every response to limiting factors and every tolerance range, will be subject to a range unique to that species or that particular population within a larger species. Tolerances are genetically determined and passed on from generation to generation, subject to alterations in the genetic material, the genome of individuals, and the genetic pool of the population. Because population genetics is statistically dependent on the genomes of the individual members of the population, two ranges actually exist. One is the range characteristic of the population, in which most of the members will fall. The other is that effected by the actual genome of the individuals. There will be occasional individuals who are beyond the minimum and maximum for their population, and this outsider status may be detrimental or beneficial to the individual.

The detriments arise when the individuals cannot tolerate a condition in which its fellow organisms survive even when they do not thrive. The benefits arise when individuals can survive or even thrive in conditions beyond either extreme. The capacity to meet environmental contingencies can ultimately lead to a more resilient population or to actual speciation, as will be explored in the next chapter.

Significantly, at least simple populations can be studied under controlled laboratory conditions. Here, group attributes lend themselves to measurement, and therefore environmental factors can be imposed and the results on those attributes described in qualitative and quantitative terms. Such relationships are not readily isolated for clear analysis in natural populations.

Table 12.2
The Continuum of the Components of Behavior

Pattern of Behavior		Representative Organisms Mediating Stimulus;
Component	Characteristics	Comment
Tropism	Directed movement, coordinated by hormones	Organisms lacking a nervous system
Taxis	Directed reaction to, from, or transverse to mediating stimulus	Protozoa (chemicals) Moth spp. (light) Bee spp. (orientation)
Reflex	Innate	Organisms with a central nervous system (mediated at level of organ or organ system)
Instinct	Innate	Strict, genetically determined pattern relatively fixed and associated with a minimum of learning
Learned Behavior	Acquired	Organisms with an organized brain
Reasoning	Acquired	Limited to humans with likelihood in other primates and so-called higher organisms

The Role of Behavior[4]

In earlier discussions, the importance of the third spatial dimension, height, in addition to the two horizontal dimensions, was emphasized. Similarly, the importance of the fourth dimension, time, has been repeatedly emphasized. Neither ecology nor the practice of the various environmental sciences is complete without those two dimensions. They are ignored at the risk of the quality of analysis and, where a political or legal decision affecting the ecosystem rests on that analysis, at the peril of the ecosystem.

Another "dimension" characterizing the biota is equally important yet subject to neglect: behavior. Behavior is a complex of the phenotype and is just as dependent on the genome as more easily studied features. Behavior is not limited to animals, although in animals it is complex to the point of limited predictability, especially among species with highly developed brains. Behavior is an attribute of the simplest organism, and the highly developed animal brain is nothing more or less than the other extreme of a continuum (see Table 12.2).

Behavior is an attribute of all organisms and occurs on a continuum ranging from tropisms of plants to the profound ability to reason that is attributed to humans and to other organisms humans consider to be their companions high on the scale of complexity approaching intellect. In fact, these components of behavior tend to blend from one to the next, with unique leaps in taxons sporting central nervous systems and boasting the next step, an organized brain.

Tropisms are readily observed in the higher plants. A tropism is a movement or orientation mediated by hormones. Plants exhibit three kinds of tropism. Geotropism causes roots to grow downward into the soil, and the remainder of the plant to grow upward. Heliotropism—particularly apparent in sunflowers—and phototropism cause herbaceous plants to move with the sun and with light, respectively.

Taxes are manifested by single-celled organisms and by organisms as complex as insects. A taxis is a directed reaction to a physical or chemical stimulus. Different kinds of protozoa move toward, away from, or in a direction transverse to a chemical stimulus or a physical one such as light. Moths are drawn to light, and bees orient themselves under the stimulus of polarized light.

Both tropisms and taxes are innate to the organisms manifesting them and may or may not require a central nervous system. Also innate are reflexes, but here, cells and tissues must be organized into organs or organ systems. One familiar reflex is salivation at the sight or, more intensely, the scent of food, a reflex that can be conditioned, a simple form of learning. Another familiar reflex is the (original) knee-jerk reaction—the sudden, uncontrollable snap of the lower leg when a sharp tap is administered just below the bent and relaxed knee. (The figurative knee-jerk reaction associated with political affairs is presumably conditioned but requires no well-developed brain.) A more subtle reflex is the spontaneous removal of the hand from a surface that might be hot. This reflex, about which the "victim" may grin sheepishly with a shake of the head upon "remembering" that the stove or iron or whatever was not on at the time, is identified as a spinal reaction. The stimulus need not reach the brain; the reflex is mediated by nerves in the spine. There is actually a selective advantage to the speed associated with such reflexes.

The components of behavior identified as instinct, learning, and reasoning are subject to substantial controversy. While scientists prefer to label such phenomena and then place actual manifestation of them neatly in the labeled categories, realities are not so amenable to labels or categories.

Instincts, which are stereotyped behavior patterns fixed by the gene pool of the taxon and essentially immutable once stimulated, are actually complex patterns of behavior that are subject to some level of learning determined in some part by the complexity of the nervous system. The distinction between instinctual and learned behavior is not an easy one.

There are those who will argue that human behavior is all learned without resort to any instincts. But there are others who maintain that there are human instincts. Those who recognize human instincts include these innate, programmed responses among human behavior patterns. Here, there is special reference to behavior associated with primal needs, notably including thirst, hunger, and sexual drive. Of all the organisms, humans are the most likely to temper both learned and any instinctual behavior with reasoning.

All of these intraspecific interconnections are simultaneously participating in those occurring among and across populations to give rise to the community.

COMMUNITY ECOLOGY[5]

Aggregations and even associations among individuals of a population could be no more than fortuitous, but ecological research has revealed interactions causing population patterns. If, like the organism and the population, a community is a legitimate biological system and identifiable level of organization, what questions are appropriately applied to it? The first and most obvious question is, What identifies an aggregation of populations as a community, an *association* among populations?

How is a community organized, and how do its component populations interact? These questions raise the next one: How is a community effectively analyzed? Finally, what does community analysis reveal of the ecosystem, and to what extent can the revelations be applied to ecosystems generally? What do they tell us of the biosphere? For the environmental professional, what are the practical implications of community ecology?

At the simplest level, the community is the living component of an ecosystem. A community is an organized assemblage or association of populations in a prescribed area or a specific physical habitat. While assemblages can be no more than fortuitous with no associations among organisms, a community is defined by physical, chemical, and biological connections. Community or ecosystem boundaries may be sharply defined and separated from others, or one may gradually blend into another.

The most immediate question is the extent to which a community is more real than an artificial construct merely serving the convenience of the observer. That lines are no more simply drawn at this level of organization than elsewhere is reflected in the "closed" and "open" communities of ecologists. These designations are a reflection of interconnections across whatever lines may be drawn around ecosystems.

Every ecosystem is intimately connected with at least contiguous ones, and all are ultimately connected with the biosphere. In attempting to draw lines distinguishing the real from the artificial, there is one governing principle: The efficiency and stability manifested in a community of organisms increase in direct proportion to the degree of evolutionary adjustment marking relations among populations. An aggregation of organisms among which there are highly organized interactions giving rise to perceivable efficiency and homeostasis at least suggests the existence of a legitimate level of organization—in short, a biological system.

Relationships within a community can be described in terms of correlation. A mere aggregation of randomly distributed organisms will reveal zero correlation. Relationships, on the other hand, are described in terms of positive or negative correlations and in terms of the strength of either correlation.

The most extreme evolutionary adjustment is coevolution to the point of obligate association in which pairings between species or other combinations represent mutual interdependence. This mutualism includes a range of interactions. Certain flowers are pollinated by certain insects, and fruits may be distributed by herbivores for later germination. More intimately, lichens are an obligate combination of an alga and a fungus. Ruminants and termites depend on internal microorganisms capable of digesting cellulose. In their roots, legumes support populations of the bacterial genus *Rhizobium*, whose species fix nitrogen for biological assimilation and distribution.

Significantly, patterns of mutualism probably evolved from antagonisms such as parasite and host, predator and prey, or plant and herbivore. The opposite extreme is independence, a most unlikely situation in nature where individuals of each species would be randomly distributed with respect to those of other species. Between the two extremes are a variety of patterns of association.

Community Organization

A community is an organized unit at least to the extent it exhibits characteristics above and beyond those of its individual and population memberships. Like those biological and ecological units, a community functions as a unit through coupled metabolic transformations. In the case of the community, those transformations are based in the effect on populations of products of metabolism and catabolism of others in addition to the more obvious direct interactions at the individual and population levels.

Major communities are so characterized on the basis of sufficient size and completeness of organization to allow for relative independence. Major communities need only the externality of the sun's energy for support. They are relatively independent of the resources (outputs from) and requirements (inputs to) of adjacent communities. Minor communities, then, are characterized by a greater dependence on neighboring aggregations.

Each community is so organized as to manifest definitive functional unity, based in a characteristic trophic structure and associated patterns of energy flow. There is some compositional unity, that is, a definitive array of taxons. In other words, there is an expectation of the presence together of certain organisms, but species are to some extent replaceable by others over space and time in the ecosystem. The niches, however, are relatively fixed and open to a limited array of organisms.

The community defining a specific ecosystem, whether a seral stage or a climax community, starts with the abiotic environment. Whether that community represents a seral stage, the climatic climax, or an edaphic climax will be determined in the first instance by environmental gradients in such familiar features as latitude, altitude, and climate, both regional and local.

Between ecosystems, unique communities may also exist. The ecotone represents a transition habitat separating one ecosystem from another. An ecotone community may include organisms (possibly distinct ecotypes) from adjoining systems and characteristic populations that may be limited to niches found only in such transitional settings.

Interspecies Relationships and Community Analysis

Interspecies relationships in a community may be sharply defined and separated from others or may blend into one another. The overall result of interactions within a community can, as has already been described in some detail, be measured and qualified in terms of standing crop as well as in terms of overall community metabolism. Since the most conservative estimate would acknowledge the presence of hundreds of thousands of individual organisms in a community, focal points of analysis are essential. In selecting such points of departure for purposes of analysis and comprehension, the assumption is that relatively few of those organisms exert the major controlling influence through their numbers, size, or production. Moreover, representatives of those few are enough to provide meaningful information for purposes of ecology or the environmental sciences. This, after all, is the major premise behind statistics and the applications of biostatistics in science and law.

The observer seeks out ecological dominance and species diversity to characterize a community. Ecological dominance is categorized as the concentration of influence in one, several, or many species. Indices of dominance are based in major structural features, physical habitat, or functional attributes. Species diversity is measured in terms of ratios between the number of species or individuals in a species present and the total number of individuals present. Higher diversity is associated with longer food chains, more symbiosis among species, and greater feedback control, all of which serve ecosystem homeostasis by reducing oscillations and increasing stability among and within populations. Diversity is believed to be high in older communities and low in newly established ones.

Community Development

The development of an individual community will follow the strategy of ecosystems previously discussed. Still, every community will be unique within genetic and abiotic constraints. Moreover, each community will be the result of any perturbations afflicting the ecosystem directly or indirectly.

Other than the matter of inherent value of this biological system, what are the practical implications of communities and their respective organizations? The answers lie in the aphorism, As the community goes, so goes the organism, and its numerous corollaries.

CONNECTIONS: LESSONS AND IMPLICATIONS FOR THE ENVIRONMENTAL PROFESSIONAL[6]

Environmental professionals can learn much from what research ecologists have been asking of ecosystems in recent years, starting with an ecologist's view of the minimum requirements for meaningful experiments into community components as elsewhere. They are threefold: knowledge of initial conditions, adequate controls, and replication. For both researchers and environmental professionals addressing questions raised in a politicolegal context, the most common failing in studies lies with inadequate descriptions of the preexperimental situation. Significantly and somewhat ominously, this failure cannot be overcome without a sufficient period dedicated to the collection of baseline data, the status quo ante.

Similarly, controls are a ubiquitous problem but most particularly for the applied ecology practiced by most environmental professionals. Under most circumstances, a discharge or other pollution event will be into a receiving environmental medium (an ecosystem or portion thereof) for which there simply is no control. In lieu of more traditional controls, an effort is made to work from relevant literature to project what would have happened in that ecosystem absent the anthropogenic intrusion. In the absence of acceptable controls, similar conjectures must be made in deciding whether to attribute any alteration in the ecosystem to the intrusion in question.

These sorts of problems can be clarified with reference to microcosms representing population or community ecology. For example, the role of controls is clarified in an experiment to determine whether two species in the same genus are competing in a habitat. In seeking an answer, the researcher must set up experimental plots distributed throughout the habitat.

In one series of plots, one species will be removed in the expectation that the other will increase if the hypothesized competition is in effect. In a second series of plots, the other species will be removed in the same expectation. In a third series, neither species will be removed.

Thus, if one species does indeed increase in its experimental plots, the effect of competition on that species is demonstrated. Or is it? What if a comparable increase occurs in the control plots?[7] The control plot is only one control here. Equally important is the fact that each condition, the control and two experimental ones, is the subject of more than one plot. This is an effort to accommodate any subtle differences imposed from place to place in the habitat as identified. It is also essential for purposes of internal replication.

Replication is yet another obstacle to sound experimentation for ecologists and environmental scientists. It is literally impossible to find identical locations for experimental comparisons because of the pervasive variability in natural systems. The resultant uncertainty is whether unrecognized systematic differences are present among the locations.[8] Replication of the application of experimental conditions is at once a kind of control and internal replication of the experiment. A second and equally important kind of replication is that of the experiment itself in the same habitat, elsewhere, and by the same or different researchers.

In designing research programs, research ecologists have publication in mind, while most environmental professionals have missions with externally imposed deadlines to meet. There may be a crucial difference here: The researcher may be motivated simply to understand the subject system and will manipulate it for that purpose, while the environmental professional may be motivated or constrained by factors that are not compatible with the realities of the system. One often hears the argument that the information sought is crucially important and must be put to immediate use in the marketplace or under the law. The usually unstated premise is that anything is therefore better than nothing. But that premise is highly suspect. If the information is critical, time is not the sole factor to be considered. Certainly, the accuracy of the information is equally essential, if not more so.

Despite the complexity of real ecological systems in comparison to their laboratory counterparts, there is considerable pressure to devise ways to study natural systems for the reason that their very complexity makes them far more real. They will provide a more nearly "real" answer to the question at hand. A related practical problem is the matter of explaining the result that fails to substantiate the underlying hypothesis. There are no less than four potential explanations for failure to confirm a hypothesis in a natural system. All are worthy of contemplation by the environmental professional.

1. The expected phenomenon is irregular in occurrence.
2. The experimental design was inadequate.
3. Experimental execution was inadequate.
4. *The hypothesis is wrong.*[9]

It is worth remembering here that almost all of science, including ecology and the environmental sciences, is a matter of inference. The first and foremost inference is that events are not purely random. There is a cause-and-effect relationship in some form or in a variety of interactions. Scientists often use the Null Hypothesis to advance theories. By this process, the disproof of a variety of alternative explanations of an event or phenomenon serves to advance the "preferred" hypothesis. The process is necessary because logically one cannot prove the premise by the occurrence of the expected conclusion; one can only disprove the premise by the failure of the expected conclusion. With this limitation in mind, scientists go about reinforcing hypotheses by approaching the hypothesized premise from a variety of intellectual directions.

Statistical probabilities are a kind of Null Hypothesis used to establish that a phenomenon has not occurred at random or by chance and is instead more likely to be somehow related to a specified phenomenon as predicted. Thus, to be as complete as possible, a researcher must show at least three things:

1. The phenomenon could be causally related to the hypothesized premise.
2. The phenomenon has not occurred by chance.
3. The phenomenon is not attributable to some other cause (including one or more causes of the hypothesized premise).

A subtle difficulty arises whenever an experiment is performed. To what extent is the result attributable to or altered by the experimental technique itself? Notorious examples are "cage effects," whereby isolating the experimental system itself affects the system positively or negatively. Specific situations include the ability of predators to follow investigators' trails to the subject (prey) organism and the existence of "trap-happy" individuals in a population. These are organisms capable of learning that a desired object is available in the trap without expenditure of energy to search it out elsewhere and without risk of harm.[10]

With particular reference to community ecology, the conventional wisdom is that the greater the diversity, the healthier and more stable the ecosystem. Is this conventional wisdom supported with experimental results? The hypothesis is that as species are added to the community in the course of the sere, each takes up a unique portion of the niches that have been established by successional predecessors. Thus is each niche enriched, and the loss of a portion of it need not spell doom for related niches and eventually the ecosystem itself. The fluctuations to which earlier invaders were subject are reduced, and homeostasis is protected.

The question to be raised through appropriate experiments is whether there is any evidence to the effect that fluctuations are any less dangerous to small populations than to large (and what the answer means to the ecosystem). The related hypothesis is that smaller populations are at greater risk of extinction than larger ones. Can the competing hypotheses be reconciled?

How are causes and effects to be sorted out in this situation? Is it that stability enhances diversity?[11] Are there points in a sere where cause and effect actually reverse? Is this a matter of positive feedback? Is positive feedback of indefinite duration, or can there be a point at which feedback turns from positive to negative? Such questions are not subject to immediate answers, for all their significance to the research ecologist and the environmental professional.

Of equal importance to both is the matter of diversity. It has been observed that a pattern of abundance exists in nature. In any given area, a few species are abundant, while many are rare. An unfulfilled mission of ecological research is to devise a formula for a statistical model or a statement of that phenomenon for the purpose of guiding comparison among communities. Any "index of diversity" would be a declaration of the richness of the community. The results would represent hypothetical community organizations against which actual communities could be compared for fit.[12] How can matters or issues before the environmental professional that turn on diversity be addressed or resolved in the absence of such models?

Overall, there are instructive conclusions to be drawn from ecological experimentation in the field. Generally, however, a major caveat holds: "[E]ach kind of environment should be considered separately, because there are few, if any, specific statements about ecological processes that will be true across all environments."[13]

The great coherence among conclusions is associated with forest communities. There, experiments within trophic levels yield consistent results, and relationships between trophic levels are consistent with those within. For example, it has been shown that interspecific competition is significant among decomposers. Negative interactions occur among species in almost all systems, and interference competition is consistently demonstrated. In the grazing cycle, distribution of herbaceous species is determined by distribution of nutrients or toxic ions. Trees adapt to herbivore damage, but adaptations to those defenses by herbivores is both effective and ubiquitous.[14]

In successional communities, relationships within and between most trophic levels are less consistent than in forests. Decomposers are an exception in that they are always in competition. A related phenomenon is that "accumulation of organic matter in most terrestrial situations is too slow to be of importance in preventing competition among the fungi and bacteria."[15] There is also some suggestion of mutualisms: "In the process of chewing the dead plant matter, the detritus feeders create smaller particles and thus larger surface areas for the true decomposers to colonize."[16]

A series of conclusions of some relevance to the applied ecology of environmental professionals have followed from research among successional plants:

1. Competition is sometimes present.
2. When competition is present, it is weak or diffuse.
3. Some studies show that herbivores have an important impact.
4. At least minimal competition occurs among herbivores.
5. Predation has a significant effect on populations of some herbivores.
6. Competition among predators is difficult to demonstrate.[17]

Because when the exigencies of the marketplace and of the politicolegal system are imposed on this kind of natural conundrum far more questions are raised than answered, the environmental professional may well cringe in the recognition that the legal profession is not the only one to whom "weasel-words" are attributed.

The foregoing questions as presented are hypothetical ones.[18] But they can be of critical importance in the professional settings of environmental practitioners. Yet the questions are not answered in this chapter or anywhere in this volume. Instead, the principles and discussions provide the tools by which the answers and others like them can be sought effectively in terms of scientific ecology, presumably the foundation of environmental protection in all its forms.

There are two relevant observations to be heeded by the environmental professional: As the organism goes, so goes the community, *and* as the community goes, so goes the organism. Hence, in order to "manage"— encourage or discourage—a specific organism, it may be more effective to manipulate the community or some portion of it rather than the target organism itself.

NOTES

1. The principal sources for population ecology are Odum, chapter 7; Smith, chapters 14–16 and at 473–481; and *Journey*, chapters 37 and 39.

2. Recognition of a species as a population of organisms capable of interbreeding obviously is prone to circularity. The definitions of population, species, and speciation all use the other concepts in making the requisite distinctions among them. Although the taxon known as species has a basis in evolutionary, taxonomic, and ecological reality, sanity is served by an acknowledgment of some degree of artificiality for the purpose of reasoned analysis.

For purposes of this discussion, a population is a naturally occurring group of potentially interbreeding organisms of relatively uniform life history, behavior patterns, conformation, anatomy, biochemistry, and physiology. Because they are interbreeding, they share a gene pool. Over time, the individuals making the population may become genetically diverse to the point of speciation of the population—that is, the evolution of two or more different populations as defined here. (See Chapter 13 for an expanded discussion of adaptation, speciation, and extinction.)

3. It is worth noting at this point that ecologists recognized not four but six seasons in analyzing natural variations in populations and communities: hibernal (winter), prevernal (early spring), vernal (late spring), aestival (early summer), serotinal (late summer), and autumnal (fall). *See* Odum, at 157.

4. *Id.*, at 247–249.

5. The principal sources for community ecology are *id.*, chapter 6; Smith, chapter 24; and Ricklefs, chapters 20 and 21.

6. The principal source for this section is N. Hairston, *Ecological Experiments: Purpose, Design, and Execution* (1989).

7. *Id.*, at 25.

8. *Id.*, at 27.

9. *Id.*, at 57–58.

10. *Id.*, at 34–36.

11. *Id.*, at 15–16.

12. *Id.*, at 21.

13. *Id.*, at 316.

14. *Id.*, at 316–317.

15. *Id.*, at 318.

16. *Id.*

17. *Id.*, at 319.

18. For more, *see, e.g.*, R. Lewin, "Biologists Disagree over Bold Signature in Nature," 244 *Sci.* 527 (May 5, 1989) (contrasting great biological diversity in tropics with scant in arctic); and J. Brown and B. Maurer, "Macroecology: The Division of Food and Space among Species on Continents," 243 *Sci.* 1145 (Mar. 3, 1989) (analyzing empirical patterns among populations with implications for environmental professionals). *Science*, the weekly journal of the American Association for the Advancement of Science (AAAS), is a valuable resource for articles and items addressing both scientific and political ecology.

13

Ecology, Adaptation, and Evolution

Ecological successes and failures are related to diversity among organisms, adaptation of and among biological systems, evolution, and extinction. Primary inquiry into these interrelationships seeks mediating mechanisms. Ecology and evolution are related through the concept of species as expressed through populations. What happens when a single species is introduced to an area with open niches? What happens when there are comparable open niches in physically separated regions?

ADAPTATION, ECOLOGICAL AND EVOLUTIONARY

Adaptability commonly incorporates two concepts, for simplicity, distinguished as ecological and evolutionary adaptations. Throughout its life, an individual adapts to an array of environmental conditions or suffers the consequences of failing to do so. Such an *ecological* adaptation is founded in the genotype that individual has inherited. Similarly, populations, whole communities, and even the larger ecosystem are constantly adapting to environmental circumstances. None of these ecological adaptations calls for alteration in the gene pools of the affected biotic aggregations. All are relatively temporary.

But adaptation is also used in a frankly evolutionary sense applicable only at the population or community level, despite necessarily being expressed through outstanding individuals. At any given point in time, living species and higher taxons reflect adaptations to enduring environmental circumstances. These evolutionary adaptations have been mediated by genetic alterations allowing for survival of generations of organisms and becoming fixed in gene pools at least for the duration of the corresponding selective pressure. In contrast to the purely ecological sense of the word, evolutionary adaptation tends to be permanent, fixed in the genetic code.

There is a relationship between these two kinds of adaptation, expressed through individuals. In the first instance, evolutionary adaptations include individual ability to adapt to constantly altering circumstances. More important for future generations, if a population encounters environmental challenges (selective pressures) exceeding its range of tolerance, individuals limited to existing ecological adaptations will be eliminated along with their genes. Only those members genetically endowed for tolerance beyond the extreme will survive to produce offspring bearing their genes. These offspring will carry that genetic endowment into the future. The number of affected individuals will increase relative to the rest of the population until the more tolerant individuals compose the whole of the population. The population has adapted in the evolutionary sense and may have undergone speciation in the process.

The surviving species is adapted to a new niche. Evolutionary adaptation has resulted in ecological adaptation. In both cases, homeostasis is the immediate strategy. Significantly, the strategy of the species is survival over generations rather than survival of either the individual or of even a single generation.

Even though adaptation in both senses may be expressed at any number of levels of organization, the result is based in molecular responses. Examples include alterations in the structure of enzymes when temperatures are high, the breakdown of photosynthetic pigments in excessive light, and altered configurations in protein molecules with variations in salt content of the environment. Every adaptation requires energy. Once again, ecology comes full circle, linking the holistic to the reductionist. Synecology and autecology are not severable.

In order to begin answering the opening and related questions, it is necessary to return to a reductionist approach. It is necessary to consider the individual organism and the species in the ecosystem. Genetics is an informative point of departure for establishing linkages among ecology, adaptation, and evolution. Adaptation and evolution represent ecological success, while extinction represents failure. Genetics can explain both.

CONNECTIONS: THE SCIENCES OF GENETICS AND TAXONOMY

All living beings, extant as well as extinct, share two features: All are based on the chemistry of carbon, and all share one of two specific molecules in common—DNA and RNA. These genetic molecules, by which traits are passed on from generation to generation, paradoxically represent both the unity and the diversity of life.

Genetics of the Individual[1]

Genotype and Phenotype. The individual organism is the expression, phenotype, of the genotype, the genetic basis of identity and function of all organisms. Each individual is the expression of the code incorporated in its genome. That genome is unique to the individual within the constraints of the taxons to which it belongs. The species is defined genetically by the number and structure of its chromosomes, the bodies on which the genes are located. At the molecular level, those genes are an expression of the order in which four bases[2] appear along the strands of DNA making up each individual chromosome. The process by which phenotype emerges from genotype can be summarized as follows:

$$DNA \rightarrow RNA \rightarrow amino\ acid\ sequences \rightarrow proteins$$

Genes are expressed in the somatic (body) cells of multicellular organisms.

In actuality, a specific complement of genes, not necessarily on the same chromosome, will be expressed in an elaborate pattern of protein synthesis with the exquisite timing required for the cell to function properly as a whole. If the organism is a single cell or an association of like cells, coordination and timing need go no further. In multicellular organisms, especially those composed of interacting tissues, organs, or whole organ systems, the expression of individual gene complexes acting together will be serving the needs of the whole organism.

Obviously, there is far more to an organism as it functions in the ecosystem than has yet been fully revealed in the above sequence; and in fact, the complex of molecular events lies far outside the scope of this discussion. Suffice it to say that the basis of the complexity we know as life is ultimately the result of individual genes switching on and off, with consequent molecular changes occurring intracellularly. Those molecular changes are very precisely integrated for expression at the cellular, extracellular, and organismal levels.

Moreover, in the somatic cells, there is a precise division of labor supporting in these multicellular organisms the structure and function of tissues, organs, and organ systems, all the way up to the organism itself. As will be discussed below, this division of labor is the basis of physiology, taxonomy, ethology, and both ecological and evolutionary adaptation.

Sexual Reproduction. Among organisms that reproduce asexually by the simple fission of cells into daughter cells, there is limited opportunity for genetic variability. Instead, in bacteria, for example, genes can be turned on and off to meet the exigencies of the environment, with special reference to altering chemical content. Bacteria adapt readily to altering nutrient supplies as well as to an altering toxic environment. Moreover, these and other organisms undergoing asexual reproduction tend to have very short generation times. Rapid division alone can allow for the distribution of new phenotypes from generation to generation. But even bacteria occasionally exchange genetic information between organisms in a kind of forerunner of sexual reproduction. This exchange of information allows for enhanced variability that tends to expand the environmental horizons of those who participate.

Sexual reproduction is a considerable advancement, if only in terms of genetic variability and environmental adaptability. Most members of the plant and animal kingdoms engage in sexual reproduction and possess specialized gametogenic cells in addition to their somatic, or body, cells.

If each organism is the subject of a specific and unique genotype passed on through all its generations, how is the genotype distributed? How is it that the chromosomes do not all pile up and crowd out all the rest of the intracellular components?

Cytogenetics. Molecular genetics, molecular biology, and cellular physiology are all "visible." The visibility is the subject of the science of cytogenetics. Cytogenetics has revealed that at certain intervals each cell of an organism provides a microscopic picture of genetic processes. Upon division, the chromosomes in each cell "materialize" and proceed in a "dance" of extraordinary precision.

Each somatic cell contains the diploid number of chromosomes characteristic of the species. The diploid number for humans is forty-six, or twenty-three pairs. Each parent contributes one set of the paired chromosomes. Moreover, there is a karyotype; that is, the chromosomes have shapes and sizes even more precisely characteristic of the species than the diploid number alone. Each chromosome also has a characteristic structure, including a centromere, a "swelling" that occurs at a specific location along the length of the chromosome. Cytogeneticists can identify an organism by its karyotype and even find certain kinds of gross genetic abnormalities represented by extra or missing chromosomes or misshapen ones.

Every time a somatic cell divides, it first goes through the process of mitosis. Within the nucleus, each chromosome has been duplicated during interphase, when the chromosomes are diffusely distributed as chromatin. Just before cell division, the doubled chromosomes materialize and begin to line up end to end in the center of the nucleus. In humans, all forty-six doubled chromosomes, each consisting of two chromatids, line up at random, and then each chromatid is drawn away from its partner by its centromere. Simultaneously, the nuclear membrane commences to indent and causes a split in the nucleus between the separating chromatids until the two sets of forty-six chromosomes are fully separated. Both the nuclear membrane and the cellular membrane pinch off to result in two new ("daughter") cells, each with an intact cellular membrane and a nucleus in which the chromatids fade into the dispersed chromatin of interphase.

The forty-six chromosomes will each again be duplicated into two chromatids during the subsequent interphase. Thus, under normal circumstances, each cell of a multicellular organism has a complete set of the genetic information identifying that organism. But any mistakes in the code will also be duplicated in subsequent generations of cells.[3]

If each parent is to contribute only half the genome to offspring, a mechanism must exist to accomplish that reduction in the gametes, or germ cells—the sperm and ova of multicellular organisms. The mechanism is the process of meiosis, which generates haploid gametes.

Like their somatic counterparts, germ cells go through a nuclear interphase during which, using the human example again, the forty-six chromosomes are doubled into chromatids connected by their centromeres. In the course of meiosis, two cellular divisions will occur in rapid succession.

This time, however, the chromosome from one parent will pair with its counterpart from the other parent. The result in the first meiotic division is the lining up of paired chromosomes so that there are four chromatids aligned lengthwise in the center of the nucleus. Here, the forty-six chromosomes are randomly distributed along the line in twenty-three pairs; each member of the pair, consisting of two chromatids, is separated by its centromere. Each of the two daughter cells has a full complement of forty-six chromosomes, each consisting of the two chromatids. Those from each parent, however, have been randomly distributed. Some of the forty-six are from one parent, others from the other parent.

Now, instead of entering interphase, a second cellular division occurs. The forty-six chromosomes of mixed parentage again line up in the two daughter cells, and the two chromatids separate, resulting in a total of four gametes, each with the haploid number of twenty-three chromosomes. When the gametes combine to initiate development of the offspring, the two sets of the halpoid karyotype are reunited in the diploid cell, which proceeds through division and differentiation to form the new organism.

This whole process allows for variation attributable to genetic differences in the parents and still greater variation through mutation and exchanges of genetic information between paired and doubled chromosomes. Such variation accounts for individual differences within a species and can also account for failures of some young to survive and for speciation when such an alteration meets the needs of selective pressures in the environment.

Population Genetics[4]

Genetic variation among its individuals represents the genetic content of the species, the population's gene pool. This gene pool is a qualitative and quantitative description of the population. A kind of biological "law" holds that under specified circumstances the gene pool will not be altered but will remain stable from generation to generation.

This Hardy-Weinberg Equilibrium is a mathematical description of how genes, including any that have mutated or otherwise been modified, are distributed in the population. Once established, the percentage of individuals expressing a new gene will stabilize and thereafter remain constant over any number of subsequent generations.

The Hardy-Weinberg Equilibrium thus describes a population that is undergoing no quantitative alteration in ratios among genes in its gene pool. The ratios of individuals carrying any given genotype will remain constant. Neither negative nor positive effects would influence the ecological status of the population. But for the stability of this theoretical equilibrium to be realized, several factors must be in operation:

1. The population must be closed, without gains from or losses to any other population.
2. (Additional) mutations either do not occur or do not disturb the established ratio of genotypes.
3. Reproduction is at random.
4. The population is large enough that chance alterations in frequency are insignificant.
5. No natural selection is occurring.

One need be neither geneticist nor ecologist to be aware that this particular array of conditions is highly unlikely in any ecosystem, even assuming it is closed to immigration or emigration. Mutations, harmful and beneficial, will be occurring spontaneously. Moreover, their effect may alter substantially as alterations in the ecosystem occur. An inherited feature that was neutral or detrimental can become beneficial, and all kinds of permutations or changes in environmental circumstance can occur as the ecosystem undergoes natural alterations or perturbation. All the array of ecological interactions will impinge on the gene pool and the implications of any given mutation transform accordingly, with corresponding alterations among ratios.

Reproduction is almost certainly never at random, and indeed, mate selection and reproductive success from individual to individual will be major factors in the status of the gene pool and the population. Adaptation, speciation, and evolution itself will all depend on this reality. Natural selection will be present to some degree.

Taxonomy and Reality[5]

Clearly, ecology of both the individual and the species depends on, or at least can be explained in terms of, physiological processes in cells and whole organisms. Molecular biology, once the antithesis of ecology, is now recognized as a source for ecological events and for the structure and

Table 13.1
Taxonomy: Organization of Living Beings—A Typical Example

Taxon	Identification
Kingdom	Animalia
Phylum	Chordata (Vertebrata)
Class	Tetrapoda (Mammalia)
Order	Primata
Family	Hominidae
Genus	*Homo*
Species	*sapiens (sapiens)*

function of the ecosystem. It is truly astonishing that the basis of inheritance among all of life in all its possible diversity of life—extant, extinct, and yet to evolve—is mediated by four simple molecular entities, the bases of the DNA molecule.[6]

From photosynthesis to respiration to the buildup and distribution of biological chemicals to their catabolism and elimination, cellular physiology is at work. Even death represents physiological processes that not only define the boundary between life and death but also participate in biogeochemical cycles. The ecologist, then, cannot safely ignore the detail of biochemistry, which parallels the wealth of detail encountered at the ecosystem level. Even adaptation, evolutionary as well as ecological, is ultimately mediated, or at least explicable, at the molecular level. Here is a true emergence of phenomenal order out of complexity beyond most imagination. Taxonomy is the biological science charged with extracting the order from the chaos of complexity. The interconnections are expressed and utilized in reconciling reality with perceived taxonomic relationships.

Taxonomy seeks to establish what might be called familial relationships among living organisms. Taxonomy also seeks to find family lines linking existing organisms to their evolutionary pasts and to reveal familial relationships among organisms known only from the fossil record. Taxonomy is also responsible for identifying every organism with an array of taxons from kingdom to species and subspecies (see Table 13.1).

Note that there is a structure here, and it is not far removed from the

Theory of Integrative Levels. As taxons move from kingdom to species, each step is more specific than the last. But, at the same time, that which defines the higher taxon is retained throughout the lower.

The human being has been defined, not entirely facetiously as a featherless biped. In taxonomic terms, *Homo sapiens sapiens*[7] is a member of the animal kingdom, distinguished today not only from the plant kingdom but also from Monera (bacteria), Protista, and fungi. Animals are multicellular organisms characterized by a cellular membrane but lacking the cell wall of plants. Animals are incapable of photosynthesis, but all of them respire.

Homo sapiens sapiens is among those animals with a chord of nerves protected by the bony structure of a backbone. This phylum places humans among the animals that are bilaterally symmetrical. Humans are vertebrates, a subphylum of all chordates. Humans have four limbs; they are tetrapods. As mammals, they are warmblooded, bear live young, and provide nourishment for the newborn by secretions of the mammary glands. Most have hair, a specialization of cells in the organ called skin. Humans are primates; their limbs are specialized in two sets for locomotion and for grasping, respectively, and they possess particularly large brains of a unique configuration giving rise to high intelligence.

There is one extant genus of human, *Homo*. There is also one extant species, *sapiens*. That extant species is distinguished from all its predecessors as the subspecies identification, the second *sapiens*. We distinguish ourselves from all other primates and any other species in our genus in terms of our intellect, especially as manifested in the cultural organization of our populations.

There was a time when taxonomy was held by some, especially nontaxonomists, to be entirely artificial, a mere convenience in aid of communication among biological scientists. Based essentially on morphology and other relatively obvious similarities and differences in the outward appearance and some behavior patterns, any correlation between taxonomic identification and actual relationships among taxons was dismissed as fortuitous. Now, those obvious criteria are accompanied by distribution of biochemical pathways, relationships among karyotypes, and actual molecular structure of DNA in efforts to sort out members of the biota into taxons reflecting evolutionary accuracy.

CURRENT EVOLUTIONARY THEORY

Neo-Darwinism

Neo-Darwinism explains Darwin's concepts of survival of the fittest and origin of species in terms of the full array of biological sciences, including ecology. Ecological and evolutionary adaptation constitute a crucial component of neo-Darwinism, which now recognizes genetics, mutation, and population genetics as the mechanisms of evolution. The preceding discussions of individual and population genetics represent the underlying foundation.

Punctuated Evolution

The current theory of the extinction and origin of species goes beyond neo-Darwinism in recognizing that the slow processes associated with population genetics cannot fully explain the fossil record. This slow process is "punctuated" with sudden losses of major taxons (most notoriously, the dinosaurs) and unusually rapid emergences of others. These periods of punctuation are attributed to a variety of phenomena not far removed from cosmology and the sciences associated with comprehending our galaxy, solar system, and planet (see Chapter 9). Once again, the natural sciences come full circle as evolution affects ecology and is explained in terms of phenomena beyond the global.

Evolution and Ecological Niche

How organisms adapt and evolve to fill ecological niches is pieced together from a variety of sources almost exclusively by inference. Inferences are derived from interpretations of the entirely empirical sciences of paleontology in combination with current field studies, in which some experimentation can clarify empirical findings. Some laboratory analyses can also contribute to relevant inferences.

The pattern is perceived as one of rapid diversification among organisms with concomitant geographical expansion of their ranges and territories. With that expansion comes adaptive radiation—"formation of two or more new species, macromolecules, or physiological pathways, adapted to different ways of life, from one ancestral species, molecule, or pathway"[8]— followed by internal extinctions, with the survivors becoming highly specialized.

Examples of the diversification stage are familiar ones. Insects and microorganisms fill every known habitat. Reptiles invaded terrestrial habitats, marsupials invaded Australia, mammals invaded the whole of the biosphere with the extinction of large reptiles, and birds invaded the whole globe with their ability to fly. In each case, diversification followed closely upon the invasion.

Adaptive radiation is followed by intervals of little evolutionary change. Extinct species will be replaced by close taxonomic relatives. Such evolutionary conservatism is advantageous—until the next important perturbation. Thereupon the process is reinitiated: adaptation and evolution or extinction.

APPLICATIONS IN THE ENVIRONMENTAL PROFESSIONS

Whenever we step into an ecosystem, we are taking a chance and may be misguided even before we take action:

We tend to think of familiar natural landscapes as frozen in time, like the image in a photograph, to remain unchanged. To preserve the area as we see it, we protect it against fire, insect attack, and other events we consider harmful. In doing so we change it, because we fail to comprehend that nature is not constant, that disturbance is the means by which landscape diversity is maintained.[9]

In the end, "[a]n environmentally induced modification of a character is not inherited. What is inherited is the ability of the organism to modify such a character."[10]

Biological Diversity and Endangered Species

We may be able to discern evolution in process. But how do we observe extinction in process? Ordinarily, the answer is that we do not. For one thing, extinction is extremely infrequent over the history of life. For another, it is extremely difficult to predict with useful reliability. Finally, extinction is the last event in a long sequence of subtle ecological and evolutionary processes acting in concert. Instead, we turn to the fossil record for clues into the processes of the past in expectation of bringing the lessons into the present and even taking them into the future. But "fossils open only a tiny obscured window on biological communities of the past."[11]

Biological Diversity. Biological diversity is explained in terms of genetic variability. With greater specificity, the breadth of diversity based in profoundly simple chemistry is the result of sexual reproduction; structural alterations in karyotype; and chemical changes, mutation, within the DNA molecule. Traits are inherited and passed on to future generations, subject to selective pressures in the environment that favor specific phenotypes over others. Survival and reproduction depend on the ability to adapt to those pressures.

Speciation or Extinction?[12] The fossil record suggests that virtually all taxonomic lineages have become extinct without leaving any descendants in the form of new taxons. Extinction may well be the inevitable fate of every species. We have recently discovered that even cells extinguish themselves.[13] In fact, today's millions of living species are believed to have derived from only a small fraction of those living at any time in the distant past. Extant species represent less than 1% of those alive some 600 million years ago.

Actually, there are levels of what scientists identify as extinction. Small, localized populations may die as a result of severe local conditions or the introduction of a particularly efficient predator. Such a local—ecological—extinction would not necessarily lead to extermination of a whole taxonomic lineage.

Larger local or full global extinctions also occur, especially in the face of competition from an ecologically similar species, because no two species can simultaneously exist indefinitely in the same niche. One species will be replaced, and community structure will undergo ecological or evolutionary adaptation. Even larger extinctions have occurred, presumably in a punctuating event such as that which wiped out the major taxon containing the dinosaurs.

The Endangered Species Act

In the year 1810, passenger pigeons numbered in the billions in this country. Just over a century later, they were extinct. Why? Because the passenger pigeon was known to gourmet and gourmand as squab. The human predator preyed on the population until it was eliminated from the ecosystem.

Some 200 years ago, taxonomists observed that certain extinctions had occurred in recent times at the hands of humans. Among these extinctions were fifty-three species of bird and seventy-seven of mammals. Exploitation was not the sole anthropogenic cause. Some species were destroyed as pests; others were subjected to depredation by domestic animals or by organisms like the rat, which enjoys an embarrassing relationship with humans. Still other species were eliminated through the destruction of their habitat.

Ecology and the Statute. Among the federal statutes with an ecological foundation, the Endangered Species Act (ESA) 16 U.S.C.A. 1531–1544, is intended to provide a means of conserving those ecosystems upon which endangered species depend (ESA sec. 2(b)). Although ecological and scientific values of species are only two of the bases for protection (sec. 2(a)(3)), ecological concepts are prevalent in statutory provisions. The essential role of habitat is expressly recognized (secs. 3(5) and 4(b)(2)). An ecological foundation for protective measures is apparent where protective mechanisms include predator control and protection of both habitat and food supply (sec. 4(b)(a)(A)). Ecological tools are also to be used to determine the effectiveness of conservation efforts (sec. 3(3)). How effective this statute will be ecologically and politically depends on a number of *human* factors, only partially revealed in the statute itself, in the regulations,[14] and in evolving case law.[15]

Despite the obvious attention to ecological principles and concepts, some congressional credibility is lost for lack of practical distinction between natural and anthropogenic causes of extinction. A serious ecological argument can be made for limiting politicolegal response to only those species placed in jeopardy by human intrusions, including those altering habitats. Natural extinctions are presumably within the natural realm of ecosystem and perhaps biospheric strategy. Can we really make a sound case for intruding?

POINTS TO PONDER

What is the environmental professional to do upon observing that a species is faced with the choice of adaptation, evolution, or extinction, especially the latter? For example, one might "[s]uppose an impassable barrier cuts off gene flow between two populations that inhabit areas of somewhat different climates. What change in the two populations' gene pools would you expect to observe as time passes?"[16] The ecologist might ask whether there is a single species or at what point two species might be recognized. Any interested observer might inquire into the evolutionary implications of the loss of one of the species. It is for the environmental professional to inquire into the propriety of and choice among political steps.

In this context, it may be relevant to make yet another inquiry at an entirely new level:

What is the effect on the human gene pool of the [advancement] of expensive medical treatments that permit individuals with previously lethal phenotypes to live? Should society permit research to find ways to treat more such conditions?[17]

Also of interest is the matter of deliberate elimination—"extermination" replaces "extinction"—of vaccinia, the smallpox virus.

When does ecology cross the intellectual line into ethics or morality? To what extent are the science and the philosophy coextensive, and to what extent, compatible, if not coextensive? What strategies are at work in the two situations referenced above? The answers go beyond the province of the environmental professional and enter into the niches being filled by humans.

NOTES

1. The science of genetics can be extracted from *Journey*, part 2, at 144–243. For the history of genetics, *see* A. Sturtevant, *A History of Genetics* (1965) or *Classic Papers in Genetics* (J. Peters, ed., 1959). For a more contemporary view of genetics, *see* 252 *Science* (Frontiers in Biotechnology) (Jun. 21, 1991).

2. The DNA molecule is a skeleton of a five-carbon sugar and phosphate, constantly repeating. Along the sugar-phosphate skeleton are arrayed the four bases adenine, guanine, thymine, and cytosine, paired as adenine-thymine and guanine-

cytosine. A "triplet" of three bases represents a nucleotide, or codon, specifying one amino acid. The four bases are quite simple chemically and consist of carbon, hydrogen, oxygen, and nitrogen. The carbons and some of the nitrogens are in six-member ring configuration. *See Journey*, at 149–151.

3. Significantly enough, the Toxic Substances Control Act (15 U.S.C.A. 2601–2671, at sec. 4(b)(2)(A) and elsewhere), addresses toxicity in the form of mutagenesis (alteration of genetic information), teratogenesis (defects occurring in the course of fetal development), carcinogenesis (morbidity arising from abnormally rapid division of cells often resulting from mutagenesis), behavioral disorders, and cumulative or synergistic effects. These specific toxic effects obviously correspond to damage in biological systems from the cellular to the organismal level.

4. *See Journey*, at 266–287.

5. Major sources for the science of taxonomy are *Journey*, chapter 18; and Odum, at 10–11. *See also Journey*, chapters 19–21.

6. A fifth base, uracil, replacing thymine in RNA, must be added in order to include in life those viruses that carry RNA instead of DNA.

7. The use of Latinized terminology allows a scientist from any culture to recognize taxons without resort to the language of another.

8. *Journey*, Glossary, at G–1.

9. Smith, at 665.

10. *Id.*, at 294.

11. Ricklefs, at 363.

12. The discussions of extinction here and in the next section are taken from *id.*, at 362–363.

13. D. Stipp, "Scientists Probe Cellular Suicide to Fight Illness," *Wall St. J.*, Feb. 24, 1993, at B1.

14. *See* 50 C.F.R. 17.1, 50 C.F.R. 424.01, and 60 C.F.R. 227.1.

15. *See, e.g.*, J. DeBlieu, "Could the Red Wolf Be a Mutt?" *NYT Magazine*, Jun. 14, 1992, at 30; and R. Rose, "A Plucky Family Fights for Survival in a Montana Valley," *Wall St. J.*, Nov. 6, 1990, at 1.

16. *Journey*, at 288.

17. *Id.*

PART VI

ECOLOGY AND THE POLITICOLEGAL SYSTEM: THE CULTURAL DIMENSION

14

The Niche of *Homo sapiens sapiens*

THE SPECIES, UNIQUELY UNIQUE?

Throughout history and in a variety of contexts, the question has come up: Just what is the human species? A notoriously superficial answer to what a human is relates to the elements of which the human body is composed. Like all organisms, we are composed mostly of carbon, nitrogen, hydrogen, and oxygen, with the last element constituting nearly two thirds of our total weight. In fact, if sodium, calcium, phosphorus, potassium, chlorine, sulfur, and magnesium are added, 99.9% of our constituents have been taken into account. An array of heavy metals from aluminum to zinc represents the remaining minute percentage.[1] This litany of chemicals, however, is not much of a start on any definition of this species.

By definition, every species is unique, but is there something about *Homo sapiens sapiens* that actually makes this species *uniquely* unique among species? Many of the contexts in which this question arises are well outside the scope of a quasi-scientific ecology text. But two contexts are particularly relevant: the scientific and the political. Ecologically, the human species occurs as one or many populations distributed throughout the globe and occupying the most flexible niche of any species. Politically, the human species is perceived as a particularly devastating organism potentially capable of destroying whole ecosystems and perhaps the biosphere itself.

We may be unique in our ability to adapt to an extraordinary range of environmental conditions, not through physiological or other "purely" biological means but through intelligence and our ability to communicate abstract ideas, including concepts of the past and future. We can learn from the past of our species as well as from personal experience. We can plan for the future, often by applying past history. Language, writing, culture, and both an individual and a political sense of morality may be features that render our species quantitatively and qualitatively unique in a sense no other species is unique. Our minds represent a new level of organization as profound a leap from life as life is from physicochemistry.[2]

Human horizons are constantly expanding, literally scaling new heights and exploring new dimensions. We see ourselves as Lilliputians, poised precariously on a very small planet. But through intellect, we "have the extraordinary ability to examine and comprehend the structure of the universe. This [alone] truly distinguishes us from less-evolved animals."[3] The potency of the human mind is one lesson from contemporary astronomy.[4]

With this recognition combined with concepts of the Gaia Hypothesis or of deep ecology comes a paradox for all of us but most particularly for environmental professionals. If our species is a part of nature, our actions cannot be other than natural, no matter how detrimental to our ecosystems. If our cultural organization distinguishes us from other life forms, how can we be bound exclusively to follow "nature's way"?[5]

In the end, it would seem that evolution has led to human nature, which has led to culture; culture has enabled the behavior that is believed by many to impair nature's integrity. We face a quandary in that any return to nature for us would contravene our nature and our history.[6]

In seeking a way out of our quandary, it is worth contemplating the ecologically sound assertion placing populations beyond good and evil. It is the nature of every population to grow to fill its ecosystem. When too numerous, organisms either die out or transcend themselves. Those that transcend "find new ways to procure room, carbon, energy, and water." But they produce new wastes, which test them.[7]

At what stage is the human population? *Are* we too numerous? If so, are we at the brink of extinction? Or are we about to transcend ourselves?

THE POPULATION ECOLOGY OF
THE HUMAN SPECIES[8]

At least one ecologist holds the human species unique in our capacity to alter our niche seemingly at will. We can increase the sources of niches in deriving energy from something other than complex organics we ingest, and we can use novel materials and systems unlike any other species.[9] Another scientist finds the combination of size of brain, social structure, speech, and the use of tools to be what sets humans apart. In other words, the biological system we call culture is unique to us and a new level of organization. It is culture that allows us to manipulate our environment in ways that are both purposeful and anticipatory.[10] It is in culture that our unique capacity for abstract reasoning—from mathematics to aesthetics—comes to its culmination.[11] The strategy of human cultures, each a supra-population, is to improve the quality of life for one or more future generations.[12]

Sometimes our biological nature and our cultural one are in conflict. Biologically, it was expedient when some thousands of years ago we attained the capacity for which every species is striving: the ability to alter the environment to eliminate other species. Morally, we are beginning to take a second look. Doing so does not come easily. Has Garrett Hardin's "tragedy of the commons" placed us in need of "lifeboat ethics"? Must some individuals be denied a place on the global lifeboat for the sake of those already on board?[13]

Indeed, we may not yet have escaped our first niche. We started out as wandering ice age foragers, and our physiques, temperaments, desires, and patterns still reveal that beginning.[14]

There are those who consider humans either an unnatural population or, perhaps more accurately, a supranatural population. There are others who perceive urban human aggregations as akin to a climax community. Whatever the scientific reality and whatever the political, economic, and social ramifications of those realities, *Homo sapiens sapiens* is a particularly important biological system to environmental professionals.

If one is to analyze humanity in ecological terms, one of the first questions to arise is whether the species is subject to limiting factors. Or does that seemingly infinite capacity to adapt into expanding ranges of tolerance, through seemingly infinite expansions of consumption, have a maximum? Maximum or not, can human populations thrive under near-optimum conditions without compromising either the carrying capacity of their respective ecosystems and ultimately the biosphere itself? Are we really jeopardizing other species in some "unnatural" sense, or are we merely manifesting the traits of all species in filling and expanding our niche?

Significantly enough, we may be the only species capable of asking such questions and moved by a sense of obligation associated with the answers.[15] As Odum has observed, we must *transcend* the principles of general ecology because of our unique abilities to control our immediate surroundings, and our tendency to develop culture independently of environment.[16]

First, we must recognize that human populations are parts of widely ranging biotic communities and ecosystems. Superimposed on that status is the reality that our ecology goes beyond mere demographics—the statistical functions of any population. Causes and effects driving our populations demand closer analysis than statistics alone can provide. Finally, internal dynamics as well as relationships to external factors must be taken into account. Where biological regulation may not succeed, cultural regulation may be demanded.

We are responsible for any number of perturbations in ecosystems. Among the most frequently recognized are nutrient enrichment, acidification, toxification, nutrient depletion, habitat modification and outright destruction, and both the elimination of native species and the introduction of alien species. Above and beyond assumption of our niches, our intrusions into ecosystems can be stimulatory or inhibitory or can impose structural alteration.

In considering the ecology of human populations for purposes of application, most particularly in the marketplaces and in law and policy, it is essential to expand the questions and any answers derived beyond ecology into the cultural fields that do make us "uniquely unique." When we perceive anthropogenic ecological perturbation, the first step is to comprehend the ecological results of that perturbation. But before we can turn to cultural institutions to prevent consequent harms or to protect or restore the ecosystem, we need to explore the cultural implications of the perturbation, of its ecological results, and of available responses. Only then can we begin to take effective action.

When we do act, we must always remain sensitive to ecological complexity. We must heed the lessons of past intrusions into ecosystems, whether taking the form of intervention or representing a perturbation. The former is presumably, but not necessarily, beneficial to the system, the latter detrimental. The truth is, we seldom are able to predict whether an action will be intervention, intrusion, or perturbation. Too often, whatever the intent or lack of it, our actions result in ecological backlashes. These are unexpected and certainly unintended ecological responses. In simple terms, ecological backlashes can be categorized as failures to secure the intended correction or as additional perturbation in the subject ecosystem or one somehow connected to it.[17]

In short, environmental professionals and, indeed, the population at large must heed all the ecological principles and concepts described here. We must take them personally! Only then are we in a position to apply our cultural selves to resolving our place in the biosphere.

SYSTEMS ECOLOGY AND RESOURCES[18]

In seeking to apply ecological principles to human activities, some rhetorical questions should lie behind those efforts. What are the practical implications of the phenomenon that the optimum for quality is always less than the maximum population that an ecosystem can sustain? To what extent are deteriorating environments attributable to cultural tendencies to be too independent of the natural environment?

Systems ecology, emergent with the analytical power provided by computer technology, is a kind of return to the black box described in the opening chapters. When attempting to analyze the ecosystem or some component thereof, the ecologist or the environmental professional is immediately confounded by the sheer complexity of the interactions at and among all the relevant levels of organization. As should be thoroughly instilled by now, every level of organization from pure mathematics to planetary ecology and beyond has something to contribute to an ecosystem's output as a result of each and every isolated input. In a very real sense, systems ecology and computer modeling are founded in the Theory of Integrative Levels.

Systems analysis is defined for purposes of ecological systems as the process of translating internal physical or biological concepts into a set of mathematical relationships that are then manipulated to predict or explain the behavior of that system. Some of the complexity can be transformed into the mathematical symbols and equations on which computer modeling depends.[19] In brief, the mathematical symbols can be a useful shorthand describing complex ecological systems. The equations can permit a formal statement (which can often be transformed into a highly effective visual presentation) of how an ecosystem's components are likely to react to change.

The model resulting from the mathematics derived through systems analysis remains a mathematical system. However valuable, it will always present an imperfect and abstract simplification of the real world. The challenge, of course, is to work with that relatively simplistic representation while recognizing its imperfections in order to serve the ecosystems upon which we depend for life. As every research scientist can avow, even tentative answers open the way to a fuller understanding of how the natural world functions, allowing for predictions and some degree of control.

But it is the real world that is correct, if there is any conflict between the answers and the underlying reality reflected in the information provided by the natural sciences.[20] Wrong answers and other "failures" serve to reveal flaws in the conceptual framework and may point the way to corrections in the modeling process. If applied to a living system, however, wrong answers can do more harm than good, intentions notwithstanding.

The criteria to be applied in evaluating models are threefold: realism, precision, and generality. Realism is the degree of correlation with the biological concepts represented by the model. Precision is expressed through the ability to predict quantitative change and to mimic the data upon which the model is based. Generality is the breadth of applications the model fits. Models are also characterized in terms of resolution and wholeness. The former expresses the number of attributes included in the modeling process; the latter, the interactions recognized between levels of organization.

Allegedly, ecological models are noted more for their generality than for their precision. There is an argument to the effect that a model cannot at once be general and precise. Any improvement in the one is matched by a loss in the other. Moreover, an ecological model should be expected to be unrealistic in terms of lower levels of organization because of the lack of complete information concerning input and output at those levels, the sum of which are ultimately being expressed at the level of interest.

Whatever the tools of the environmental professionals, it is important to remind ourselves constantly to expand our thinking and to take care in imposing restrictions in that technology alone is not enough. "[M]oral, economic, and legal constraints arising from full and complete public awareness that man and the landscape are a whole must also become effective."[21] Environmental professional or private citizen or both, it is essential further to heed the ecological principle that the optimum for quality for a population is always less than the maximum quantity that can be sustained. Another ecological principle that must be heeded is that the more we demand of an ecosystem, large or small, the less energy is retained by that system for maintenance. Has *Homo sapiens sapiens* been justifiably labeled a parasite on the environment at large? Are we truly as destructive to our host as most parasites?

HUMAN NATURE AND U.S. ENVIRONMENTAL PHILOSOPHIES

Science, the Mind, and Culture

Throughout the history of the human species, environmental philosophy has played a major role. That role has, however, undergone profound alteration, especially in Western civilization as it is manifesting itself and merging with others here in the United States. We have gone from hunter–gatherer to tiller of the soil to industrialist to scientist to the age of information. Both our niche and our intellectual relationship to our ecosystems have altered accordingly. Emerging from the status of one more primate species in the wild, we have learned to fear the natural world. It is in our nature to seek conquest of whatever we fear. Some may believe human populations have conquered the natural world, but most of us realize that our place as conqueror is tenuous at best. In recent years, we have come to realize that we may represent a unique hazard not only to our ecosystems but to the biosphere as a whole. We are rediscovering our niche and the habitats in which it is active.

When humans left the forests and fields to enter into agricultural and later societies, they came to fear the wilderness. When North America was invaded by representatives of Western civilization, the frank intent was to conquer those usurping the land—wild beasts, howling wilderness, and hellish fiends. This vast wilderness was a place of evil as well as one of physical danger.[22] Conquest was a moral imperative.

The contemporary environmental movement in the United States traces its most recent roots to the conservation and preservation movements in the early twentieth century. In fact, early conservation helped shape the notion of "commons" as a public domain in resources that are held not susceptible to private appropriation.[23] Conservation seeks to ensure the preservation of a quality environment in company with a continuous yield of useful plant, animal, and natural materials—natural resources. Conservation, then, tends to be more anthropocentric than preservation, which tends more toward biocentrism or ecocentrism.

Our literature and the popular arts in the United States are rich in images identifiable as personal ideas of wilderness, conservation, and preservation. Among the best known of the writers is Aldo Leopold, who spoke of conservation as a "state of harmony between men and land"—his "land ethic," an ecological conscience.[24]

Ecological health, according to Leopold, lies in the land's capacity for self-renewal. Conservation arises from efforts to understand that capacity in order to preserve it.[25] The land ethic is a major concept incorporated into the contemporary environmental movement.

The Contemporary Environmental Movement

What Is It? In the early 1960s, the environmental movement in the United States still took the form of conservation or preservation. In the 1970s, the shock of gross pollution and disappearing landscapes moved us to a kind of grim pleasure expressed in part as cultural and individual ambivalence toward progress. The environmental movement provided one outlet for our malaise.[26] Whatever our individual relationship to the movement, we can all probably agree that the role of culture is not to overcome nature but to be open to its potential.[27] A primary lesson from ecology is that all "poverty" is attributable to unrestrained population growth.[28] The environmental movement, then, is seeking ways to alleviate the results of population growth, unrestrained at least at the local level, and thus to relieve ecological poverty in whatever biological systems in which it is being expressed.

An Ecological Perspective. To the extent Odum can be cited for the ecological perspective, he has observed that ecologically sound conservation, one of the missions of contemporary environmental policy, is neither a matter of hoarding resources nor one of total rejection of development. Instead, the objective should be one of rejection of unplanned development in violation of ecological laws. In the past, such ecologically unsound development has rightfully been attributed to ignorance as well as to short-sightedness and advancement of parochial interests. Today, there is no excuse for development characterized by any of those three factors. In the United States, at least, there is a very real movement toward integration of all the factors supporting development that is ecologically responsible. It is a youthful movement, however, and subject to all the excesses of youth. At least we are moving away from all three impediments to environmental quality.

One of the major problems, and one that may be insurmountable, is the nearly total focus on the human perspective. We tend to speak in terms of environmental quality in association with products, recreation, and aesthetics. We seek to ensure continuous yields of useful plants, animals, and materials. Not until we act on the knowledge that ultimately it is only healthy environments that are healthful are we likely to change our ways in an ecologically sound manner.

As environmental professionals seek to serve what is sometimes called stewardship of ecosystems and of the biosphere itself, some turn to cultures not ordinarily included in that of mainstream America. For example, some assert that we should heed the injunction of certain Native Americans to consider the effects of our actions through seven generations. All too often, we have barely thought beyond the current generation. Another lesson to take from Native American peoples is the notion that we cannot preserve ecological systems by the sole expedient of dictating by law. There instead must be a profound alteration in the way each of us relates to the world around us.[29]

NOTES

1. H. Blum, *Time's Arrow and Evolution* (3d ed., 1968), at 84.

2. R. Augros and G. Stanciu, *The New Story of Science: How the New Cosmology Is Reshaping Our View of Mind, Art, God . . . and Ourselves* (1984), at 11–12.

3. W. Kaufmann, *Black Holes and Warped Spacetime* (1979), at 66.

4. *Id.*

5. M. Oelschlaeger, *The Idea of Wilderness: From Prehistory to the Age of Ecology* (1991), at 296–297.

6. *Id.*

7. L. Margulis and D. Sagan, *Microcosmos: Four Billion Years of Evolution from our Microbial Ancestors* (1986), at 243.

8. The principal source for the discussion of human ecology is Odum, chapter 21.

9. P. Colinvaux, *Why Big Fierce Animals Are Rare: An Ecologist's Perspective* (1978), at 219 and 221.

10. J. Lovelock, *Gaia: A New Look at Life on Earth* (1987), at 132.

11. S. Gould, *Wonderful Life: The Burgess Shale and the Nature of History* (1989), at 320.

12. W. Tucker, *Progress and Privilege: America in the Age of Environmentalism* (1982), at xv.

13. G. Hardin, "The Debate over Growth" (1972), *in American Environmentalism: Readings in Conservation History* (R. Nash, ed., 3d ed., 1990), at 237.

14. Colinvaux, *supra* note 9, at 219.

15. For a biologist's view of humans as moral animals, *see, e.g.*, G. Simpson, *The Meaning of Evolution* (Mentor rev. and abridged ed., 1951), at 144.

16. Odum, at 512.

17. For those who argue the risks of being wrong in taking action are far outweighed by the risks of being wrong in taking the much-maligned attitude of "wait and see," there is a counterargument. The contrary position takes into account not only the risk of ecological backlash but also the matter of the resources to be dedicated to prompt action. The same resources may be wasted or squandered, should a backlash result from their application. These resources might be put to better use in advancing some better understood ecological need or upon deferring their application until the situation has been clarified.

18. The principal source for this discussion is Odum, chapter 21.

19. There is an insidious hazard here. Even those most meager and inaccurate data can result in a compelling picture generated by a computer. The hoary adage, "Garbage in, garbage out" was never so critical a caveat as it is here. In order to appreciate what any application of computerized systems ecology can and cannot reveal, one must be aware of the quality of the data and of the processes whereby they were generated.

20. Deep ecologists are only one of the newest voices reminding us that there is more than one realm to be taken into consideration. Here, we are limited principally to the realm of the natural world. The spiritual realm is separate and outside the scope of this work, although for many the spiritual realm is an authoritative source that can and should inform the natural, just as the natural can and should inform the spiritual. *See, e.g.*, Oelschlaeger, *supra* note 5; G. Snyder, *The Practice of the Wild* (1990); and B. Devall and G. Sessions, *Deep Ecology: Living As If Nature Mattered* (1985).

21. Odum, at 406.

22. L. Mighetto, *Wild Animals and American Environmental Ethics* (1991), at 2.

23. S. Hays, "From Conservation to Environmentalism" (1987), *in* Nash, *supra* note 13, 144, at 148–149.

24. A. Leopold, *A Sand County Almanac: With Essays on Conservation from Round River* (Ballantine ed., 1966; original copyrights 1949 and 1953), at 243 and 258.

25. *Id.*, at 258.

26. Tucker, *supra* note 12, at xiv and 6.

27. D. LaChappelle, *Earth Wisdom* (1978), at 137.

28. Colinvaux, *supra* note 9, at 222.

29. Hunbatz Mien, a Mayan elder, *in* S. McFadden, *Profiles in Wisdom: Native Elders Speak About the Earth* (1991), at 234.

15

Ecology and the Politicolegal System

CONNECTIONS: ODUM'S "GREAT IDEAS IN ECOLOGY"[1]

Scientific literacy is high on the lists of needs compiled by many observers of the contemporary scene.[2] Certainly, science courses intended for those who will never enter the ranks of scientists are essential in today's world. In fact, lists of the "top hits" in science have been compiled and recommended as the foundation of general science courses. Notable on any such list are the two laws of thermodynamics with which the science in this volume opens. Other members of the "top twenty" are ecological: " 'everything on earth operates in cycles,' 'all forms of life evolved by natural selection,' and 'all life is connected.' "[3]

With considerable justification, Odum has long contended that ecology has emerged from among the biological sciences as

a separate discipline that integrates organisms, the physical environment, and humans—in line with *oikos*. . . . From this view, the ecosystem level becomes the major focus. Populations are considered as ecosystem components and landscapes as associations of interacting ecosystems. This viewpoint is now generally accepted . . . [as is indicated by listings of the most important ecological concepts, in which] [t]he ecosystem was the concept most frequently listed.[4]

In keeping with such recognition, Odum was recently moved to compile the twenty great ideas in ecology, which are the foundation of these concluding considerations. None of the ideas should come as any surprise. Eighteen are presented here as a kind of review of all that has gone before from the ecosystem to human populations.

The Ecosystem

1. *Ecosystems are thermodynamically open.* They do not constitute an equilibrium. Thus, the future of an ecosystem depends on external life support. In this sense, at least, a city can be viewed as an ecosystem.

2. *Energy is required not only for energy flow and initiation of material cycling but also for ongoing maintenance of the two phenomena.* In fact, as communities and other biological systems become larger and more complex, they demand more of the available energy (which may take the form of biological chemicals—or more).

3. *Large ecosystems tend to be more homeostatic than their components.* Larger ecosystems tend to be characterized by slower interactions. For this reason, interactions among species that are unstable, transient (not in equilibrium), or chaotic tend to be constrained. Moreover, short-term interspecific interactions tend not to be oscillatory or cyclic. At the holistic level, large complex systems such as the oceans, the atmosphere, soils, and large forests all tend toward order out of chaos and exhibit more steady-state characteristics.

4. *Ecosystem feedback is internal but without a fixed goal.* That is, there is no one, single feedback mechanism directly serving the ecosystem as such. Instead, feedback at the ecosystem level is the net result of the array of ongoing internal feedback processes within, each serving its own biological system. For those systems, probably from the organism on down, cybernetic processes are externally stimulated and move the system toward a set point. "Ecosystem control, where manifested, is the result of a network of internal feedback processes as yet little understood."[5]

5. *In a food web, indirect effects may be as ecologically important as direct interactions, and such indirect effects may contribute to network mutualism.* In an aquatic system, for example, plankton support planktiverous fish, which are in turn eaten by bass. Indirectly, then, the plankton support the bass, while the bass reduce predation on plankton.

6. *Heterotrophs may serve to control energy flow throughout food webs.* This idea may seem to contradict or at least limit the importance of primary producers to the regulation of energy flow through an ecosystem. In warm waters, for example, bacteria may be an energy sink. In effect, these microorganisms can be "short-circuiting" energy, leaving less to reach the ocean bottom and to support fish populations in that habitat. In cool waters, where bacteria are less active, more of the energy fixed by primary production reaches the ocean floor. Small heterotrophs seem to play a comparable controlling role in terrestrial ecosystems.

7. *An ecosystem's carrying capacity is two-dimensional.* The "dimensions," number of individual organisms sustained and the intensity of per capita use, are reciprocal. Whenever either increases, the other necessarily decreases.

Between Biological Systems

8. *Source-sink phenomena are in operation.* Restated, this idea is that one area or population exports to another. The exporting system is the source; the importing one, the sink. This observation applies as well at the ecosystem level. In fact, it almost certainly applies at every level of biological organization. An example is the salt marsh that feeds adjacent coastal waters. Any excessive numbers in a marsh population constitute or reflect recruitment in another ecosystem.

Strategy in the Sere

9. *Since the origin of life on earth, organisms have adapted to physical conditions and modified their immediate environment in ways that have proved to be beneficial to life.* This crucial interaction is manifest at the levels of microcosm, ecosystem, and biosphere. The strategy works locally and, ultimately, on the global scale. This strategy can be viewed as a kind of modified Gaia Hypothesis. Elements in the strategy are to be found throughout an ecosystem, but particularly startling are the major roles played by microorganisms in vital nutrient cycles and the phenomenal homeostasis maintained by the atmosphere and in the oceans.

10. *Ecosystem development effected through autogenic succession occurs in two phases; one stochastic or at random, the other mediated through greater self-organization.* The early or pioneer invasions are relatively random in nature, as opportunistic organisms first arrive and colonize. Later in the sere, that which has gone before determines what is present and the direction (and species content) of later seral stages.

Evolution

11. *Natural selection may occur at more than one level in an ecosystem.* In sum, coevolution, group selection, and traditional Darwinism fortuitously acting together compose a hierarchal theory of evolution.

12. *Two kinds of natural selection are in progress.* In one process, one species is pitted against another in competition. In the other process, the individuals within a species are pitted against the environment. Mutualism can be the successful result of this process. Mutualism arises from a cooperative adaptation to or modification in either the abiotic or biotic component of the ecosystem. The biotic alteration occurs at the community level.

13. *Competition leads either to extinction or to diversity.* The ability of populations to shift their niches is associated with increased diversity. It is extinction that is believed to be the exception in this situation.

14. *The evolution of mutualism increases as resources become scarce.*

Significant situations leading to this ecological response result when resources are bound into the biomass or whenever the soil or water is poor in nutrients.

Biodiversity

15. *The concept of biodiversity should be expanded beyond species diversity to include both genetic and landscape diversity.* The inclusion of genetic diversity is obvious, but it is possible that the importance of landscape diversity remains more obscure (notwithstanding the emphasis on interactions between biota and abiota throughout this text). In reinforcement, Odum states the obvious: The "variety of species in any given region depends on the size, variety, and dynamics of [ecosystems] and corridors."[6]

Perturbation

16. *The first signs of environmental stress usually occur at the population level, especially among sensitive species.* In an ecosystem where sufficient redundancy among species exists, another species may fill the niche of a sensitive species. In this context, it is worth noting that the parts are less stable than the wholes to which they contribute. On the practical level, ignoring an early warning can lead to an effect detectable at the ecosystem level only when the whole has already been placed in jeopardy. Early warning actually occurs at the level of individual organisms but is infrequently observed, much less heeded.

Pollution and Human Populations

17. *"Transition ["indirect"] costs are always associated with major changes in nature and in human affairs."*[7]

18. Homo sapiens sapiens *remains parasitic on the planet.* Significantly, the survival over time of any parasitic species depends on a reduction in the virulence of its parasitism and on an establishment of a "reward" feedback benefiting the host.

THE ECOLOGY OF OIL SPILLS

History and Ecology

Oil spills did not commence with the *Exxon Valdez*, and ecological analyses of this perturbation have been in progress for years. Oil from a September 1969 spill off Buzzards Bay, Massachusetts, lingered at least ten years, as did its effects. Less than a year later, a spill occurred off Nova Scotia. Tarred beaches began to clear in six years, but higher concentrations persisted below the surface. Following a March 1978 spill in the English Channel, heavy waves entrapped oil in the water column and produced unexpectedly high mortality manifested in subtidal organisms. Oil reaching shore was buried in sediments and became further entrapped in salt marshes.[8]

Through the years, serious ecological studies have been pursued in the effort to understand the full impact of oil spills for more effective response. One such study was reported only weeks before the *Exxon Valdez* spill.[9] In 1986, a spill had occurred in the Caribbean, affecting tropical coastal habitats of mangroves and coral reefs. For once, considerable baseline data were available for oiled and unoiled populations. A lack of data detailing normal ecological relationships is one reason so little is known of the effects of oil on populations.

Recovery in the Caribbean had already commenced within a year and a half, but there were unpredicted as well as predicted results in that interval. Generally, the degree of oiling varied greatly, in part with depth of water and with the extent of extreme low tides and higher-than-normal high tides. Algal cover seaward on reefs was reduced but regained or exceeded typical abundance by the time of the study, as did sessile populations of animals. Some shrimp were destroyed, but survivors benefited from decreased competition for cavities within the coral, in defense of which they ordinarily fight. Nevertheless, immediate damage was of greater magnitude than expected, and extensive sublethal effects were identified as potential sources of long-term effects possibly more significant than early mortality. For example, some coral was expected to be more susceptible to disease because of oiling.

Presumably, studies will continue in the Caribbean as well as in temperate and subpolar waters where spills have occurred to provide insights into the full ecological effects of spills and to reveal the extent to which affected ecosystems restore themselves. This knowledge will aid in decisions regarding the transportation of oil and in selecting the most promising response on behalf of environmental amenities. Certainly, substantial ecological analysis has proceeded in Prince William Sound and other waters affected by the *Exxon Valdez* spill.

The *Exxon Valdez* Experience

This March 1989 spill is reportedly the worst in U.S. waters. In addition to the vast amounts of oil released, weather conditions, among other factors, impeded response and churned the oil into a mousse, an emulsion, even more difficult to control than oil itself.[10] Within a week, the slick covered nearly 900 square miles, in some places six inches deep. The immediate public focus was turned to appalling images of birds and marine animals drenched in oil, but to ecologists the greatest concern was accumulation in the benthos that would increase the time needed for a recovery already expected to be prolonged by the subarctic cold water and diminished light.[11]

As was reported at the time, surprisingly little is known about long-term effects. Publicity aside, only a half dozen spills have been studied at length, and they were in temperate waters. Limited experience has shown enormous variance in severity and duration of effects. Only the broadest predictions were possible for Alaskan ecosystems.[12]

One method proposed to enhance the degradation of oil was to spread fertilizers rich in nitrogen and phosphorus as nutrients for natural bacterial populations. The enrichment was expected to increase their assimilation of the oil. Without increased assimilation, the oil was expected to break down in five to seven years. Enrichment was expected to reduce the interval to two to five years. Unfortunately, there was limited relevant ecological research behind the claim. In the first instance, significant biodegradation was already in progress, although active species had not been identified. Enrichment would be affected by reduced air and water temperatures. Finally, the fertilizers carried the risk of toxicity to larvae of sea urchins, oysters, and mussels.[13] In short, it would seem there was ample opportunity for ecological backlash.

A major series of ecological studies in and around Prince William Sound is in progress at the direction of the Natural Resources Trustees, agencies of the federal and Alaskan governments, pursuant to CERCLA and the Clean Water Act, among other laws. The studies are grouped under five perspectives and ten categories. The perspectives are immediate injury, sublethal or latent effects, long-term alteration of populations, habitat degradation, and effects at the ecosystem level. The ten categories focus on chemistry, habitats, and major communities.[14] The intent goes beyond assessment of ecological damage to include restoration. Even a cursory review of specific studies among populations, communities, and habitats reveals a strong sense of ecological priorities and a recognition of major gaps in data and in knowledge of affected ecosystems. Better comprehension of ecological structure and function may prove a benefit that will someday be attributed to this spill.

LESSONS FOR THE FUTURE

Odum's listing of great ecological ideas forms a lengthy synopsis of the ecological principles presented here. Some of his ideas are seemingly simple statements of the obvious. Others are more subtle or bear subtle implications. The synopsis with which this concluding chapter opens reveals many questions that environmental professionals might well add to the research ecologist's agenda of experimentation. Where no questions are immediately raised, each ecological idea not only reflects considerable ecological study and analysis but also provides much food for thought among environmental professionals.

It is clear that there must be effective communication between ecologists and environmental professionals seeking application of ecological information to matters of immediate social or political concern. Moreover, the disciplines represented by these scientists and other professionals must be effectively communicated to legislators, regulators, and other members of the politicolegal community. Similarly, those responsible for advancing environmental policy and practice have an obligation to communicate their questions and needs to environmental professionals in a manner calculated to elicit meaningful ecological answers.

NOTES

1. E. Odum, "Great Ideas in Ecology," *Land Rep.* (44) (Summer 1992), reprinted from 42 *Bioscience* (7) (1992). The ideas are not in the order in which Odum organized them. Instead, they are intended to follow the organization of the text. Two of the ideas seemed out of place, even given the contemporary interaction between ecology and environmental protection. Of these two, one asserts an urgent need for bridging contemporary gaps between manufactured and naturally occurring goods and services supporting life. This urgency attaches particularly in the *apparently* divergent contexts of tropical forests, agricultural ecosystems, and cities. The other idea asserts that management of input is the only way to address nonpoint pollution. Under the law, nonpoint pollution is the entry of anthropogenic contaminants (physical as well as chemical) into environmental media (usually bodies of water) from diffuse sources rather than from specific, confined sources such as a pipe, stack, or other conduit.

2. *See, e.g.*, D. Howell, *Scientific Literacy and Environmental Policy: The Missing Prerequisite to Sound Decision Making* (1992). *But see also* H. Bauer, *Scientific Literacy and the Myth of Scientific Method* (1992).

3. Odum (1992), at 15.

4. *Id.*

5. *Id.*

6. *Id.*, at 16.

7. *Id.*

8. L. Roberts, "The Legacy of Past Spills," 244 *Sci.* 22 (Apr. 7, 1989).

9. J. Jackson, *et al.*, "Ecological Effects of a Major Oil Spill on Panamanian Coastal Marine Communities," 243 *Sci.* 37 (Jan. 6, 1989).

10. E. Marshall, "Valdez: The Predicted Oil Spill," 244 *Sci.* 20 (Apr. 7, 1989).

11. L. Roberts, "Long, Slow Recovery Predicted for Alaska," 244 *Sci.* 22 (Apr. 7, 1989).

12. *Id.*, at 22.

13. M. Crawford, "Exxon Bets on Bugs in Alaska Cleanup," 245 *Sci.* 704 (Aug. 18, 1989).

14. *The 1991 State/Federal Natural Resource Damage Assessment and Restoration Plan for the Exxon Valdez Oil Spill, Vol. I: Assessment and Restoration Plan Appendices A, B, C,* at 1.

Glossary

Abiotic   Refers to the nonbiological components of the environment, including energy sources such as sunlight, physical agents such as wind and temperature regimes, and the inorganic and organic chemicals present in forms that may be available and unavailable to the biological components.

Acclimation   Ability of an individual organism to accommodate relatively minor alterations in its environment through changes in metabolism or behavior patterns; also the process of that accommodation (can also refer to other levels of biological systems).

Acid (n.), *acidic* (adj.)   Inorganic or organic compound that dissociates in aqueous solutions to release hydronium ions (H_3O^+); the condition of the resultant solution.

Adaptability (ecological)   Ability of a biological system to accommodate itself to alterations in the environment through genetically mediated responses ranging in scale from the molecular through individual behavior to the community at large.

Adaptability (evolutionary)   Ability of an organism to alter its phenotype to acclimate "permanently" to alterations in its environment that would otherwise jeopardize its long-term survival; can refer to comparable long-term alterations in other levels of biological systems.

Aerobe (n.), *aerobic* (adj.)   An organism that requires molecular oxygen as the basis of energy assimilation; aerobic organisms respire oxygen from the air or water and produce CO_2 as a "waste" product.

Age distribution   The number of individuals in the several age classes composing a population; a statistical function characterizing populations.

Alga (n.), *algae* (pl.), *algal* (adj.)   Relatively simple plant taxons, occurring in monocellular and simple multicellular forms; also an individual taxon or organism within each higher taxon.

Amino acids   An organic acid ($R-COOH$) with an $-NH_2$ on the carbon atom adjacent to the carboxyl (COOH) group; certain amino acids constitute the building blocks of the proteins of all organisms.

Anaerobe (n.), *anaerobic* (adj.)   An organism that thrives in the absence of oxygen as a source of energy; anaerobic fermentation replaces respiration.

Anatomy   The organization and structure of the physical components of an individual organism within the limitations set by the morphology of its taxon.

Anthropogenic   Refers to phenomena, especially those observed in ecosystems, caused by or as a result of human activities.

Anthropomorphic subclimax   *See* disclimax.

Ash   The inorganic component of biomass.

Assimilation   The entry of energy or material into a living system with any necessary conversion(s) for utilization or incorporation by or into the system.

Atmosphere   The mass of gases surrounding the earth and separating the planet from the relative vacuum of interplanetary space; the atmosphere is a major contributor to the evolution of the biosphere and of the evolution and succession of ecosystems. *See* hydrosphere; lithosphere.

Autecology   The study of ecology from the perspective of the relationship of the individual organism or component to its environment.

Autotroph (n.), *autotrophic* (adj.)   Organism capable of metabolizing complex organics of life solely from inorganics, given an appropriate energy source.

Available   Refers to an inorganic or organic chemical present in the environment in a form and location suitable for direct incorporation in biological systems or readily converted chemically or physically for incorporation.

Base (n.), *basic* (adj.)   An inorganic compound that dissociates in aqueous solution with the release of hydroxide (OH^-) and metal ions; also one of the four organic moieties of the DNA or of the RNA molecule, the order of which along the molecule constitutes the genetic code.

Baseline (n. or adj.)   The status of an ecosystem or other biological system prior to experimental or other intrusion; baseline studies are often performed to determine the qualitative or quantitative nature of a system or its components prior to an intrusion to act as a time control ("before" to the resultant "after").

Benthos (n.), *benthic* (adj.)   Underwater sediments and their biotic components.

Biochemistry   The study of metabolic pathways in organisms or their internal systems; also the representative pathways of metabolism and catabolism for a chemical entity in an organism or specific subcellular system.

Biogeochemical cycle   The pattern whereby a chemical element essential to one or more living organisms is transferred through the abiotic and biotic components of the biosphere and specific ecosystems; each step in the process is mediated by physical forces, chemical reactions, or the metabolism and catabolism of individual species or other taxons; said pattern constitutes a cycle through which the element continuously passes over some unit of time.

Biomass   The weight of the biotic component of a system, ordinarily measured as wet weight, dry weight, or ash.

Biosphere   The ecosphere and its biota.

Biota (n.), *biotic* (adj.)   The living component of an ecosystem.

Biotic potential   Maximum reproductive power of a population; a statistical function characterizing populations; will be limited externally by the ecosystem's carrying capacity and further reduced by biotic factors imposed by the community.

Birth rate *See* natality.

Carbohydrates Class of organic compounds consisting of carbon chains bearing multiple hydroxy (OH^-) groups; includes sugars, starches, and cellulose.

Carbon Nonmetallic element capable of a vast variety of tetravalent bonds; the basic element of organic chemistry—the chemistry of carbon chains and cyclic compounds with characteristic bonds predominantly with hydrogen and oxygen, hence, the basis of biochemistry; the carbon cycle is a major biogeochemical cycle.

Carbon dioxide A major gaseous component of the atmosphere and necessary for life; assimilated into the organic component of green plants in the process of photosynthesis, thus entering the food webs of ecosystems; expired during the respiratory process of organisms.

Carnivore An organism that depends on the consumption of animals for its energy and nutrients.

Carrying capacity The maximum capacity of an ecosystem to sustain one or more populations; will be imposed on each population's biotic potential and distributed among populations competing for space, energy, or material.

Catabolism The breakdown of complex organics through the physiological and biochemical processes.

Catalyst (n.), *catalyze* (v.) A chemical entity that alters the rate of a chemical reaction without being consumed in the process of the reaction; enzymes are biological catalysts.

Catastrophic climax Climax community maintained through naturally occurring catastrophes, such as fire (chaparral) or biological invasion (spruce forest), which often occur in discernible cycles.

Cell (n.), *cellular* (adj.) Small package of protoplasm bounded by a semipermeable membrane containing nuclear material and other structural and physiological components of life; the basic structure of living organisms (except viruses), which may be monocellular or multicellular.

Celsius *See* Centigrade.

Centigrade Temperature scale ordinarily used in the biological sciences with the freezing point of water set of 0° and the boiling point at 100°; can be converted to Fahrenheit by the formula: $C = 5/9(F - 32)$.

Chlorophyll Biochemical entity that actually effects reaction whereby light is fixed in the process of photosynthesis; occurs exclusively in plants; responsible for green color in plants.

Chloroplast Organelle in the cytoplasm of plants that generates and contains chlorophyll and in which photosynthesis occurs.

Climatic climax Single climax community toward which a given ecosystem is theoretically progressing and which is in equilibrium with the regional climate; based on a combination of latitude and altitude.

Climax community The (predicted) terminal stabilized community of a given ecosystem.

Coenzyme The small nonproteinaceous component of an enzyme upon which the effectiveness of the enzyme depends; many vitamins function as coenzymes.

Community   Geographically limited aggregation of populations interacting to form a characteristic biological unit composing the biotic component of an ecosystem, possessing relatively stable patterns of structure and function.

Complex (n. or adj.)   (Refers to) the condition of being composed of and/or subject to multiple interacting, interdependent forces and components. (Organisms, their internal organization, and their interrelationships and ecosystems themselves each represent biological complexes not readily amenable to simplistic analyses from a single perspective.)

Control   Essential part of any experimental study that stands for the system of interest as uninfluenced by the experimental manipulations or portions thereof; there may be an overall control and/or controls for specific components of the system or of the experiment itself.

Cyclic climax   *See* catastrophic climax.

Cytoplasm   Protoplasmic component of the cell, outside the nucleus and separated from the external environment by the cellular membrane.

Death rate   *See* mortality.

Decomposition   The breakdown of complex organic materials ultimately to their inorganic components through successive steps mediated by saprotrophs, including fungi and microorganisms; an essential component of biogeochemical cycles.

Density   The number of organisms composing a population occupying a specified unit of space; a statistical function characterizing populations.

Detrivore   An organism that depends on the consumption of decaying organic material for its energy and nutrients.

Development   Successive stages in the organization and growth of an organism from conception through maturation; may also relate to the progression of seres in an ecosystem.

Disclimax   Edaphic climax maintained through human activities or those of domestic species; also "anthropomorphic subclimax."

Dispersion   The distribution of individual organisms of a population within its habitat or home range or territory; a statistical function characterizing populations.

Dry weight   The combined organic and inorganic components of biomass.

Ecological backlash   Unanticipated negative result in target or other ecosystem associated with human intervention or intrusion in the processes of an ecosystem.

Ecological pyramid   Graphic representation of energy flow or trophic relationships in an ecosystem, reflecting the numbers or biomass sustaining successive levels.

Ecological succession   Orderly process of community development that is reasonably directional and therefore predictable.

Ecology   The study of organisms as they are organized and interacting among themselves and other components composing their physical environments.

Ecosphere   The lowest two and a half miles of the earth's atmosphere, which is capable of sustaining life.

Ecosystem   The characteristic complex of physical, chemical, and biological components in and with which an organism interacts; a structural and functional unit; each ecosystem is theoretically approaching a characteristic climax community through an identifiable sere, a climax determined primarily by climate, latitude, and altitude.

Ecotone   Transition between diverse adjacent communities.

Ecotype   Genetically stabilized, distinctive phenotype of a species or other taxon localized in a given ecosystem or microenvironment.

Edaphic climax   One of several possible intermediate climax communities occurring under conditions precluding succession to the single climatic climax community of a given ecosystem.

Energy   The ability to do work; in ecosystems, the initial source of all energy is sunlight, biologically fixed by green plants and certain other autotrophs; wind, water currents, and climate represent additional (and intermediate) abiotic sources of energy.

Entropy (n.), *entropic* (adj.)   A measure of the disorder in a system; the loss of energy, usually in the form of heat, that accompanies biological reactions; *see* the Second Law of Thermodynamics.

Environment   A generalization for the physical, chemical, and biotic situations in which an organism or groups of organisms exist(s); depending on context, can refer to a microcosm, an ecosystem, a subdivision thereof, a series of closely related ecosystems, or the biosphere at large.

Enzymes   A class of proteins that catalyze chemical reactions in living organisms; enzymes make it possible for reactions, which might not otherwise proceed at all, to proceed under conditions and at rates suitable to life in general and responsive to immediate physiological needs of the system.

Eutrophication   Natural evolutionary process through biological enrichment and succession whereby a waterway is transformed into a terrestrial sere.

Evolution   The gradual alteration in type marking the establishment of new species of living organisms through alterations in phenotype and genotype under the influence of selective pressures exerted by the abiotic and biotic features of the environment; also the progression of ecosystems through stages approaching the climax community (measured in years); progression of events resulting in the existence of the biosphere (measured in geological time).

Extinct   Refers to a species or higher taxon that has died out and no longer exists in one or more of its natural habitats.

Fahrenheit   Commonly used temperature scale with the freezing point of water set at 32° and the boiling point at 212°; can be converted to the Centigrade (Celsius) scale by the formula: $F = 9/5C + 32$.

Feedback   Positive or negative influence of external factors or of the results of a biological process itself on the rate or continuation of that process.

First Law of Thermodynamics   A statement of the empirical law of physics that matter or energy can neither be created nor destroyed but can be transformed from one form into another.

Fixation (biological)   The conversion by one or more taxons of an otherwise biologically ineffective physical or chemical entity into a form that can be utilized by that taxon and others; for example, photosynthesis is the biological fixation of light energy into the organic chemicals that participate in plant biochemical processes, chemicals that in turn can proceed through higher trophic levels or be broken down by saprotrophs; the conversion of N_2 from the atmosphere into

NO_2 by certain bacteria is the biological fixation of molecular nitrogen, which other organisms are unable to assimilate.

Food chain   A simplified pattern of consumption among organisms in an ecosystem representing the successive trophic levels of that ecosystem.

Food web   The patterns of consumption between and among the organisms in an ecosystem, representing the complete network of trophic relationships.

Gene pool   The collective genotype represented by all the individuals in a population; the source of the range of "population phenotype" and of the capacity for adaptation, ecological and, through extremely tolerant individuals, evolutionary.

Genetics   The study of the chemistry, structures, and mechanisms of inheritance in offspring of the physical, chemical, and behavioral characteristics of parental organisms.

Genotype   The unique genetic complement establishing the molecular identity of the individual within the limits of the basic nature of the species; the chemical basis of phenotype.

Genus, genera (pl.)   Taxon made up of closely related species within a taxonomic family of organisms; for example, the family of cats contains the genus *Felis*, which includes the species *catus*—the common domesticated cat; the family Hominidae includes the genus *Homo*, consisting of a single living species, *sapiens*; and the family Liliaceae contains the genera *Lilium* and *Allium*, which, respectively, include several species of lilies and the onion, *A. cepa*.

Geological time   Time frame representing the age of the earth and measured in millions of years.

Growth form   The characteristic pattern of distribution of members of a population as it progresses from immaturity through senescence; a statistical function characterizing populations.

Habit   Characteristic morphology, growth form, and function in the community of a given taxon; *see* habitat; niche.

Habitat   The physical space or conditions in which a specific taxon is ordinarily located; *see* niche.

Herbivore   An organism that depends on the consumption of green plants for its energy and nutrients.

Heterotroph (n.), *heterotrophic* (adj.)   Organism requiring one or more external sources of complex organics in order to survive; that is, one unable to metabolize those organics from their inorganic constituents.

Home range   The physical area ordinarily occupied by an individual animal as it engages in its daily patterns of behavior.

Homeostasis   A state of relative stability maintained by an organism or other biological system against limited alterations in environmental conditions and perturbations.

Hydrogen   Nonmetallic element; the simplest element; capable of bonding with oxygen to form water, the essential medium of life and life processes.

Hydrosphere   The entire body of surface and underground waters, ice, and gaseous water in the atmosphere of earth.

In situ   Refers to phenomena, observations, or experimentation occurring or conducted in the actual, naturally occurring biological system, for example, in the
living cell or in the ecosystem.

In vitro   Refers to phenomena, observations, or experimentation in the laboratory,
usually in the absence of the corresponding intact biological system; literally,
"in glass."

In vivo   Refers to phenomena, observations, or experimentation occurring or
conducted in an intact biological system, usually the organism itself.

Inorganic (n. or adj.)   The branch of chemistry or the chemicals limited to minerals, elements, and their molecules and their reactions, specifically excluding
carbon in combination with hydrogen or oxygen and hydrogen.

Integrative Levels, Theory of   Statement of the empirical concept that each level
of physical, chemical, and biological organization—from subnuclear physics
through basic chemistry into biological levels and through ecosystems—can be
comprehended at its own level only in part through a comprehension of the
properties of the preceding levels; each successive level exhibits features that
are more than the sum of its parts.

Ion   A dissociated component of a compound that carries an electrical charge;
H_3O^+ and OH^- are the ions of water.

Kinetic energy   Forms of energy that actually accomplish work.

Liebig's Law of the Minimum   Statement of empirical observation to the effect
that under steady-state conditions the material available in an ecosystem in the
amount most closely approaching the critical minimum of a population will tend
to be the limiting material for that population; *see* limiting factor.

Limiting factor   An abiotic or biotic component of an ecosystem that restricts the
biological functioning of an individual, population, or the community; *see* Liebig's
Law of the Minimum.

Lithosphere   The outer sixty miles of the earth's crust, the upper ten miles of
which is composed of igneous and sedimentary rock, in turn covered with subsoil
and topsoil.

Macronutrient   A chemical requirement of a biological system for which relatively
large quantities are demanded.

Maximum   Refers to the upper limit of tolerance in a given taxon for a specific
physical, chemical, or biological component of its immediate environment.

Metabolic pathway   Specific series of subcellular biochemical reactions whereby a
macro- or micronutrient is assimilated, distributed or utilized by, or eliminated
from a given organism or taxon.

Metabolism   The complex of precisely organized biochemical reactions by which
organisms assimilate energy and inorganic and organic materials from the environment or other organisms and convert those raw materials into mass and
energy for their own utilization.

Microenvironment   A locally distinct horizontal or vertical segment of an environment, where the complex of physical, chemical, and biological factors will
be unique within the larger environment.

Micronutrient   A chemical requirement of a biological system for which relatively minute quantities are demanded; often inorganic components of enzymes or coenzymes.

Minimum   Refers to the lower limit of tolerance in a given taxon for a specific physical, chemical, or biological component of its immediate environment.

Molecular biology   The study of life processes at the subcellular level with an emphasis on the chemistry and physics of individual molecular species as each proceeds through the array of metabolic pathways associated with assimilation, conversion, utilization, and excretion.

Monitoring   The process of following changes in a(n) (eco)system over time.

Monocellular   Refers to organisms naturally existing as single cells.

Morphology   The form unique to individuals within species and higher taxons; ranging from the subcellular (for example, viruses) to the multicellular (for example, colonial algae, fungal mycelia and fruiting bodies, higher plants, and animals).

Mortality   The death rate in a population; a statistical function characterizing populations.

Multicellular   Refers to organisms existing as aggregations of cells in varying degrees of organization ranging up to higher plants and animals composed of cells organized in tissues, organs, and organ systems.

Natality   The birth rate in a population; a statistical function characterizing populations.

Neo-Darwinism   Currently viable theory of evolution through speciation mediated through alterations in genotype that become "fixed" in a population in response to selective pressures.

Niche   Characteristic complex of habitat, habit, and functional role within community and position within environmental gradients for a given taxon.

Nitrogen   Gaseous element capable of bonding with carbon and other elements to form inorganic and organic molecules essential to life; the nitrogen cycle is a major biogeochemical cycle.

Optimum   Refers to the most advantageous quantitative measure of a specified physical, chemical, or biological component for an organism or taxon (often with reference to given stages in its life cycle or metabolic condition); *see* Shelford's Law of Tolerance.

Organ   Physically distinct structure organized from diverse tissues in a higher organism, usually an animal, and committed to one or more specific functions serving that organism.

Organ system   Complex structure in a higher organism, usually an animal, composed of more than one organ and committed to physiologically or structurally related functions serving that organism; for example, the respiratory, nervous, digestive, and reproductive systems.

Organelle   A subcellular structure in the cytoplasm of a cell and serving a specific function in that cell for it or for the larger organism; for example, a mitochondrion or a chloroplast.

Organic   Refers to the chemistry and the chemicals of carbon and its compounds, with special reference to those including hydrogen and oxygen; the basis of biochemistry—the chemistry of life.

Oxidation-reduction   Class of chemical reactions involving the transfer of electrons; a major component of biochemical processes; oxygen is the major oxidizing agent, and hydrogen is the major reducing agent in the biosphere.

Oxidizing agent   A chemical species that accepts electrons in an oxidation-reduction reaction.

Oxygen, molecular (O_2)   The stable form of oxygen that is essential to respiration in most living organisms, including both plants and animals.

Ozone (O_3)   An unstable molecule of oxygen; in the upper atmosphere, it provides a shield against damaging ultraviolet radiation, thus protecting living organisms.

Perturbation   Externally imposed disturbance of an ecosystem.

Phenotype   The expression of the genotype in the individual from its physical chemistry through its morphology and anatomy to the full array of its behavior patterns.

Photosynthesis   The biological fixation of light energy and CO_2 by green plants and certain microbial species with the release of O_2 (as a waste); the step in the carbon biogeochemical cycle transforming inorganic carbon into organic carbon and providing energy for the biotic components of an ecosystem.

Physiology   The biological science of the chemical and physical phenomena occurring in living systems.

Population   Geographically limited aggregation of organisms of the same species, composing a biological unit subject to unique description and predictions associated with patterns; geographically limited aggregations of two or more interacting species are known as communities.

Potential energy   Forms of energy that are not accomplishing work but have the inherent capacity to do so.

Primary consumer   Organism that feeds on the primary producers in an ecosystem; the herbivores are primary consumers.

Primary producer   Organism that biologically fixes the energy of sunlight, thus incorporating that energy into the biotic component of an ecosystem; green plants and certain autotrophic microorganisms are primary producers.

Primary succession   Sere that occurs in an area not previously occupied by a natural or anthropogenic community.

Productivity   The assimilation and storage of the energy of the sun in the form of organic material in green plants and hence available for circulation through the food webs of an ecosystem.

Proteins   A class of extremely complex organic molecules synthesized by living organisms by precise combination of certain amino acids; protein composes the protoplasm of cells and includes such molecules as insulin, all enzymes, and hemoglobin.

Protoplasm   The highly organized complex of organic chemicals in aqueous solution that is the basic chemical stuff of life; organized within individual cells; the internal "environment" of cellular metabolism, isolated from the external environment by the cellular membrane, itself an active structure of the protoplasm.

Punctuated evolution   Currently viable enlarged theory of evolution in which large-scale perturbation causing intervals of relatively rapid extinctions and radiative adaptations is superimposed on Neo-Darwinism.

Redox   See oxidation-reduction.

Reducing agent   A chemical species that donates electrons in the course of an oxidation-reduction reaction.

Respiration   Assimilation of molecular oxygen by organisms, with the release of carbon dioxide (CO_2); significant step in the carbon biogeochemical cycle and in the flow of energy through the biota.

Salt   An inorganic or organic compound formed upon the neutralization of an acid or a base.

Science   An analytical approach to comprehension of the natural world and its components through structured study based on observation, experimentation, the formulation of hypotheses, and their testing; the body of knowledge of any scientific discipline developing through scientific method as applied to that discipline's entities and phenomena.

Scientific method   The means whereby science and scientific analyses are conducted; specifically, the formulation of natural laws, theories, and hypotheses based on observation and controlled experimentation.

Second Law of Thermodynamics   Statement of the empirical law of physics that energy tends to dissipate from higher concentration to lower, more dispersed concentration; no process of energy transformation will occur spontaneously unless there is a corresponding degradation of energy; some energy is always required or lost in any transformation.

Secondary consumer   Organism that is feeding on primary consumers in an ecosystem; the carnivores that feed on herbivores are secondary consumers.

Secondary succession   Sere that occurs when natural communities invade an area from which a preexisting community has been eliminated, usually conveys an implication of human activity.

Selective pressure   Abiotic or biotic influence in the environment through which certain genetic characteristics provide advantages for the long-term survival (or alteration) of a species.

Senescence   The process or state of aging after maturity; applies to individual organism or to a population.

Sere   Sequence of community succession in a given ecosystem; comprises ecological succession.

Shelford's Law of Tolerance   Empirical statement to the effect that each organism depends on an intricate network of qualitative factors present in precisely quantitative relationships to survive and thrive in its ecosystem.

Species, species (pl.)   Genetically isolated aggregation of interbreeding organisms; a dynamic biological unit reflected in the more static (and probably synthetic) concept of biologists; composed of relatively similar individuals; a geographically limited aggregation of a single species is known as a population; the taxon or taxons composing a genus.

Steady state   That condition of a natural system that is characterized by apparent constancy; a state of equilibrium; nontransient.

Strategy   A perceived direction in a sere or in the behavior patterns of organisms and taxons.

Subcellular   Refers to natural biological organization below the cellular level.

Symbiosis "Living together"; the close association of two or more species, each dependent on the other(s) for energy, nutrients, or protection.

Synecology The study of ecology from the perspective of isolatable groups of organisms interacting with their environment.

Taxon A given level of organization of similar organisms; the animal, Protista, bacterial, fungi, and plant kingdoms are the highest (most general) taxons, species (or subspecies) are the lowest (most specific).

Taxonomy The study of relationships among groups of organisms, living and extinct, based on a combination of genetics, physiology, and molecular biology and, to a lesser extent, on morphology; purports to reflect actual biological relationships and evolutionary patterns.

Tertiary consumer Organism that is feeding on secondary consumers in an ecosystem.

Territory A home range that is ordinarily subject to active protection by the individual animal occupying it.

Tissue A distinct complex of two or more types of cells having a specific structural or physiological purpose in a multicellular organism.

Tolerance The relative ability of a taxon or individual organism to withstand the presence or absence of, or extremes in, the presence of a physical, chemical, or biological component in its environment.

Trophic level Position in food chain determined by the number of steps in energy transfers from energy incidence to that position.

Trophic structure The pattern of trophic levels present in a given community.

Unavailable Refers to a chemical bound up chemically and/or physically in the abiotic components of the biosphere or an ecosystem to the extent that the chemical cannot be assimilated by components of the biota and is not readily incorporated into an active biogeochemical cycle; the extreme of unavailability includes chemicals located deep in the lithosphere, but there can be degrees of unavailability—a chemical may be in physical proximity to a population that can assimilate it but present in a form not readily metabolized by that population.

Virus A class of subcellular, strictly parasitic organisms composed of nucleic acid (DNA or RNA) and a protein coat and requiring entry into specific living cells to complete their reproductive cycle.

Wet weight The combined weight of water, organics, and inorganics composing biomass.

Principal Sources and Suggested Readings

PRINCIPAL SOURCES

Arms, K., and P. Camp. *Biology: A Journey into Life*. 2d ed. Philadelphia, PA: Saunders College Publishing, 1991. Basic introductory text in biological sciences, soundly and effectively organized and enhanced with superb photographs and drawings; particularly lucid and even fascinating presentation of molecular biology and other scientific esoterica.

Odum, E. *Fundamentals of Ecology*. 3d ed. Philadelphia, PA: Saunders College Publishing, 1971. The most recent edition of a classic of ecology; no loss of relevance with the passage of time; the author used the substantially smaller second edition as an undergraduate in her first (undergraduate) ecology course in the late 1950s.

Ricklefs, R. *The Economy of Nature*. 2d ed. New York, NY: Chiron Press, Incorporated, 1983. A second recent edition of a basic ecology text; in some ways more accessible than Odum but with its own intimidating passages.

Smith, R. *Ecology and Field Biology*. 4th ed. New York, NY: HarperCollins Publishers, 1990. Opens with an instructive history of the relatively recent discipline of ecology; somewhat more accessible to the lay reader than Odum or Ricklefs.

SUGGESTED READINGS

Science

Augros, R., and G. Stanciu. *The New Story of Science: How the New Cosmology Is Reshaping Our View of Mind, Art, God . . . and Ourselves*. New York,

NY: Bantam Books, 1984. An entry in the literature of the New Age but worthy of the attention of anyone curious about how science and the natural world work and how scientists relate to their work and to the human experience.

Bauer, H. *Scientific Literacy and the Myth of the Scientific Method*. Chicago, IL: University of Chicago Press, 1992. The myth is not the existence of the methods of science but in popular images that would restrict scientific methodology; instructive description of the sociology and human practice of science with all its inspiration and foibles.

Gribbon, J. *Blinded by the Light: New Theories about the Sun and the Search for Dark Matter*. New York, NY: Harmony Books, 1991. Popular version of current cosmology commencing with our sun as a point of departure; the paradox is that this closest star has been as mysterious as distant galaxies.

Hull, D. *Philosophy of Biological Science*. Englewood Cliffs, NJ: Prentice-Hall, Inc., 1974. As a "philosophy" text bridges any gaps separating ecology from the natural and biological sciences by asking whether there is a single philosophy serving all of science or one for each discipline.

Kaufmann, W. *Black Holes and Warped Spacetime*. San Francisco, CA: W. H. Freeman and Company, 1979. Relatively early popularization of cosmology with particularly lucid presentations of arcane theory and abstract hypotheses.

Ecology and Environmental Sciences

Allen, J. *Biosphere 2: The Human Experiment*. A. Blake, ed. New York, NY: Penguin Books, 1991. Provides ecological basics and history of industrial and scientific influences in addition to describing the steps toward establishing Biosphere 2, a synergy between natural and engineering laws.

Anonymous. *Coping with an Oiled Sea: An Analysis of Oil Spill Response Technologies*. Washington, DC, OTA-BP-O–63, 1990.

Attenborough, D. *Life on Earth: A Natural History*. Boston, MA: Little, Brown and Company, 1979. One among numerous highly appealing recent natural histories intended for the armchair ecologist.

Blum, H. *Time's Arrow and Evolution*. 3d ed. Princeton, NJ: Princeton University Press, 1968. Exploration of the relationship between the Second Law of Thermodynamics ("time's arrow") and organic evolution, asserted to be the meeting ground between biology and philosophy.

Bramwell, A. *Ecology in the 20th Century: A History*. New Haven, CT: Yale University Press, 1989. Origins and ideas behind ecological movement from 1880 to 1980s; "political and spiritual history" of the ecological movement's "tributary streams."

Colinvaux, P. *Why Big Fierce Animals Are Rare: An Ecologist's Perspective*. Princeton, NJ: Princeton University Press, 1978. Readable compilation of ecological thinking from an offbeat perspective calculated to draw the most reluctant reader's attention; provides insights into the existence of controversies in ecology more as a science than as an exercise in natural history or field studies.

Dobzhansky, T. *Mankind Evolving: The Evolution of the Human Species*. New

Haven, CT: Yale University Press, 1962. One approach to human nature and niche.

Florkin, M., and E. Schoffeniels. *Molecular Approaches to Ecology*. New York, NY: Academic Press, 1969. Early recognition of the connections in science, here between the seemingly disparate molecular biology and ecology.

Hairston, N. *Ecological Experiments: Purpose, Design, and Execution*. New York, NY: Cambridge University Press, 1989. Particularly informative compilation of ongoing research for the environmental professional; provides the insights possible from a "disinterested" perspective.

Moore, J. *The Changing Environment*. New York, NY: Springer-Verlag, 1986. An ecology text intended for environmental professionals with chapters addressing contemporary issues associated with the environmental movement.

Simpson, G. *The Meaning of Evolution*. (Mentor rev. and abridged ed.) New York, NY: Mentor, 1951. A classic popularization by a renowned evolutionary biologist.

Applied Statistics

Barnes, D. *Statistics as Proof: Fundamentals of Qualitative Evidence*. (paperback ed.) Boston, MA: Little, Brown, 1983. Intended more for lawyers than for scientists and thus blessedly light on theory and heavy on practical application of statistics in the politicolegal context; two approaches, descriptive and inferential.

Finkelstein, M., and B. Levin. *Statistics for Lawyers*. New York, NY: Springer-Verlag, 1990. The title speaks for itself!

Science, Theology, and Philosophy

Schrödinger, E. *What Is Life?: And Other Scientific Essays*. (Anchor paperback ed.) New York, NY: Doubleday Anchor Books, 1956. Ruminations of a scientist–philosopher with no loss of relevance over some forty years; includes such chapters as "Science and Humanism: The Spiritual Bearing of Science on Life."

Schroeder, G. *Genesis and the Big Bang: The Discovery of Harmony between Modern Science and the Bible*. New York, NY: Bantam Books, 1990. For those who may be curious, concerned, or intrigued with regard to the relationship between scientific and Judeo-Christian approaches to cosmology, the biosphere, and natural strategies; lucid presentation of the natural history underlying ecology.

Thomas, L. *The Fragile Species*. New York, NY: Charles Scribner's Sons, 1992. A study of the human species in ecological and expanded contexts: neither as evocative nor as convincing as Lewis's earlier *The Lives of a Cell*.

———. *The Lives of a Cell: Notes of a Biology Watcher*. New York, NY: Viking Press, 1974. Highly evocative entrée into the biological sciences as philosophy as well as science.

Deep Ecology and Its Relatives

Snyder, G. *The Practice of the Wild*. San Francisco, CA: North Point Press, 1990. Anecdotal critique of contemporary U.S. approaches to ecosystems, with a degree of mysticism based in some part on aboriginal relations with nature and in some part on personal reiminiscences.

Index

ABOUT THE AUTHOR

DOROTHY J. HOWELL, Assistant Professor at the Environmental Law Center, Vermont Law School, started her career as an ecologist in 1969, becoming an environmental lawyer in 1975. She is also the author of *Intellectual Properties and the Protection of Fictional Characters* (Quorum, 1990) and *Scientific Literacy and Environmental Policy* (Quorum, 1992).